PSYCHOLINGUISTICS AND READING

By the same author: *Understanding Reading*

FRANK SMITH

The Ontario Institute for Studies in Education

PSYCHOLINGUISTICS AND READING

HOLT, RINEHART AND WINSTON, INC.

New York   Chicago   San Francisco   Atlanta
Dallas   Montreal   Toronto   London   Sydney

Preface

"Psycholinguistics", a relatively unfamiliar word in the language at large, is rapidly becoming part of the jargon of English language instruction, especially in reading. A growing number of psycholinguists—theorists and researchers in the scientific study of the uniquely human skills of language learning and use—are turning their attention to the uncertainties of reading. Their interest is reciprocated by many educators seeking new insights to further the development of children's reading abilities. The label "psycholinguistic" is also being used more and more in educational merchandising to promote an assortment of instructional notions, many of which owe as much to the scientific study of language as "miracle" detergents owe to the benign intervention of supernatural agencies.

In the present volume I provide a brief descriptive introduction to psycholinguistics and then examine at some length a number of aspects of reading in the new light that psycholinguistics offers. I have particularly drawn upon topics that will be of practical interest to teachers and others concerned with the basic nature of reading, whether from the point of view of classroom instruction or from the more fundamental standpoint of increasing knowledge of how the human intellect functions. In particular I have tried to present and extend the debate upon three radical insights which are strongly supported by contemporary linguistics and cognitive psychology. (No great originality can be claimed for the insights themselves—very little in psychology or education is startlingly new—but they have been out of fashion for some time, partly because they are not compatible with the kind of technological educational assault that I shall presently discuss.) The insights are:

1. Only a small part of the information necessary for reading comprehension comes from the printed page.
2. Comprehension must precede the identification of individual words.
3. Reading is not decoding to spoken language.

The present book is broadly an elaboration of one or another of these three themes viewed from a variety of theoretical positions and supported by a diversity of empirical data. In part I have tried to achieve this

428.4
Sm56 p

elaboration by presenting my own views and my interpretation and synthesis of evidence and ideas that others have provided. But in some of the chapters I have, with the kind permission of authors and publishers, reprinted papers which I think make notable contributions to the understanding of reading.

I can by no means claim to have exhausted the field in my selection of relevant materials upon psycholinguistics and reading. A number of papers and extracts that I originally hoped to reproduce have reluctantly been excluded for considerations of space or to avoid extensive repetition. Such sources are included in the list of references at the end of each chapter and in the suggested further readings. The papers that I have reprinted—accounting for about half of the book—are those of particular individual interest and importance which I thought could not be justly reflected in paraphrases or brief quotations. These papers, not always easily accessible to many readers, provide at least a flavor of the different approaches that lead to substantially the same conclusions.

The present volume complements my earlier *Understanding Reading* (Holt, Rinehart and Winston, 1971); I have tried to ensure that neither book is a prerequisite for reading the other. *Understanding Reading* is basically an overview of relevant aspects of linguistics, cognitive and behaviorist psychology, information theory, developmental psycholinguistics, and the neurophysiology of eye and brain, together with an analysis of three aspects of reading: letter, word, and meaning identification. The present volume goes into far more detail on the relation between visual and nonvisual aspects of reading, at a rather more controversial level and with rather closer attention to implications for reading instruction.

There is also, I must confess, a deeper polemical thread underlying my selection and organization of material for the present volume. At the conclusion of *Understanding Reading* I make the point that a deeper understanding of what is involved in reading, and in learning to read, is far more important for the reading teacher than any expectation of better and more efficacious instructional materials. Nevertheless I am frequently pressed to elaborate upon what I think are the implications of psycholinguistics for reading instruction, as if psycholinguists have a responsibility to tell teachers what to do. Many teachers have difficulty in accepting that a child might have a better implicit understanding of his intellectual needs than the producers of educational methodology or technology. This reliance on technique is so antithetical to insights we have gained into reading that I shall use the privileged space of a preface to expand a little on my personal feelings.

To many people today—children, parents, teachers, researchers, and politicians—reading is a *problem*. There are innumerable books and papers and conferences on the topic of the *problem* of teaching reading. And almost invariably the solution to this problem is seen in terms of "improved" methods of instruction.

The pressure—and very likely the problem also—will get worse as a burgeoning educational industry tries more and more to persuade schools to rely on technology rather than on understanding in order to teach reading. Already some schools have contracted out to private groups of "educational consultants" who *guaranteed* to get groups of children up to certain levels of proficiency by a certain time and who would be paid only by results—an experiment that the Office of Education decided was a failure. These levels of proficiency are inevitably related to standardized *tests* rather than to individual needs, interests, or abilities of a child. There are contemptuous attempts to produce "teacher-proof" materials. Programs bruited as "individualized instruction" are little more than automated reflexes to scores on a multitude of arbitrary tests. Sophisticated electronic gadgetry is often paired with naive ideas about how learning takes place and about the subject being taught.

At national and international levels there seems to be no doubt that a reading problem exists. In the United States the "Right To Read" has become a national goal for the 1970s, replacing moon landings as the focus of a monstrous national effort. It has been decided that an ideal technology of reading instruction can be found provided sufficient resources are allocated to systematic development. The decision is an act of faith similar to that of the space program that a systematically organized effort could develop a technology to put man on the moon.

But the idea that the level of literacy will be raised, and learning to read made easier, by the development of new materials or a more complex technology is in fundamental contradiction to everything that new knowledge and common sense tell us about reading and learning. Man had never journeyed to the moon before technology took him there, but children have been learning to read for centuries. We have failed even to consider the possibility that when children learn to read today it may be despite all our sophisticated educational gimmickry, rather than because of it. Such a huge variety of materials has been produced for the purpose of helping or encouraging children to read (or of attracting schools to purchase) that it seems unlikely that any radically new type of material could be produced.

Obviously, I think that psycholinguistics has something to offer teachers of reading that systems analysis and operations research cannot supply, and that is an understanding of what reading is all about. But I must admit that I feel a growing anxiety about the word "psycholinguistics" itself. Already there are signs that "psycholinguistic" is becoming one of those faddish labels that suffer a brief career of indiscriminate application in education in order to deceive, dissemble, or convey an image of totally false authority. Reading instruction has been a frequent victim of such adjectival oversimplification, the offence typically compounded by the use of the definite article to imply a completely unwarranted uniqueness, as in *the* linguistic method, *the* language experience technique, or *the* phonics approach. Now the stage is set for *psycholinguistic* methods and approaches —or even *the* psycholinguistic method or approach. At least one publisher has advertised explicitly the expectation for which a large segment of the communications industry is evidently tooling up—that "psycholinguistics" is the coming word in education.

There can no more be one "psycholinguistic" method of teaching reading, or even of theorizing about reading, than there is a unique "medical approach" to treating sore throats or an exclusive "culinary method" of baking cakes. There is more on this theme in a chapter with the ironical title: "On the Psycholinguistic Method of Teaching Reading".

In the final chapter I have conceded at least in part to the frequent challenge to specify what psycholinguistics has to tell teachers about reading instructional practices. While still refraining from telling teachers what to do (except to try to understand better the reading process) I point to some common classroom practices for which I can find little rational justification.

Finally, acknowledgements. My thanks to Carol Chomsky, Ken Goodman, Debbie Holmes, Paul Kolers, George Miller, Susan Poritsky, Paul Rozin, Raina Sotsky, and Jane Torrey—the authors who permitted me to reprint from their work. My thanks also to the anonymous others to whom all authors are indebted—to those who said so much of it first, or who collected so much of the data—and to so many colleagues, students, teachers, and friends (overlapping categories).

Once again Connie Tyler deserves special mention for her exceptional secretarial tolerance and expertise. And the final thank-you is for my agent, collaborator, and friend, Mary Marshall.

Toronto, Canada   F.S.
July 1972

Contents

x   *Contents*

PSYCHOLINGUISTICS AND READING

1

Psycholinguistics and Reading

The first word in the title to be examined is the smallest. The "and" in *Psycholinguistics and Reading* implies only that we will be dealing with the intersection of two broad areas of study, not that both areas will be covered exhaustively. Just as there is much more to psycholinguistics than reading, so there is more to reading than psycholinguistics. On such important topics in reading as taste, preference, enjoyment, appreciation, persistence, and motivation as well as more formal aspects of individual differences such as testing, diagnosis, and remediation, pyscholinguistics is largely silent. Psycholinguistics is relevant to reading, but it is by no means the last word.

Having dealt with the conjunction, we can now turn to the two heavyweights in the title. They will be less easily disposed of. Psycholinguistics, as its name suggests, is a field of study that lies at the intersection of two broader disciplines, psychology and linguistics. Linguists in general are concerned with the abstract study of language—they analyze and compare such aspects of languages as their sounds, syntax, and lexicon; they examine similarities and differences among languages, and try to trace their evolutionary development. Linguists are concerned with the nature of language as a system that is available to its users, rather than with the way in which language is acquired, produced, and comprehended by individuals. (It is sometimes asserted, however, that linguistics is a sub-field of human psychology. After all, the relatively small number of examples from any language that linguists study are all produced by individuals, sometimes by

1

only the linguist himself who in turn uses his own acquired knowledge of language in order to make his analyses. In other words, although the content of linguistics may be relatively abstract, its pursuit is distinctly psychological.)

Psychology, on the other hand, is uniquely concerned with behavior and with the conditions under which it is learned. Cognitive psychologists, whose primary focus is on the manner in which humans acquire, interpret, organize, store, retrieve, and employ knowledge, are particularly interested in the manner in which language is developed and used. Language is obviously central to human mental behavior, and it has often been remarked that many of cognitive psychology's greatest questions might be resolved if a full understanding could be gained of how we comprehend language through reading. However, a complete understanding of the reading process still appears to be a long way off (by implication, it will not occur until many of psychology's greatest questions are settled). On some issues, such as the actual nature of the mental events that transpire when a person understands a statement in language, there is considerable confusion about how the question should be framed.

Psycholinguistics

Psychologists have studied language development and use for the best part of a century, although the subject fell into a certain disfavor and even disrepute with the rise of behaviorism in the second decade of the present century. For about thirty years, any interest in the comprehension of language and other phenomena of mental life was widely interpreted in the United States as being vaguely unpatriotic.

Language emerged from the psychological underground in the mid-1950s, welcomed by a number of linguists with the rather novel idea that psychology might have something relevant to contribute to their area of interest. Such interdisciplinary osmosis, reflected in the adoption of the label "psycholinguistics", marked a refreshing departure from the frequent impermeability of the boundaries between neighboring fields of study. Many psychological studies of language appear to have proceeded in complete ignorance of anything that linguists could say about what language is really like—some psychological theories in effect have concerned languages that nobody actually speaks. This insularity has been fully reciprocated by linguists whose conjectures about how individuals or the human race in general developed language have completely disregarded known constraints on how the human brain works.

The first formal transactions of psycholinguists were primarily neo-behavioristic, concerned mainly with trying to explain language phenomena in a nonmentalistic stimulus-response framework. But a larger and more dramatic psycholinguistic attack developed that was boldly mentalistic, looking for an understanding of the abstract "rules" that individuals "hypothesize" and "test" as a consequence of their "biological predisposition" to learn language. The major impetus for this cognitive approach to psycholinguistics—which underlies the present volume—came from the school of "generative transformational" linguistics associated primarily with the name of Noam Chomsky.

A survey of the shifting sands of generative linguistic theory would be time-consuming, technical, and largely tangential to our present concern. Readers inclined to a closer acquaintance with contemporary linguistics, a pursuit as fascinating as it is complicated, are offered some introductory references in a list of suggested further readings at the end of the volume. For the moment it will be sufficient to outline two particular consequences of the Chomskian linguistic influence in psycholinguistics and in cognitive psychology generally:

1. The distinction between two aspects or levels of language, its physical manifestation and its meaning, was re-emphasized—though it was by no means new. The physical aspect of a sentence or utterance—the sound waves that pass through the air, or in the case of writing the ink marks on paper—is derived from what was labelled the *surface structure*, and the information conveyed by the utterance—its meaning—was derived from a *deep* or *underlying structure*. Grammar, or syntax—the set of rules that determine how words are organized in sentences—was defined as the bridge between the surface and deep levels of language. Without syntax there can be no understanding, because meaning is not directly represented in the surface structure. As a very oversimplified example, the sentence *Man catches fish* is quite devoid of any specific meaning at the surface level; the meaning can be extracted only by the exercise of our prior syntactic (and semantic) knowledge. The words "man", "catches", "fish" could each be a noun or a verb, and their actual semantic and grammatical function in the sentence is determined only through the manner in which they are combined, that is, by their syntactic relations. Similarly, the only reason that *man catches fish* can be distinguished from *fish catches man* (or from a quite meaningless arrangement like *catches man fish*) lies in the way in which the words are ordered—the rules of syntax—and our knowledge of these rules. The argument is developed in the following chapter by Miller. A crucial psycholinguistic implication is that children cannot possibly learn to understand language by imitation or by rote because meaning is not directly represented in the sounds that they hear. Language can be understood only through the application of syntactic rules that are never formally or systematically taught.

2. The second major influence of Chomskian linguistics lay in its stress

on the creative aspects of language—the fact that a grammar can be regarded as a set of rules for generating (and recognizing) an infinite number of grammatical sentences. If the rules of grammar are in effect such a sentence-generating mechanism, and since it is a distinguishing characteristic of most human beings that they are capable of generating and comprehending an infinite number of grammatical sentences, then the complete grammar of a language—if ever one could write it—would be a very good approximation for the knowledge of language that every language user must have stored in his head. In other words, the linguist's grammar would be an excellent psychological theory.

The argument occasionally was pushed to an absurd extreme. Since the linguist's rules of grammar are never formally taught to a child, and in fact nobody knows enough about the complete set of supposed rules to say what they are, then it must be concluded that every baby is born with the rules of language already in his brain. Language is a biological bonus for man; it is innate. But there are more reasonable explanations, as I shall show.

The early Chomskian view of language so interested psychologists in syntax that for a long time it might have been a reasonable conclusion that psycholinguists thought there was nothing more to language development and use than grammar. But while an abstract grammar might be seen as capable of producing an infinite number of sentences, the actual circumstances in which language is uttered place considerable constraints on its form. Moreover sentences are produced and understood by human beings that would never be produced by the formal grammars of the linguist. As for the innateness of language, the most that can be said from any useful point of view about the kind of knowledge of language a child is born with is that he seems to know the right kind of questions to ask. He does not have expectations that language is quite different from what it actually is. But such a statement says nothing more than that language is what it is because it was invented by humans for use by humans; it would be just as appropriate to say that we have a biological predisposition for riding bicycles because we are born with an anatomy that can place itself on and around the saddle of a bicycle. Bicycles were developed with precisely the shape that they have because they were to be ridden by humans. Language, similarly, is a human invention.

The continuing influence of transformational linguistics on psycholinguistics is reflected in the fact that as the linguistic community has turned itself more and more to the question of meaning, so many psychologists have turned their attention from the question of how the grammatical structure of sentences is learned and perceived to how the information that sentences contain is expressed, stored and comprehended. As a consequence, whereas psycholinguistics was initially primarily concerned with questions linguistic, there is a growing tendency now for the linguistic enterprise to turn to matters cognitive. With this redirection of emphasis has come a greater attention to reading.

Reading

One reason for the disinclination of many psycholinguists in the past to turn their attention to reading would seem to be a profound misunderstanding of the nature of reading in the first place. I characterize this disinclination in very general terms because the misunderstanding has manifested itself in two quite extreme and contradictory forms. On the one hand it has sometimes been bluntly declared that reading is a complete mystery —that we just do not know enough about how the brain works to hypothesize how people can read with comprehension at 500 words or more a minute. On the other hand it is quite commonly asserted that there are no interesting questions to be asked about reading, that surely reading is simply a matter of decoding from written symbols into sound, and that since the code itself is relatively straightforward (the argument goes), all the interesting questions lie in a spoken language. Most of the chapters in this book offer substantial counter evidence to both the preceding propositions.

An additional discouragement to many cognitive psycholinguists to involve themselves in reading has been the incredibly confused and inconclusive state of reading research, aggravated by the fact that research into reading frequently fails to separate itself from matters of reading instruction, instructional theory, and social and educational bias.

As psycholinguists began to take an objective look at reading, and as reading theorists became interested in the insights that psycholinguists had to offer, much of the mystery and many of the underlying assumptions about reading were reformulated into manageable and productive questions. As I shall show, psycholinguistics offered a new look at reading that was dramatic and even iconoclastic. (This was about 20 years after the term "linguistic" had begun to make its mark—or scar—in education by being associated with the conceit that the best way to teach reading and writing was to turn children into miniature linguists, preferably through exercises bearing little resemblance to any language that anyone might actually read or write.)

Psycholinguists draw a clear distinction between the reading process and reading instruction, between theories of what goes on in the head and beliefs about what should go on in the classroom. Interaction between the reading theorist and the educational practitioner should be consistently positive and constructive. Neither side in fact is in a position to prove the other wrong, because each asks a different kind of question. It does not matter how radical or definitive a scientific discovery might be, it cannot make the slightest difference to anything in the past history of the classroom. Any method that worked the day before the great discovery will work the day after, no matter how illogical the underlying rationale might now appear. I frequently assert that children could not possibly learn to read through the medium of spelling-to-sound correspondence rules, which are far too cumbersome and unreliable for anyone ever to be able to use them effectively. But I do not suggest that teachers immediately stop using whatever they happen to call "phonics" in the classroom, especially if the method shows results. If children learn to read as a consequence of that instruction then the teacher must be doing something right. Somewhere there must be sufficient information for a child to get the knowledge that he needs and the opportunity to test that knowledge in practice. Of course, with new psycholinguistic theory we might get fresh insights into why some methods work better (some of the time and with some children) than others—but that is the most that theory can offer. Theorists cannot assert that something that obviously is getting results cannot possibly get results; such an assertion reflects only on the theorist.

On the other hand, educators cannot argue against theory on the basis of what their practice is. All too often we get results for reasons we do not suspect. The teacher using phonics cannot prove the researcher wrong who discovers that the number of letter-sound rules in English is well over 200, and argues that not even a computer could use them to read aloud. Similarly the fact that correlations exist between particular practices and instructional outcomes does not mean that a causal relationship exists. There is probably a high correlation between reading ability and absence of cavities, but this does not mean that tooth brushing is an essential part of learning to read.

In the following few paragraphs I shall briefly outline some of the more general aspects of the approach of psycholinguistics to reading. The particular topics are all covered in more detail in one or more of the chapters in this volume, although probably none of the other writers represented would subscribe wholly to the outline that I present.

Reading is not primarily a visual process. Two kinds of information are involved in reading, one that comes from in front of the eyeball, from the printed page, that I call *visual information*, and one that derives from behind the eyeball, from the brain, that I call *nonvisual information*. Nonvisual information is what we already know about reading, about language, and about the world in general.

Obviously reading is a visual activity, in the sense that we cannot read print with the lights out. But being able to see sentences in front of our eyes is not enough—we must also contribute nonvisual information. We must know something of the language in which the material is written, and about its subject matter, and about reading. All this might appear obvious and distinctly unimportant, except for two very important facts, neither of which received very much attention in reading until the advent of psycholinguistics. In view of the fact that there is so much under the sun that is not new, especially in the matter of reading, it is significant that these two contributions are indeed novel and potentially revolutionary. The first contribution of psycholinguistics is that there is a trade-off between visual and nonvisual information in reading—the more that is already known "behind the eyeball", the less visual information is required to identify a letter, a word, or a meaning from the text. Conversely the less nonvisual information that can be drawn upon, because the text is on an unfamiliar subject matter or because it is written in language that is not easy to comprehend, the slower reading tends to be. More visual information is needed.

The second major psycholinguistic contribution to reading is that there is a severe limit to the amount of information coming through the eye that the visual system can process. In other words, the trade-off between visual and nonvisual information is critical. The reader who relies primarily on visual information will simply overload his visual system; he will be unable to get as much information as he needs. He will read as if he were in the half-dark. (It is not without reason that we say a passage is not "clear" if we do not understand it.)

A supplementary conclusion follows—the reader who concentrates on identifying every word correctly will, unless he is already very familiar with the material he is reading, be unable to read for meaning. Contrary to the widespread belief, reading word perfectly is not necessary in order for comprehension to take place. Quite the reverse. A reader who concentrates on words is unlikely to be able to get any sense from the passage that he reads. It is only by reading for meaning first that there is any possibility of reading individual words correctly.

There is, moreover, a sound linguistic reason for the critical importance of nonvisual information in reading. The nature of written language is such that words cannot be uniquely identified and sentences cannot be comprehensibly uttered unless the meaning of the word is determined first. There is just not sufficient information in the spelling of words to read them *before* their meaning is comprehended.

In addition to the limitation on the amount of visual information that can be utilized in reading, there are also severe restrictions to the capacity of working memory. The bottleneck of working memory is critical when the question of "phonics" is reconsidered. The system of letter-sound correspondences in English is so complex, in addition to its unreliability as the sole or even major method for producing the sounds of words without first getting their meaning, that it is unrealistic to expect anyone to clutter his memory with phonics rules and bits of half-digested words and still be able to read.

One of the most dramatic discoveries in reading in recent years has been that children clearly know so much about reading right at the beginning. Children rarely attempt to sound out unfamiliar words that occur in sentences they are reading, in fact they frequently demonstrate that they are not too concerned with reading words at all. They are much more likely to get directly to the meaning and to omit or change the actual words, particularly the ones they are not too sure about. In short, they behave like fluent adult readers. A good deal of the remedial activity that is called speed reading instruction is designed to break inefficient readers of the habit of depending on words.

Organization

It is unusual to find a psycholinguistic paper about reading that deals with just one self-contained topic. Reading does not easily lend itself to compartmentalization, in fact some of the uncertainty that persists about reading might be attributed to attempts to fragment the subject unduly, for example the analysis of the relation between spelling and sound without taking meaning into account.

Nevertheless, with a certain amount of overlap and inescapable repetition, the contents of this volume do tend to cluster around the three themes that I listed in the Preface, namely:

1. Only a small part of the information necessary for reading comprehension comes from the printed page. *Chapters 2, 3, 4, 5.*
2. Comprehension must precede the identification of individual words (reading is not primarily visual). *Chapters 4, 5, 6.*
3. Reading is not decoding to sound. *Chapters 5, 6, 7, 8, 9, 10, 11.*

Chapters 8 and *10* also have something to say about spelling, and *Chapter 11* is on the important topic of dialect.

Chapters 12, 13 and *14* are primarily concerned with the process of learning to read, and *Chapters 15* and *16* with instruction, albeit in a nondirective and precautionary way.

The book has been arranged in such a way that the chapters can be read consecutively, but since a number of chapters were originally written to be published independently, it is also possible to read selectively. Most of the chapter titles are reasonably explanatory, and the reader who wishes to dip should first examine the Table of Contents in order to ascertain more about individual chapters.

Additional information will be found in the introductory comments at the beginning of each chapter, where I attempt to provide a little connective tissue, pointing up the relevance and relationship of the chapter to the major themes of the book. Where a chapter is a reprint of a paper that has appeared elsewhere, I also include in the introduction the author's original abstract, if one was provided, and the acknowledgement to the copyright holder.

I have followed the convention of listing references chapter by chapter, rather than gathering them all together at the end of the book. This method of organizing references permits the retention of the original format of the paper where a reprint is involved, and will facilitate the search for additional source materials. Readers seeking further information on a particular topic would be advised first to examine the lists of references for chapters whose titles are closest to their particular interest. In addition I have included at the end of the book a list of suggested further readings.

Occasionally the author of a chapter makes a reference to another paper that has also been reprinted in this volume. In such a case the citation in the body of the chapter has been marked by an asterisk, e.g. (Torrey, 1969*).

2

Some Preliminaries to Psycholinguistics

——GEORGE A. MILLER

The paper that forms the basis of this chapter has become a classic of psycholinguistics. Patiently and carefully, Miller demonstrates that there is much more to language than its physical characteristics, which is precisely the point underlying the theme of this book that only a small part of the information necessary for reading comes from the printed page.

Miller develops his argument in terms of spoken language, but the points that he makes are fundamental; there are two aspects of language, physical representation and meaning, and the gulf between the two is wide. Where Miller writes about "speech" and "utterances", the words "writing" and "sentences" can often be substituted, just as what Miller terms "significant differences for vocal communication" can be interpreted as "differences of meaning". Thus the first of Miller's seven ideas might be paraphrased as "Not all the visual information on the printed page is significant for reading, and not all differences of meaning are represented in writing".

This chapter also undermines the frequent assumption in the "decoding to sound" view of reading that written language becomes comprehensible to a reader the instant he transposes it into speech. Miller shows first of all that producing the sounds of speech is not enough; even if decoding to sound were possible, subsequent translation to meaning would still be required. But since in any case a reader cannot transpose from written language into speech without the use of meaning, the silent reader might just as well stop with meaning in the first place.

This chapter has a dialectic tone reflecting Miller's concern to dis-

mantle an opposing point of view about language, namely that all linguistic phenomena can be accounted for in behavioristic stimulus-response terms. Miller's frequent psycholinguistic collaborator, Noam Chomsky, had no hesitation in specifying his antagonist, B. F. Skinner, in a much more acerbic attack on the behaviorist approach to language. The relevant references for Skinner and for Chomsky are listed in the Suggested Further Readings.

George Miller, a former professor of psychology at Harvard and Rockefeller Universities, is currently at the Institute for Advanced Studies, Princeton. His paper originally appeared in American Psychologist, *1965, 20, 15–20, and is reprinted with the permission of the author and publishers.*

The success of behavior theory in describing certain relatively simple correlations between stimulation and response has encouraged experimental psychologists to extend and test their theories in more complicated situations. The most challenging and potentially the most important of these extensions, of course, is into the realm of linguistic behavior. Consequently, in recent years we have seen several attempts to characterize human language in terms derived from behavioristic investigations of conditioning and learning in animals. These proposals are well known, so I will make no attempt to summarize them here. I will merely say that, in my opinion, their results thus far have been disappointing.

If one begins the study of a new realm of behavior armed with nothing but hypotheses and generalizations based on experience in some quite different area, one's theoretical preconceptions can be badly misleading. Trivial features may be unduly emphasized, while crucially important aspects may be postponed, neglected, or even overlooked entirely. These hazards are particularly dangerous when we generalize across species, or from nonverbal to verbal behavior.

The impulse to broaden the range of phenomena to which our concepts can be applied is commendable. But when this enthusiasm is not guided by a valid conception of the new phenomena to be explained, much intelligent enterprise can end in frustration and discouragement. Human language is a subtle and complex thing; there are many aspects that, if not actually unique, are at least highly distinctive of our species, and whose nature could scarcely be suspected, much less extrapolated from the analysis of nonverbal behavior.

It was with such thoughts in mind that I decided to take this opportunity to summarize briefly seven aspects of human language that should be clearly understood by any psychologist who plans to embark on explanatory ventures in psycholinguistics. The ideas are familiar to most people working in the field, who could no doubt easily double or treble their number. Nevertheless, the seven I have in mind are, in my opinion, important enough to bear repeating and as yet their importance does not seem to have been generally recognized by other psychologists.

Without further apologies, therefore, let me begin my catalogue of preliminary admonitions to anyone contemplating language as a potential subject for his psychological ratiocinations.

A Point of View

It is probably safe to say that no two utterances are identical in their physical (acoustic and physiological) characteristics. Nevertheless, we regularly treat them as if they were. For example, we ask a subject to repeat something we say, and we count his response as correct even though it would be a simple matter to demonstrate that there were many physical differences between his vocal response and the vocal stimulus we presented to him. Obviously, not all physical aspects of speech are significant for vocal communication.

The situation is more complicated than that, however. There are also many examples—homophones being the most obvious—where stimuli that are physically identical can have different significance. Not only are physically different utterances treated identically, but physically identical utterances can be treated differently. It may often happen that the difference in significance between two utterances cannot be found in any difference of a physical nature, but can only be appreciated on the basis of psychological factors underlying the physical signal.

The problem of identifying significant features of speech is complicated further by the fact that some physical features are highly predictable in nearly all speakers, yet have no communicative significance. For example, when a plosive consonant occurs initially, as in the word *pen*, American speakers pronounce it with aspiration; a puff of air accompanies the *p* (which you can feel if you will pronounce *pen* holding the back of your hand close to your lips). When *p* occurs as a noninitial member of a consonant cluster, however, as in *spend*, this puff of air is reduced or absent. The same phoneme is aspirated in one position and unaspirated in the other. This physical feature, which is quite reliable in American speech, has no communicative significance, by which I mean that the rare person who does not conform is perfectly intelligible and suffers no handicap in communicating with his friends. Facts such as these, which are well known to linguists, pose interesting problems for psychologists who approach the acquisition of language in terms of laboratory experiments on discrimination learning.

In order to discuss even the simplest problems in speech production and speech perception, it is necessary to be able to distinguish significant from nonsignificant aspects of speech. And there is no simple way to draw this distinction in terms of the physical parameters of the speech signal itself. Almost immediately, therefore, we are forced to consider aspects of language that extend beyond the acoustic or physiological properties of speech, that is to say, beyond the objective properties of "the stimulus."

Since the concept of significance is central and unavoidable, it is important to notice that it has two very different senses, which for convenience, I shall call "reference" and "meaning."

For example, in most contexts we can substitute the phrase, "the first President of the United States" for "George Washington," since both of these utterances refer to the same historical figure. At least since Frege's time, however, it has been customary to assume that such phrases differ in meaning even though their referent is the same. Otherwise, there would be no point to such assertions of identity as "George Washington was the first President of the United States." If meaning and reference were identical, such an assertion would be as empty as "George Washington was George Washington." Since "George Washington was the first President of the United States" is not a pointless assertion, there must be some difference between the significance of the name "George Washington" and of the phrase "the first President of the United States," and, since this difference in significance is not a difference of referent, it must be a difference in something else—something else that, for want of a better name, we call its meaning.

This distinction between reference and meaning becomes particularly clear when we consider whole utterances. An utterance can be significant even though it might be extremely difficult to find anything it referred to in the sense that "table" refers to a four-legged, flat-topped piece of furniture, etc. Sentences are meaningful, but their meaning cannot be given by their referent, for they may have none.

Of course, one might argue that psycholinguists should confine their attention to the significance of isolated words and avoid the complexities of sentences altogether. Such an approach would be marvelously convenient if it would work, but it would work only if words were autonomous units that combined in a particularly simple way. If the meaning of a sentence could in some sense be regarded as the weighted sum of the meanings of the words that comprise it, then once we knew how to characterize the meanings of individual words, it would be a simple matter to determine the meaning of any combination of words. Unfortunately, however, language is not so simple; a Venetian blind is not the same as a blind Venetian.

Perhaps the most obvious thing we can say about the significance of a sentence is that it is not given as the linear sum of the significance of the words that comprise it. The pen in "fountain pen" and the pen in "play pen" are very different pens, even though they are phonologically and orthographically identical. The words in a sentence interact.

In isolation most words can have many different meanings; which meaning they take in a particular sentence will depend on the context in which they occur. That is to say, their meaning will depend both on the other words and on their grammatical role in the sentence. The meanings to be assigned to word combinations can be characterized in an orderly way, of course, but not by some simple rule for linear addition. What is required is an elaborate description of the various ways in which words can interact in combination.

As soon as we begin to look carefully at the relations among words in sentences, it becomes obvious that their interactions depend on the way they are grouped. For example, in sentences like, "They are hunting dogs," one meaning results if we group "are hunting" together as the verb, but another meaning results if we group "hunting dogs" together as a noun phrase. We cannot assign meanings to words in a sentence without knowing how the words are grouped, which implies that we must take into account the syntactic structure of the sentence.

Moreover, when we consider the psychology of the sentence, the problem of productivity becomes unavoidable. There is no limit to the number of different sentences that can be produced in English by combining words in various grammatical fashions, which means that it is impossible to describe English by simply listing all its grammatical sentences. This fairly obvious fact has several important implications. It means that the sentences of English must be described in terms of *rules* that can generate them.

For psychologists, the implications of this generative approach to language is that we must consider hypothetical constructs capable of combining verbal elements into grammatical sentences, and in order to account for our ability to deal with an unlimited variety of possible sentences, these hypothetical constructs must have the character of linguistic rules.

Language is the prime example of rule-governed behavior, and there are several types of rules to consider. Not only must we consider syntactic rules for generating and grouping words in sentences; we must also consider semantic rules for interpreting word combinations. Perhaps we may even need pragmatic rules to characterize our unlimited variety of belief systems. Only on the assumption that a language user knows a generative system of rules for producing and interpreting sentences can we hope to account for the unlimited combinatorial productivity of natural languages.

Rules are not laws, however. They can be broken, and in ordinary conversation they frequently are. Still, even when we break them, we usually are capable of recognizing (under appropriate conditions) that we have made a mistake; from this fact we infer that the rules are known implicitly, even though they cannot be stated explicitly.

A description of the rules we know when we know a language is different from a description of the psychological mechanisms involved in our use of those rules. It is important, therefore, to distinguish here, as elsewhere, between knowledge and performance; the psycholinguist's task is to propose and test performance models for a language user, but he must rely on the linguist to give him a precise specification of what it is a language user is trying to use.

Finally, it is important to remember that there is a large innate component to our language-using ability. Not just any self-consistent set of rules that we might be able to invent for communicative purposes could serve as a natural language. All human societies possess language, and all of these languages have features in common—features that are called "language universals," but are in fact prelinguistic in character. It is difficult to imagine how children could acquire language so rapidly from parents who understand it so poorly unless they were already tuned by evolution to select just those aspects that are universally significant. There is, in short, a large biological component that shapes our human languages.

These are the seven ideas I wished to call to your attention. Let me recapitulate them in order, this time attempting to say what I believe their implications to be for psycholinguistic research.

Some Implications for Research

1. Not all physical features of speech are significant for vocal communication, and not all significant features of speech have a physical representation. I take this to imply that the perception of speech involves grouping and interpreting its elements and so cannot be simply predicted from studies of our ability to discriminate among arbitrary acoustic stimuli. Such studies can be useful only in conjunction with linguistic information as to which distinctions are significant. Linguists seem generally agreed that the absolute physical characteristics of a particular phone are less important than the binary contrasts into which it enters in a given language. It is noteworthy that after many decades of acoustic phonetics, we are still uncertain as to how to specify all the physical dimensions of the significant features of speech, particularly those that depend on syntactic or semantic aspects of the utterance.

2. The meaning of an utterance should not be confused with its reference. I take this to imply that the acquisition of meaning cannot be identified with the simple acquisition of a conditioned vocalization in the presence of a particular environmental stimulus. It may be possible to talk about reference in terms of conditioning, but meaning is a much more complicated phenomenon that depends on the relations of a symbol to other symbols in the language.

3. The meaning of an utterance is not a linear sum of the meanings of the words that comprise it. I take this to imply that studies of the meanings of isolated words are of limited value, and that attempts to predict the meaning of word compounds by weighted averages of the meanings of their components—an analogy with the laws of color mixture—cannot be successful in general. In Gestalt terminology, the whole is greater than (or at least, different from) the sum of its parts.

4. The syntactic structure of a sentence imposes groupings that govern the interactions between the meanings of the words in that sentence. I take this to imply that sentences are hierarchically organized, and that simple theories phrased in terms of chaining successive responses cannot provide an adequate account of linguistic behavior. Exactly how concepts are combined to produce organized groupings of linguistic elements that can be uttered and understood is a central problem for psycholinguistics.

5. There is no limit to the number of sentences or the number of meanings that can be expressed. I take this to imply that our knowledge of a language must be described in terms of a system of semantic and syntactic rules adequate to generate the infinite number of admissible utterances. Since the variety of admissible word combinations is so great, no child could learn them all. Instead of learning specific combinations of words, he learns the *rules* for generating admissible combinations. If knowledge of these rules is to be described in our performance models as the language user's "habits," it is necessary to keep in mind that they are generative habits of a more hypothetical and less abstract nature than have generally been studied in animal learning experiments.

6. A description of a language and a description of a language user must be kept distinct. I take this to imply that psycholinguistics should try to formulate performance models that will incorporate, in addition to a generative knowledge of the rules, hypothetical information-storage and information-processing components that can simulate the actual behavior of language users. In general, limitations of short-term memory seem to impose the most severe constraints on our capacity to follow our own rules.

7. There is a large biological component to the human capacity for articulate speech. I take this to imply that attempts to teach other animals to speak a human language are doomed to failure. As Lenneberg has emphasized, the ability to acquire and use a human language does not depend on being intelligent or having a large brain. It depends on being human.

In science, at least half the battle is won when we start to ask the right questions. It is my belief that an understanding of these seven general propositions and their implications can help to guide us toward the right questions and might even forestall ill-considered forays into psycholinguistics by psychologists armed only with theories and techniques developed for the study of nonverbal behavior.

A Critique

I have now stated twice my seven preliminary admonitions. In order to make sure that I am being clear, I want to repeat it all once more, this time in the form of a critical analysis of the way many experimental psychologists write about language in the context of current learning theory.

For the purposes of exposition, I have chosen a sentence that is part of the introduction to the topic of language in a well-known and widely used textbook on the psychology of learning. After remarking that, "language seems to develop in the same way as other instrumental acts," the author says:

Certain combinations of words and intonations of voice are strengthened through reward and are gradually made to occur in appropriate situations by the process of discrimination learning.

This, I believe, is fairly representative of what can be found in many other texts. I have chosen it, not because I bear any malice toward the author, but simply because I think that all seven of my admonitions are ignored in only 27 words. Let me spell them out one by one.

First, since infants are not born with a preconception of what words are, they could hardly be expected to begin acquiring language by uttering combinations of words. Perhaps the author was not thinking of infants when he wrote this sentence. If he had been, he would probably have written instead that, "Certain combinations of *sounds* and intonations of voice are strengthened through reward and made to occur by the process of discrimination learning." In either case, however, he ignores my first admonition that not all physical features of speech are significant and not all signicant features are physical.

A child does not begin with sounds or words and learn to combine them. Rather, he begins by learning which features are significant, and progressively differentiates his utterances as he learns. It is conceivable, though not necessary, that he might acquire those significant distinctions that have some physical basis "by the process of discrimination learning," but it would require an extensive revision of what we ordinarily mean by discrimination learning in order to explain how he acquires significant distinctions that are not represented in the physical signal, or why he acquires those features (such as aspiration only on initial plosives) that are not significant and are not systematically rewarded or extinguished.

Second, as I have already admitted (too generously, perhaps), it is possible to argue that a referential relation might be established between a visual input and a vocalization "by the process of discrimination learning." I deny, however, that it is reasonable to speak of acquiring meaning in this way.

Exactly what should be included in the meaning of a word is open to debate, but any interpretation will have to say something about the relation of this word's meaning to the meanings of other words and to the contexts in which it occurs—and these are complicated, systemic interrelations requiring a great deal more cognitive machinery than is necessary for simple discrimination. Since the author says specifically that *words* are acquired by discrimination learning, and since words have meaning as well as reference, I can only assume that he has ignored my admonition not to confuse reference and meaning. Perhaps a more accurate interpretation, suggested by the phrase "occur in appropriate situations," would be that he has not really confused reference and meaning, but has simply ignored meaning entirely. In either case, however, it will not do as a basis for psycholinguistics.

There is unfortunate ambiguity in the phrase, "Certain combinations of words and intonations of voice." I am not sure whether the author meant that each word was learned with several intonations, or that we learn several intonations for word combinations, or that we learn both to combine words and to modulate the pitch of our voice. Consequently, I have been forced to cheat on you by examining the context. What I found was no help, however, because all the formal propositions referred simply to "words," whereas all the examples that were cited involved combinations of words.

Perhaps I am being unfair, but I think that this author, at least when he is writing on learning theory, is not deeply concerned about the difference between words and sentences. If this distinction, which seems crucial to me, is really of no importance to him, then he must be ignoring my third admonition that the meaning of words are affected by the sentences in which they occur.

My fourth admonition—that the syntactic structure of a sentence imposes groupings that govern the interactions between the meanings of its words—is also ignored. No matter how I interpret the ambiguous phrase about, "Certain combinations of words and intonations of voice," it must be wrong. If I read it one way, he has ignored the problem of syntax entirely and is concerned only with the conditioning of isolated word responses.

Or, if I put a more generous interpretation on it and assume he meant that combinations of words are strengthened and made to occur by discrimination learning, then he seems to be saying that every word and every acceptable combination of words is learned separately.

By a rough, but conservative calculation, there are at least 10^{20} sentences 20 words long, and if a child were to learn only these it would take him something on the order of 1,000 times the estimated age of the earth just to listen to them. Perhaps this is what the word "gradually" means? In this interpretation he has clearly violated my fifth admonition, that there is no limit to the number of sentences to be learned, and so has wandered perilously close to absurdity. Any attempt to account for language acquisition that does not have a generative character will encounter this difficulty.

Sixth, from the reference to responses being "strengthened" I infer that each word-object connection is to be characterized by an intervening variable, along the lines of habit strength in Hull's system. This is a rather simple model, too simple to serve as a performance model for a language user, but it is all our author has to offer. As for keeping his performance model distinct from his competence model, as I advise in my sixth admonition, he will have none of it. He says—and here I resort to the context once more—that language "is a complex set of responses [*and*] also a set of stimuli." It may be defensible to talk about speech as a set of responses and stimuli, but what a language user knows about his language cannot be described in these performance terms.

A language includes all the denumerable infinitude of grammatical sentences, only a tiny sample of which ever have or ever will occur as actual responses or stimuli. The author would blush crimson if we caught him confusing the notions of sample and population in his statistical work, yet an analogous distinction between speech and language is completely overlooked.

Finally, we need to make the point that the kind of reinforcement schedule a child is on when he learns language is very different from what we have used in experiments on discrimination learning. No one needs to monitor a child's vocal output continually and to administer "good" and "bad" as rewards and punishments. When a child says something intelligible, his reward is both improbable and indirect. In short, a child learns language by using it, not by a precise schedule of rewards for grammatical vocalizations "in appropriate situations." An experimenter who used such casual and unreliable procedures in a discrimination experiment would teach an animal nothing at all.

The child's exposure to language should not be called "teaching." He learns the language, but no one, least of all an average mother, knows how to teach it to him. He learns the language because he is shaped by nature to pay attention to it, to notice and remember and use significant aspects of it. In suggesting that language can be taught "by the process of discrimination learning," therefore, our author has ignored my final admonition to remember the large innate capacity humans have for acquiring articulate speech.

In summary, if this sentence is taken to be a description of the fundamental processes involved in language acquisition, it is both incomplete and misleading. At best, we might regard it as a hypothesis about the acquisition of certain clichés or expressive embellishments. But as a hypothesis from which to derive an account of the most obvious and most characteristic properties of human language, it is totally inadequate.

This completes the third and final run through my list of preliminaries to psycholinguistics. If I sounded a bit too contentious, I am sorry, but I did not want to leave any doubt as to why I am saying these things or what their practical implications for psycholinguistic research might be.

My real interest, however, is not in deploring this waste of our intellectual resources, but in the positive program that is possible if we are willing to accept a more realistic conception of what language is.

If we accept a realistic statement of the problem, I believe we will also be forced to accept a more cognitive approach to it: to talk about hypothesis testing instead of discrimination learning, about the evaluation of hypotheses instead of the reinforcement of responses, about rules instead of habits, about productivity instead of generalization, about innate and universal human capacities instead of special methods of teaching vocal responses, about symbols instead of conditioned stimuli, about sentences instead of words or vocal noises, about linguistic structure instead of chains of responses—in short, about language instead of learning theory.

The task of devising a cognitive production model for language users is difficult enough without wearing blinders that prevent us from seeing what the task really is. If the hypothetical constructs that are needed seem too complex and arbitrary, too improbable and mentalistic, then you had better forgo the study of language. For language is just that—complex, arbitrary, improbable, mentalistic—and no amount of wishful theorizing will make it anything else.

In a word, what I am trying to say, what all my preliminary admonitions boil down to, is simply this: Language is exceedingly complicated. Forgive me for taking so long to say such a simple and obvious thing.

3

Psycholinguistic Universals in the Reading Process

——KENNETH S. GOODMAN

One of the most controversial issues in contemporary linguistics concerns the extent to which all the languages of the world share common features, called "universals", whose occurrence cannot be accounted for by either logical necessity or cross-cultural borrowing. A basic universal, for example, would appear to be that every human society has a spoken language, although other forms of language communication can and do exist. All the "natural languages" that the world's populations speak show the twin aspects of deep and surface structure, although this again is not a logical necessity since computer languages and those of formal logic and mathematics function with one level only. All the world's natural languages seem to limit their range of significantly different sounds (called phonemes) to between about thirty and fifty, although there is no logical or physiological reason why a language should not have as few as two sounds, like Morse code or the binary language of computers, or many hundreds. The orderly manner in which children acquire language (Chapter 12) is sometimes regarded as a linguistic universal.

There is more than a theoretical interest attached to the matter of universals because it would seem a reasonable assumption that any universal in human behavior must reflect something fundamental about the way in which the human organism, and particularly the brain, is constructed. Goodman surmises that all written languages, whatever their visual characteristics, have both deep and surface structure, and that reading always involves sampling from the physical representation in order to confirm or disconfirm predictions about meaning. As Goodman's abstract puts it: "Literate speakers in any language have two *alternative surface language forms which are realizations of the same deep structure and which represent alternate encodings of the same meaning. For the proficient reader, written language becomes parallel to speech and not a secondary representation of it. Listening and reading are processes in which the language user may sample, select, and predict from the available signal. The essential characteristics of the reading process are universal."*

The notion that visual information (Goodman's "graphic signal") is sampled rather than exhaustively analyzed suggests the mechanism by which comprehension can be achieved without prior word identification. The meaning that the reader will eventually derive originates in his head rather than on the page, and he utilizes only as much visual information as he requires to confirm a correct prediction.

Goodman's paper is written compactly and he makes one statement that requires some elaboration, or at least debate. His remark that printed English must be scanned from left to right holds for only the slowest reading. More fluent readers can examine several lines with a single fixation, a feat far more common in our everyday reading than usually believed, while readers in the "speed reading" class of 1000 words a minute or more often read down *the left-hand page and* up *the right. A reader plodding through the text on a word-by-word basis obviously is constrained to a limping left-right progression, but such a course is a handicap rather than a help to fluent reading.*

Kenneth Goodman is a professor of education at Wayne State University, Detroit, where he is director of the Reading Miscue Center. This chapter is extracted from the paper with the same title published originally in the Journal of Typographic Research, *1970, 4, 103–110, and reprinted with the permission of the author and publishers.*

Reading is a psycholinguistic process by which the reader (a language user) reconstructs, as best he can, a message which has been encoded by a writer as a graphic display.

Through research on children reading English who are native speakers of some dialect of American English, I have evolved a basic theoretical view of the reading process. It should be understood that some of what follows is an extension of and projection of a theoretical view into dimensions that go beyond the research on which it is based. In this sense, what follows is hypothetical; other scholars are invited to test and challenge the hypotheses in terms of languages and orthographies other than English.

Generative and Receptive Aspects of Language

It is ironic that although most researchers agree that receptive control of aspects of language precedes generative control, more attention has been given to the process of language production than to the process by which language is understood.

Many linguists have assumed that listening and reading are simply the mirror images of speaking and writing. They have assumed that since generative processes begin with meaning and result in a fully formed phonological or graphic display that receptive processes begin with the encoded display and reverse the process, step by step, to get back to meaning.

In this too simple view, not enough consideration has been given to the variant nature of the productive and receptive tasks that are involved in language use. *In producing language*, the language user has thoughts which he wishes to express. In a transformational view, he creates a deep language structure which represents his meaning, applies a set of compulsory and optional transformational rules, and generates a surface structure. If the language user is literate, this surface structure may utilize a phonological signal and require the application of a set of phonological rules, or it may utilize a graphic signal and require use of a set of orthographic rules. The choice will be dictated, of course, by the language user's purpose.

The *receptive* process does start with the phonological or graphic display as input, and it does end with meaning as output, but the efficient language user takes the most direct route and touches the fewest bases necessary to get to his goal. He accomplishes this by *sampling*, relying on the redundancy of language, and his knowledge of linguistic constraints. He *predicts* structures, *tests* them against the semantic context which he builds up from the situation and the on-going discourse, and then *confirms* or disconfirms as he processes further language.

Receptive language processes are cycles of *sampling, predicting, testing,* and *confirming*. The language user relies on strategies which yield the most reliable prediction with the minimum use of the information available.

Neither listening nor reading is a precise process and, in fact, even what the language user perceives is only partly what he sees or hears and partly what he expects to see or hear. This is necessarily so not only because of the prediction in which the language user engages but also because he has learned to organize his perceptions according to what is and is not significant in the language. The language user must not simply know what to pay attention to but what not to pay attention to.

The producer of language will be most successful if the signal he produces is complete and well-formed. With such a signal, the receiver of language is free to utilize his sampling strategies.

The necessary concern for oral language which had been neglected for so long caused many scholars to dismiss written language—without adequate consideration—as a secondary representation of oral language. But written language in a literate culture is not simply a way of preserving and recording oral language. It designates streets, places, and directions; it labels and classifies. It makes communication possible over time and space. A key difference between oral and written language is that speech is most commonly encountered within the situations in which it is most relevant. Speakers may rely on the situational context to make referents explicit. Listeners may infer from the situational context and from the movements, actions, and gestures of speakers a great deal of semantic information to augment and constrain what they derive from the language.

Written language tends to be out of situational context. The writer must make referents and antecedents explicit, he must create contexts through the language to replace those which are not present. He must furthermore address himself to an unseen and frequently unknown audience. He gets no immediate linguistic or visual feedback to cue him as to whether his communicative efforts are successful.

Written language is perfectable in that the writer may edit it to be sure he has said exactly what he wished to say. It isn't perishable in the sense that oral language is.

These differences should not obscure the basic similarities between the alternate language forms for literate language users, but they should make clear that reading and listening will employ variant psycholinguistic strategies to cope with the variant characteristics of the two forms. Reading employs a strategy of regression to reread, for example, whereas listening cannot employ a comparable strategy. The listener must ask the speaker to repeat and that is not always feasible.

One misconception which has caused considerable confusion in dealing with the reading process is the notion that meaning may be derived only from oral language. It is assumed by some that readers engage in a process of recoding graphic input as aural input and then decoding. While this may, in fact, take place in beginning stages of the acquisition of literacy among some learners, it is not necessary or characteristic of proficient reading. An analogy can be found in the early stages of learning a second language. The learner may be going through a process of continuous translation into his first language before he decodes. But eventually he must be able to derive meaning directly from the second language with no recourse to the first. Just so, the proficient reader becomes as skillful at deriving meaning from written language as he is from the aural form with no need to translate one to the other.

It must be remembered that oral language is no less an arbitrary code than written language. Neither has any direct relationship to meaning and the real world other than that which its users assign it.

Alphabetic writing systems have a number of virtues among which is that there is a built-in correspondence to the units and sequences of the oral language form. But this is not an unmitigated blessing. A writing system which is directly related to ideas and concepts has the virtue that it can be used for communication by speakers of different languages. The system of mathematical notation has that advantage. $6 + 9 = 15$ is a mathematical statement that will be immediately understood by speakers of a wide range of languages, whereas *six and nine equal fifteen* can only be understood if the reader knows English.

The Chinese writing system may indeed have its faults but it has the virtue of being understood by speakers of oral languages which are not mutually comprehensible. And, of course, the Chinese writing system— once it is mastered—does function quite well for its users. Alphabetic writing systems are not in fact necessary for literacy.

The Reading Process

The readers of English I have studied utilize three cue systems simultaneously. The starting point is graphic in reading and we may call one cue system *graphophonic*. The reader responds to graphic sequences and may utilize the correspondences between the graphic and phonological systems of his English dialect. I should point out that these are not phoneme-grapheme correspondences but in fact operate on morphophonemic levels (that is spelling patterns relate to sound sequences).

In English as in other languages the spelling system is fixed and standardized. This means that correspondences will vary from dialect to dialect and that over time changing phonology will loosen the fit of even the tightest alphabetic system.

The second cue system the reader uses is *syntactic*. The reader using pattern markers such as function words and inflectional suffixes as cues recognizes and predicts structures. Since the underlying or deep structure of written and oral language are the same, the reader seeks to infer the deep structure as he reads so that he may arrive at meaning.

The third cue system is *semantic*. In order to derive meaning from language, the language user must be able to provide semantic input. This is not simply a question of meaning for words but the much larger question of the reader having sufficient experience and conceptual background to feed into the reading process so that he can make sense out of what he's reading. All readers are illiterate in some senses, since no one can read everything written in his native language.

These cue systems are used simultaneously and interdependently. What constitutes useful graphic information depends on how much syntactic and semantic information is available. Within high contextual constraints an initial consonant may be all that is needed to identify an element and make possible the prediction of an ensuing sequence or the confirmation of prior predictions.

Proficient readers make generally successful predictions, but they are also able to recover when they produce miscues which change the meaning *in unacceptable ways.*

No readers read material they have not read before without errors. It must be understood that in the reading process accurate use of all cues available would not only be slow and inefficient but would actually lead the reader away from his primary goal which is comprehension. In fact in my research I have encountered many youngsters who are so busy matching letters to sounds and naming word shapes that they have no sense of the meaning of what they are reading. Reading requires not so much skills as strategies that make is possible to select the most productive cues.

These strategies will vary with the nature of the reading tasks. For example, literature has different characteristics than discursive language. The writer will use unusual terms and phrases rather than the more trite but also more predictable ones which would be used to express the same meaning in everyday conversation. The reader needs strategies that adjust to the very different constraints in literary materials.

Because reading involves visual input, characteristics of the visual system do affect the reading process. The material must be scanned from left to right, as English is printed, and the eye must focus at specific points since it cannot provide input while it is in motion. At each fixation a very small circle of print is in clear, sharp focus. Some have argued that only print in sharp focus can be used in reading. But there is a large area of print in the peripheral field at each point of fixation which is not seen clearly but is sufficiently seen to be usable in the sampling, predicting, confirming aspects of reading. The reader can, in fact, work with partial, blurred, even mutilated, graphic input to a considerable degree.

That, too briefly, is what my research has told me about the process of reading English among native American speakers. I have no reason to believe that this process would vary except in minor degrees in the reading of any language. Whether the graphic sequence is from left to right, right to left, or top to bottom would be of little consequence to the basic reading process. The reader needs to scan appropriately but he will still sample and predict in much the same way.

With alphabetical orthographies the regularity of correspondence rules for letter-sound relationships is not nearly as important as many people have believed. Readers are able to use syntactic and semantic cues to such a considerable extent that they need only minimal graphic cues in many cases. They can tolerate a great deal of irregularity, ambiguity, and variability in orthographies without the reading process suffering. There is, in fact, a wide range in which an alphabetic orthography may exist and still be viable. Only minor adjustments in the reading process are required to deal with any unusual correspondence features.

An example in reading English is the variability of vowel representation. This is particularly confused since the unstressed vowel schwa may be spelled by any vowel letter. Readers learn to rely more heavily on consonants, particularly initial ones, for their minimum cues and to use vowel letters only when other information is inadequate.

I confess to know nothing about problems of reading nonalphabetic writing systems, but I strongly believe that readers of languages which employ them will still be sampling using minimal graphic cues to predict grammatical structures.

Grammatical patterns and rules operate differently in each language, but readers will need to use their grammatical competence in much the same way. Some special reading strategies may result from particular characteristics of the grammatical system. Inflections are relatively unimportant in English grammar but positions in patterns are quite important. In a highly inflected language the reader would find it profitable to make use of inflectional cues. In English such cues are not terribly useful.

Semantic aspects of the reading process cannot vary to any extent from one language to another, since the key question is how much background the reader brings to the specific reading.

To sum up, it would seem that the reading process will be much the same for all languages with minor variations to accommodate the specific characteristics of the orthography used and the grammatical structure of the language.

4

Three Stages
of Reading*

——PAUL A. KOLERS

Paul Kolers has made a number of important studies in the areas of pattern recognition and bilingualism, two topics that may at first glance appear somewhat remote from the major concerns of this book. But as the present chapter will show, the range of Kolers' work permits him to speak with insight and authority on reading. In particular he demonstrates the limitations on the rate at which visual information can be utilized in reading, and the compensatory extent to which nonvisual information—the syntactic and semantic systems to which Goodman referred in the previous chapter—can be employed.

Kolers raises a question that causes a good deal of concern to many teachers, namely the tendency of beginning readers especially to confuse word pairs like was *and* saw, chum *and* much, *just as they confuse letters such as* p, b *and* d. *A common instructional strategy is to introduce intensive drill on these letters or words in isolation, the teacher not realizing that the task is being presented in the most difficult manner possible. As Kolers observes, even fluent readers make mistakes of seriation if letters are presented piecemeal.*

In normal reading, the words was *and* saw *will rarely be confused for the simple reason that only one of them will make sense in most con-*

* This work was supported principally by the National Institutes of Health (Grant 1 PO1–GM–14940–01) and in part by the Joint Services Electronics Program (Contract DA 28–043–AMC–02536 [E]), at the Research Laboratory of Electronics, Massachusetts Institute of Technology. I thank Mrs. Kathryn Rosenthal, who collected and scored many of the data.

texts. Both words could be completely obliterated from most texts with a minimal effect on intelligibility. Similarly, no reader who is reading for meaning will mistake dog *for* bog, *or* pig *for* dig, *because the dissimilarity in meaning is far more important than the visual similarity. Reading teachers confronted by children who make "reversals" might well consider minimizing the difficulty by presenting troublesome words in meaningful contexts.*

Paul Kolers is a professor of psychology at the University of Toronto. "Three Stages of Reading" is taken from Chapter 7 of Basic Studies on Reading, *edited by Harry Levin and Joanna P. Williams, © 1970 by Basic Books, Inc., Publishers, New York, and is reprinted by permission of the author, editors, and publishers.*

If anything is true of reading, it is that it is one of our most complex forms of information processing. This assertion is so obvious that it should not need proving. Merely consider the difference between a reader's picking up a page written in a language foreign to him and a page in a language he knows. The page in a foreign language is a visual design, a set of abstract shapes laid out on a surface. It has texture, organization, contour; a person may even, as with an ink-blot plate, see figures in the array. Yet, almost none of these visual properties is perceived when the page is written in a known language and held at reading distance. Then, one sees words, meanings, messages, and it is only when the page is held in a way that makes it illegible (too distant or parallel to the plane of the visual axis) that its pictorial aspects are seen.

Despite the obvious complexity of the reading process, the greater number of investigators have sought relatively simple, strictly causal explanations of it. By strictly causal, I mean such simplistic theses as reading is principally the activating of conditioned meanings, reading is principally a matter of discriminating the geometry of letters, and reading is a matter of translating graphemes into sounds. There have been few efforts since Huey's masterpiece in 1908 to deal with the whole phenomenon, to account for the variety of events that go into reading. The late J. Robert Oppenheimer (1956) once remarked that a characteristic of a developing area in science is the discovery that the units of analysis employed are too small. Surely this observation is appropriate to the study of reading, indeed, to the study of psychology generally. Without claiming that the "real units" for the study of reading have been captured, this chapter describes three different levels, or stages, of competence in the skilled reader that are revealed by the material he is working on and the task set him.

The experiments described were performed with temporal and geometrical transformations of text. In some cases, the subjects named letters, and in others, they read text. The description of the data is designed to illuminate three levels of performance and some of the differences between them: (1) perception of characters, or visual operations, (2) perception of syntax, or sensitivity to grammar, and (3) direct perception of the meanings of words. The description is relevant to a general model of the reader.

. Visual Operations

Naming Sequences of Letters

In one experiment (Kolers and Katzman, 1966), words were presented one letter at a time so that every letter appeared on the same part of the viewing screen as every other. The experiment was restricted to sequences six letters long, and three kinds of six-letter words were used. One type of sequence, an "ambiguous" group, can be seen as one six-letter word or as two three-letter words, for example, *cotton, carrot;* another group was formed from six-letter words whose first three letters or last three make a word, for example, *single, before*, or which cannot be divided into three-letter words, for example, *dollar, knight;* and a third group came from pairs of unrelated three-letter words, for example, *six, row*. We made the stimuli this way because we were interested in the effect on their perception of interposing a blank interval of time between the third and fourth letters. The results of many psychophysical experiments suggest that whether a presentation is perceived as one word or two should vary markedly with the length of that interval.

When we varied the amount of time for which the letters were presented and also the interval between the third and fourth letters, we found that blank intervals that lasted as long as 22 per cent of the time taken to present six letters did not greatly affect whether one word or two was seen. When six letters were presented serially for 250 milliseconds each, for example, virtually identical results on perception were obtained from a pause between the third and fourth letters of 83 milliseconds as from a pause of 250 milliseconds. Clearly, sequences of letters are grouped by the nervous system in a way different from that in which sequences of simple geometric forms are grouped. The psychophysics of item perception cannot be generalized uncritically to the psychophysics of word perception.

We found also in this experiment that the likelihood that all six letters would be identified correctly increased as the duration of the individual letters was increased; but even at 250 milliseconds each, all the letters were not identified perfectly. Thus, serially presented letters must appear for something more than one-quarter of a second each (actually, between one-quarter and one-third of a second) in order for correct identification to occur. If normal reading proceeded by a serial scan on a letter-by-letter basis, its maximum rate would be between three and four letters per second, or, because English words average about five to six letters in length, between thirty and forty-two words per minute. Because college students read on the average at a rate of 300 words per minute, it must be clear that they do not proceed in such a serial way. One other comparison bears on this assertion.

When the letters were presented for 125 milliseconds each and the subjects were required to name the letters or to name the word they spell, subjects did better naming words than letters. But when the letters were presented for 250 milliseconds each, the reverse was true. That is to say, when the letters came very quickly, subjects could make out words better than they could letters; but when the sequences were slower, subjects could identify all the letters in a sequence better than they could the word it spelled. Sometimes one can make out a word when its letters are individually unidentifiable, and sometimes one can identify letters better than words, even though the sequences presented are identical in the two cases. It follows, then, that the recognition of words has only a limited dependence on the recognition or "discriminability" of the individual letters.

Seriation

When letters were presented at shorter durations—say 125 milliseconds each or less—the subjects would sometimes report all the letters correctly, but in the wrong order. For example, if we represent the sequence as *a-b-c-d-e-f*, the subjects would sometimes report *b-a-c-d-f-e* and other distortions. What is particularly interesting about these disorders of seriation is that they never occurred at longer letter durations, even though subjects sometimes failed to identify letters correctly under those conditions. These results identify two distinguishable processes in the perception of sequence: item identification and item order. Initially puzzling is the fact that order errors ceased to be made as duration of the letters was increased, but identification errors continued to be made. How can the subject identify a sequence of items correctly until he has first identified the items themselves? Kolers and Katzman (1966) suggested that the two kinds of identification occurred in parallel and that each required a different amount of time to be completed. But this suggestion has certain difficulties about it, and I should like to propose an alternative explanation.

This alternative supposes that there are two aspects to the correct identification of items: an initial schematization and a subsequent impletion, or filling-in. The schematization provides only a general framework, a rough sketch, as it were, of what the visual system must construct in order to represent what has been presented. The actual work of filling in details is done later. The mechanism concerned with ordering the array works on the results of the schematization. Thus the perception of serial displays has three stages: *scanning*, to form a schema; *ordering* of the schematic elements; and *impleting* or filling in of the schematized but ordered items. This analysis implies that the identification errors that continue to occur when there are no further ordering errors are errors of the impletion stage rather than the scanning or schematization stage. Note that both the initial suggestion and this alternative explanation assume a mechanism in the visual system that is concerned specifically with ordering items. The data of Kolers and Katzman, furthermore, limit the conditions in which this mechanism will produce distortions to rates of presentation of five items or more per second, but under certain conditions (for example, when the items are of unequal duration), slower rates may also produce the effect.

Disorders of seriation are characteristic of certain kinds of reading disability wherein some words, usually short ones, are anagramatized. For example, *was* may be read as *saw*, *much* may be read as *chum*, and so on (Money, 1962). It may be the case that errors of this kind are owing to the combination of a momentarily improper fixation on the end of a word and a slow regressive eye motion, or alternatively, a leftward scan of an internalized image. However, it may also be the case, and this is worth testing, that readers who frequently make errors of this kind perform equally poorly in other tasks involving seriation. It is a reasonable conjecture that there is a specific mechanism of the nervous system concerned with the ordering of inputs and that this mechanism is defective in such people.

Naming Transformed Letters

In other experiments, I studied the ability of skilled readers to name letters that had been transformed geometrically. Eight examples of geometrically transformed material are illustrated in Figure 1, in which connected discourse rather than arrays of letters is presented. The top four pairs of rows in the figure illustrate text subjected to simple rotations in three-dimensional space: normal text (N), rotation in the plane of the page (R), mirror reflection (M), and inversion (I). The bottom four pairs repeat the top four with the additional transformation that every letter has been rotated on a vertical axis through itself, making rN, rR, rM, and rI. In one experiment, a single page of connected discourse was transformed by a computer into two kinds of arrangements, called "Letters" and "Pseudowords." In Letters, the relative frequency of the letters on the original page was preserved, but their order was scrambled. In addition, every letter was followed by a space, for example, *e r t s v a j l* and so forth. Pseudowords, too, preserved the relative frequency of the letters and also kept the lengths of the words of the original page, for example, *buoss*

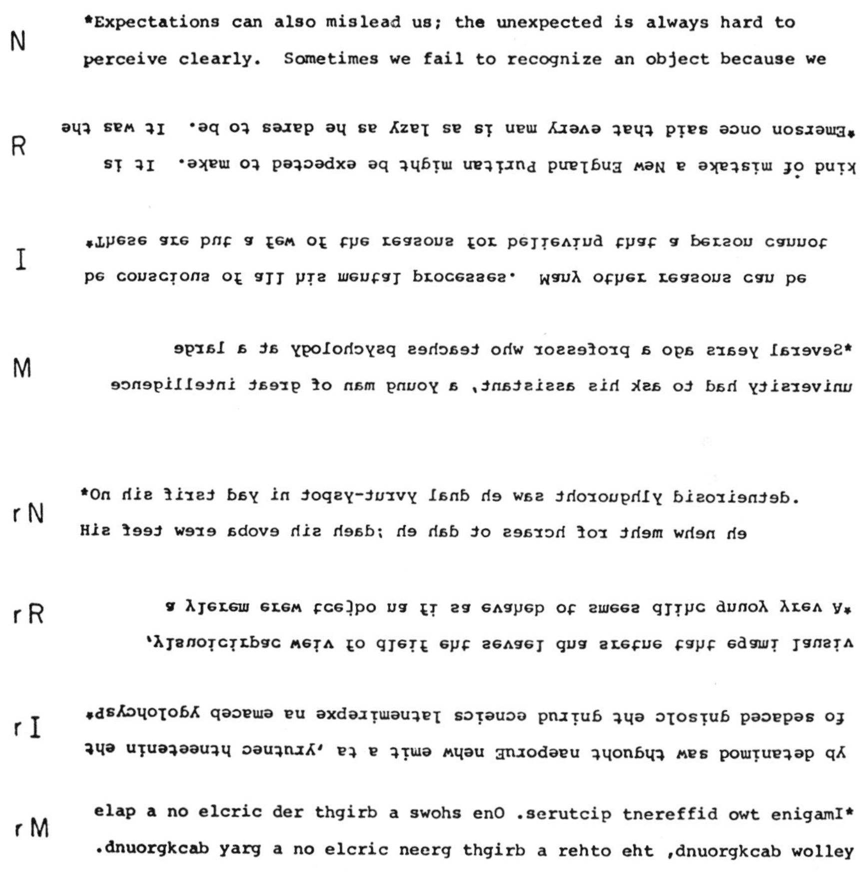

N *Expectations can also mislead us; the unexpected is always hard to
perceive clearly. Sometimes we fail to recognize an object because we

R *Emerson once said that every man is as lazy as he dares to be. It was the
kind of mistake a New England Puritan might be expected to make. It is

I *There are but a few of the reasons for believing that a person cannot
be conscious of all his mental processes. Many other reasons can be

M *Several years ago a professor who teaches psychology at a large
university had to ask his assistant, a young man of great intelligence

rN *On his first day in Psych-Intro Paul he was thoroughly disoriented.
His feet were above his head; he had of keep for that when he

rR *A merely view telco an it as evaded of smees glttic quoy very y
visual image that leaves and learned that each lamp casual

rI *to sedaes gnitud ecnetal sotenuc purng the otosunc ygolohcysp*
the nineteenth century, a ta a time when thorough was meticulously

rM *Imagine two different pictures. One shows a bright red circle on a pale
yellow background, the other a bright green circle on a gray background.

Figure 1   Examples of geometrically transformed text. The upper
four pairs of lines are rotations in three-dimensional space; the lower four add
the transformation of letter reversal to the upper four. The asterisk shows where
to begin reading each pair.

ra mgerf csltpekr and so on. With both kinds of materials, subjects named
the letters of the geometrically transformed sequences aloud as rapidly as
they could. There were 832 letters on each page of Letters and about 1,170
letters on each page of Pseudowords. In both cases the amount of time
taken was measured after the last letter on the first line had been named.
Intuition would suggest that the different transformations require different
amounts of time for their recognition; and intuition is correct, as the data
of Table 1 show. The transformations are arranged as four pairs of geometrically identical characters. The upper member of each pair was named
from left to right and the lower member from right to left. Data are shown

Table 1 Geometric Mean Times To Name Letters (Minutes)

Transformation	Letters	Pseudowords (800 LETTERS)	Pseudowords (FULL PAGE)
N	4.61	4.49	6.42
rM	5.64	6.13	9.11
rN	6.94	7.76	11.49
M	7.15	7.84	11.07
rI	7.14	8.23	12.03
R	6.69	7.48	10.56
I	7.90	8.57	12.54
rR	8.50	9.32	14.27

for the 800 letters measured on each page of Letters, for an equivalent 800 letters of Pseudowords, and for full pages of Pseudowords minus the first line. Note that, although individual letters within a pair of transformations are identical, the time taken to name them varies with the direction of scan. Thus, it is not the geometry or discriminability of the letters alone that affects their recognition. The times, however, are not the main concern here; the patterning of errors is.

The subjects made many errors when they named geometrically transformed letters. Table 2 shows the percentage of occurrence of those letters on which the greatest number of errors was made and the percentage of errors. The thirteen letters illustrated comprised 52 per cent of the total number presented in Letters and 51 per cent in Pseudowords, yet more than 90 per cent of the errors were made on these letters in the two conditions. The errors themselves, of course, are not distributed haphazardly, nor are they distributed proportionately to their frequency of occurrence in the text. For example, *b* appeared 2.5 per cent of the time in Letters, but on 31 per cent of the occasions it appeared it was misidentified. Conversely,

Table 2 Distribution of Letters in Text and of Errors (Per Cent)

	Printed Letters													
SOURCE	A	B	C	D	F	G	I	N	P	Q	S	T	U	FREQUENCY
Letters														
distribution	7	2.5	2	3	2	2	7	6	2	0.1	6	8	3	2944/5600 = 52%
errors	6	31	0	29	3	18	3	18	35	67	4	10	8	2337/2506 = 93%
Pseudowords														
distribution	7	2	2	3	2	2	7	6	2	0.1	6	8	3	4154/8190 = 51%
errors	9	46	1	42	3	12	2	9	38	56	4	3	8	3641/3894 = 94%

f appeared 2 per cent of the time, but was misidentified on only 3 per cent of its appearances. Clearly, then, frequency of occurrence and the associated opportunities for error thus provided are not the basis of making errors with the letters. It is the ambiguity of their appearance that establishes the likelihood of error. This is brought out in Figure 2. The figure shows the proportion of times something else was said in place of the letters that were printed. The upper half of the figure is for Letters, the lower half for Pseudowords; the left half for transformations R, M, and I, and the right half for the transformations involving letter reversal (r). Very few errors were made on normally oriented letters. Some were made with transformation rM, which is geometrically identical to N in Pseudowords but not in Letters.

Examining Figure 2 will reveal systematic patterns of substitution in the errors. When a subject makes an error, he does so by sampling from a small set of alternatives rather than by choosing an alternative haphazardly. Thus, *p-d-b-q* form one subset, *n-u* another, *t-f* a third, and so on. Although *bee-dee-pee* sound alike, *you-en, ay-ess,* and *tee-ef* do not; furthermore,

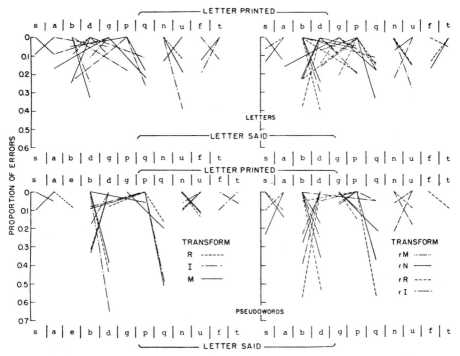

Figure 2 Maps of letter substitutions. The lines of the figure show the proportion of times another letter was said for what was printed in the two experiments, Letters and Pseudowords. The letters illustrated are examples of the type face used in the experiments.

tee sounds more like *bee-dee-pee* than it does like *ef*, but was never called *bee, dee,* or *pee*. The errors made, therefore, are based on visual appearance, not on sound similarity. For example, an inverted *p* looks like a *b* and is often called *bee*, an inverted *t* looks like an *f* with a short leg and is called *ef*, and so on.

The hypothesis to explain these results is rather complicated; it involves the subject's supposition about orientation and the existence in his mind of orientation-related reference letters. I will not go into its details now except to say that in general the data indicate that a judgment of the orientation of the letters is a precondition for their correct identification and that this judgment, an integral part of the recognition process, lapses from time to time. This assertion follows from the consideration that though all the letters of a single page appear in the same orientation, the subject sometimes calls a given letter *you*, and sometimes he calls an identical letter on the same page *en*. This kind of error clearly involves a momentary change in the subject's sense of the orientation of the material he is looking it. A close analysis of the data of Figure 2 suggests that there is an order of power in the maintenance of orientation: our subjects found it easier to maintain the sense of up-down orientation than left-right orientation. Another way to say this is that the disorders of orientation, such as those sometimes attributed to dyslexics, are not all of a piece. Left-right orientations are perceptually more labile than up-down orientations. This difference in their lability—for example, the ease with which *b* and *d* can be confused compared with the lesser confusability of *b-p* or *t-f*—suggests that the visual system may have several different mechanisms for maintaining the sense of orientation of objects.[1]

In summary, we may say that when subjects err while naming geometrically transformed letters they tend to name a letter in terms of another untransformed one (for example, an inverted *b* is called *p* or *q*) and that the patterning of these errors reveals the prior judgment of orientation of the material. Further, this judgment of orientation is not made just once for the whole transformed page, but is a continuing aspect of letter identification, which lapses from time to time.

Position Errors

It is well known that familiar words are perceived as wholes rather than piecemeal by the skilled reader. Indeed, as was shown above, if he perceived them piecemeal, he would be unable to read as fast as he does. It is well known also that in this perception, the various parts of words— beginning, middle, end—do not contribute equally to the identification.

---

[1] The subjects were tested on two days. The results reported here are for the first day only. More detailed analysis and exposition of the hypothesis suggested can be found in Kolers and Perkins (1969).

Generally, the beginning of a word conveys more information than later parts, largely, it is thought, because of the constraints built into the language. We were curious to learn whether this lesser sensitivity to the internal structure of a word than to its beginning represents some inherent difficulty in the visual system's ability to process a dense array or whether it is truly a linguistic effect. One way to examine the question is to find whether certain parts of Pseudowords are misidentified more often than other parts. If the selective sensitivity to parts of words is owing to the action of cognitive or linguistic variables, there should be no clustering of identification errors in different parts of Pseudowords; conversely, if the effect is owing to a limited ability to operate visually on a dense array, the errors should predominate in the interior of a Pseudoword.

Table 3 shows the number and location of errors subjects made in naming the letters of Pseudowords. The length of the Pseudoword is shown across the top of the table, and the location of the letter on which the error was made is indicated along the side. Scanning down any column reveals that about the same number of errors was made on every letter of a Pseudoword N letters long. Thus, the visual system does not have some special difficulty in identifying the letters in various parts of a word. The advantage to recognition of the beginning is owing to linguistic, not visual, factors. Some of these linguistic factors will be described in a later section.

Table 3   Number and Location of Errors in Naming Letters of Pseudowords

Letter Location	Number of Letters in Pseudoword																
	1	2	3	4	5	6	7	8	9	10	11	12	13	14	15	16	17
1	27	111	163	154	95	43	21	34	15	23	6	0	1				1
2		119	169	134	93	49	36	40	22	20	7	4	0				0
3			160	149	65	38	36	39	26	22	9	1	1				3
4				131	118	47	44	40	31	7	12	0	0				1
5					84	53	33	43	23	17	15	4	3				2
6						54	30	22	24	14	8	1	1				1
7							39	47	29	20	10	3	0				2
8								36	30	25	8	3	0				1
9									35	18	10	0	1				1
10										28	6	2	0				1
11											12	1	4				4
12												0	0				7
13													1				0
14														0			1
15																	1
16																	0
17																	0

In this discussion of visual operations, I have shown that the identification of letters is dependent on a prior recognition of their orientation and that the identification of orientation is a variable and continuing process. In discussing some of the temporal characteristics of letter and word recognition, I pointed out that the recognition of words cannot typically proceed by the serial integration of letters, for word recognition is often independent of letter recognition. I have also discussed the problem of seriation and suggested that seriation, like orientation, may involve the action of distinctive mechanisms in the visual system. I turn now to the reading of connected discourse and will show that just as recognizing words does not occur by the piecemeal recognition of their letters, reading connected discourse does not proceed by the piecemeal recognition of words.

Sensitivity to Grammar

In other experiments, college students read pages of text in each of the kinds of geometric transformations illustrated in Figure 1. On each of eight successive test days each of thirty-two subjects read one page in each of the eight transformations, reading different pages and in different orders on the various days. All sixty-four pages of text came from a single source (Miller, 1962).

As one may imagine, the subjects made many errors when reading the transformed text. Analyzing them reveals a good deal about the sensitivity to grammar that characterizes normal reading. The chief kind of error was the substitution of some recognizable English word for what was printed. Substitutions accounted for more than 82 per cent of the errors made on both the first and the eighth day of testing. Other kinds of errors were omissions, intrusions, neologisms, and words begun wrong but then corrected. The total number of errors made over the eight days declined by about one-third, but their relative distribution, both among kinds and among the transformations, remained the same. Approximately equal percentages of error occurred on each of the transformations, but fewer words in N were misread. Three analyses of substitution errors will be described.

Parts of Speech

The part of speech that the subject substituted for what was printed was tallied for all errors. The parts of speech used for the analysis were the eight classical ones: noun, verb, adjective, adverb, pronoun, preposition, conjunction, and article. Contemporary linguists prefer to analyze words by the functional role they play in a sentence rather than by their taxonomic categories, and, in fact, it is very often difficult to categorize a word uniquely as a single part of speech. Nevertheless, some useful information was obtained with this old-fashioned kind of analysis, even though certain ambiguities restrict its complete interpretation.

The first analysis revealed the number of times that a substitution was the same part of speech as the printed word. About three-quarters of the time, errors in reading nouns, verbs, and prepositions substituted other nouns, verbs, and prepositions. About half of the time, errors in the remaining five categories substituted identical parts of speech for what was printed. If the substitutions had been made completely haphazardly among the eight parts of speech, identity of printed and spoken form would occur only about 12 per cent of the time by chance. Thus, the actual percentages of identities are well above chance level. By itself, this coincidence in part of speech between printed form and spoken substitution shows that the reader is not reading "just words," but is sensitive as well to their grammatical category.

A second aspect of this sensitivity to grammar is revealed by considering what substitutions are not made. Table 4 shows the percentages of substitutions for all eight parts of speech. The columns of the table represent the word that was printed; the rows, the part of speech that was substituted by the subjects. Reading down the column called "noun" indicates that a noun was substituted for a noun 76 per cent of the time, an adjective was substituted 16 per cent of the time, and so forth. The bottom row indicates the number of times that a mistake was made. The table is based on a total of 721 errors—those made on the first day of testing, excluding repetitions of an error by the same subject on the same page, and excluding changes in tense and number.

Table 4 shows that adjectives are the second most likely substitution for nouns; similarly, the column marked "adjective" shows that nouns and adverbs are most likely, after adjectives, to replace adjectives. Nouns are almost never replaced by pronouns, nor are pronouns, conjunctions, or articles ever replaced by nouns. Verbs never replace articles, nor do articles replace verbs, and so on. Thus, when he makes an error the reader not only tends to replace a given part of speech with another word of the same kind (shown by the diagonal of Table 4), but even when he does not do that, there is a selective patterning to his substitution. His replacement tends to have a syntactic similarity to what is printed. The precise degree of patterning cannot be accurately assessed, however, for the reason alluded to earlier: classifying words as parts of speech is often a delicate and is sometimes an ambiguous process. The reason for this is that just as letters do not have single sounds in English, words do not have single category memberships as parts of speech. A word ending in *ing* may be classifiable equally as noun or adjective, *your* and *our* can be pronouns or adjectives, and so on. In the greatest number of cases, of course, the categorization of

Table   4   Substitution of Parts of Speech (Per Cent)

Said	Noun	Verb	Adj.	Adv.	Pron.	Prep.	Conj.	Article
				Printed				
Noun	76	4	18	4	0	5	0	0
Verb	3	82	0.5	6	2	7	10	0
Adjective	16	2	57	12	14	4	2	5
Adverb	2	3	10	45	6	4	2	6
Pronoun	0.5	4	2	10	56	2	12	16
Preposition	1	2	6	12	0	73	10	5
Conjunction	1	2	1	4	18	6	66	22
Article	0.5	0	7	8	4	0	0	45
Frequency of errors (721)	180	163	160	61	31	61	40	25

a word into its part of speech is not ambiguous, given its context; but even when following an authority such as Curme (1931, 1935), enough ambiguities remain (about 10 to 15 per cent of the total) to make precise statements impossible. Therefore, though the overall patterning of the table is clear, some accidents must necessarily have crept into the scoring. I mention them here, but do not worry about them, and recommend anxiety-free contemplation of the tables to the reader as well.

Examining the frequencies of the last row of Table 4 might lead one to think that certain parts of speech are more likely to be erred on than others. For example, almost three times as many errors are made on nouns as on adverbs or prepositions. Is there something about a noun that induces a subject to make errors on it when reading aloud, or is this finding an artifact of the statistical distribution of parts of speech in the written language? To answer the question the same criteria were applied to pages of the printed material that had been applied to the errors in order to find the frequency of occurrence of parts of speech in the original. The findings were clear-cut: the frequency of errors in Table 4 is in good accord with the frequency of occurrence of parts of speech in the original. The errors are made according to their opportunities for being made rather than according to a selective bias by the reader. Thus, readers make part-of-speech-preserving errors, but are indifferent to the part of speech they choose to err on.

Grammatical Relations

Functionally, grammar is a matter of sequences rather than isolated words, that is, the relations that parts of speech have to each other rather than the parts themselves. The thesis of this chapter is that the reader, even when reading aloud, is doing much more than identifying or discriminating letters, or translating them into sounds, or even recognizing the internal structure of words. The preceding analysis showed that the reader is sensitive to the grammatical category of words taken individually. I will now show that he is sensitive also to the relations words have to those that come before and to those that follow what he is saying at any time. To do so I will again deal with the substitution errors the subjects made when they were reading transformed text aloud.

Imagine that the sentence to be read is *Emerson once said that every man is as lazy as he dares to be* and that it was misread in the following ways by different subjects:

1. Emerson once paid that . . .
2. Emerson once bias that . . .
3. Emerson has said that . . .
4. Emerson once suggested that . . .
5. Emerson once say that . . .

Errors 1, 3, and 4 are grammatically acceptable at the place they occur: 1 could be the first part of a sentence describing Emerson's payment of a bill; 3 merely changes the tense of the verb; and 4 offers a synonym for the verb. However, though 3 and 4 remain grammatically correct when the remainder of the sentence is considered, 1 violates both syntax (it is the wrong kind of verb) and sense. Error 2 violates syntax and semantics of the preceding words; and error 5 violates syntax but preserves meaning. These examples illustrate the way errors were evaluated for their grammaticality: with respect to the words preceding the substitution and with respect to the whole sentence.

The words *paid* and *bias*, furthermore, look somewhat like *said* when it has been transformed geometrically, but *has* looks different from *once*, and *suggested* looks different from *said*. Therefore, the substitutions can also be evaluated for their visual similarity to the printed word. And finally, the readers sometimes corrected their errors and sometimes did not. These three variables make a $2 \times 2 \times 2$ table for classifying substitutions: whether they were corrected or not; whether or not the substitution looked like the original; and whether or not they were grammatically adequate with respect to preceding words and with respect to the sentence as a whole. Grammatical adequacy, in turn, has two components: syntax and semantics, which themselves form a 2×2 table. These five variables were used to classify the data in a manner I shall now illustrate.

Table 5 shows the data from the first test day for corrected errors that looked like the original, called "corrected visually similar errors." On that

Table   5   Analysis   of   Corrected   Visually   Similar   Errors
(Per   Cent)

	Antecedent Words		Whole Clause	
	SYN +	SYN −	SYN +	SYN −
Sem +	88	1	19	1
Sem −	9	2	20	60

day, the subjects made 714 substitutions, of which 374 fell within this
category. Eighty-eight per cent of them were syntactically and semantically
acceptable with respect to the preceding words of the sentence. Nine per
cent were acceptable syntactically but distorted the meaning of the passage
(*Emerson once paid that . . .*). One per cent preserved the meaning but
were wrong syntactically (*Emerson once say that . . .*), and the remaining
2 per cent were neither syntactically nor semantically acceptable (*Emerson
once bias that . . .*). When the whole sentence was taken into account, 19
per cent of the substitutions were considered acceptable grammatically,
whereas 60 per cent violated both meaning and syntax. It is an obvious
conclusion from such data that the error in grammar was a signal to the
subject that he had made a mistake.

There is another side to grammatical adequacy, and this is illustrated in
the complete table of data (Table 6). Comparing the data just described
with their neighboring uncorrected visually similar errors shows that
virtually the same percentage was grammatically acceptable with respect
to preceding words (89 per cent compared with 88 per cent). However,
61 per cent of the uncorrected errors were acceptable in the whole sentence
and only 23 per cent violated syntax and meaning. Thus, the other side to
grammatical adequacy is that when the substitution was grammatically
acceptable, the reader usually left it uncorrected. In other words, the reader
was more sensitive to the grammatical relations of what he was reading
than to the printed words themselves. This hypothesis is borne out by considering the lower half of Table 6. There we see that an even larger percentage of substitutions was acceptable at the place they were made (98
per cent and 100 per cent of corrected and uncorrected errors). Forty-eight
per cent of the corrected errors remained grammatically acceptable, but 89
per cent of the uncorrected ones were acceptable in the whole sentence.
Thus, the discrepancy of what he said from the printed word acted as a
signal to the reader to correct his error, but the higher percentage of visually
dissimilar errors left uncorrected (89 per cent) shows that the grammatical
adequacy of the substitution permitted errors to go uncorrected even though
the substitution did not look like the original. The skilled reader who has
not yet attained complete mastery of the visual code he is reading is never-

Table 6 Grammatical Analysis of Errors (Per Cent)

VISUALLY SIMILAR

	Corrected				Uncorrected			
	Antecedent Words		Whole Clause		Antecedent Words		Whole Clause	
	Syn +	Syn −	Syn +	Syn −	Syn +	Syn −	Syn +	Syn −
Sem +	88	1	19	1	89	4	61	2
Sem −	9	2	20	60	8	2	14	23

VISUALLY DISSIMILAR

	Syn +	Syn −	Syn +	Syn −	Syn +	Syn −	Syn +	Syn −
Sem +	98	2	48	5	100	0	89	0
Sem −	0	0	8	40	0	0	3	9

theless more sensitive to its grammatical regularities than to its appearance. He obviously is not reading words as such but, even at this stage of competence, words in terms of their grammatical relations to other words.

Grammatical Complexity

A third demonstration of the reader's sensitivity to grammar would describe the likelihood of an error as a function of the grammatical complexity of the text. I shall first discuss what we would like to do and then what we were able to do with this topic. There are several ways to decompose sentences into their tree structures, but, regrettably, these analyses work well only on sentences composed in the laboratory and not so well on sentences taken from the natural use of language. This is especially the case for decomposition of sentences into their surface structure, for many of the same problems that preclude the unequivocal classification of words into their parts of speech also preclude the unambiguous decomposition of sentences into their surface structure. Optimally, we would like to make such decompositions and then find whether the errors occur as a function of the nodal depth in the tree of the words erred on. Trees can be written far more easily for deep structure than for surface structure, but deep structure analysis leaves unclassified many words on which errors are made.

Grammatical complexity is somewhat correlated with the length of an independent clause, as the following examples show.

1. The autonomic nervous system controls the vegetative functions. (8)
2. On the other hand, so long as he does not talk, he will not contradict us. (13)

3.   The dream of a single philosophical principle that explains every-thing it touches seems to be fading before the realization that man is vastly curious and complicated, and that we need a lot more information about him before we can formulate and test even the simplest psycho-logical laws. (21)

4.   When they talk about their sensations,.they speak cautiously and try to say how their experience would appear to someone who had no con-ception of its true source or meaning. (23)

Example 1 is a simple declarative sentence; 2 has one dependent clause. Example 3 contains several dependent clauses within one independent clause; and 4 is a complex construction, with a compound verb and de-pendent clauses. The number after each of the sentences indicates the total number of errors that were made in reading it on the first test day.

Obviously, however, the length of an independent clause is not perfectly correlated with grammatical complexity. For example, *The very, very, very, very, very* . . . can be extended infinitely without adding complexity; and a string of possessives can do the same, as *John's brother's uncle's father's sister's.* . . . However, sentences of these kinds almost never appear in normal connected discourse.

In the examples cited, the number of errors increased with the complexity of the sentence; but if one believes that 4 is grammatically more complex than 3, the total number of words in the sentence is not the crucial variable in this matter. In our experiments, we have found, in general, that errors do increase with complexity, but not simply as a matter of the number of words in a clause. At the present stage of linguistic analysis, there is unfortunately no unambiguous way to define grammatical complexity, and so the analysis we wish to perform cannot yet be carried out on natural discourse. (One could, of course, require subjects to read sentences constructed according to rule in the laboratory and examine errors as a function of preestablished grammatical complexity.)

Nevertheless, certain aspects of grammar function differently in the reader's mind from others. That is to say, a sentence is not merely a string of words, as the following results will show. Most of the sentences in the text we used were declarative. The first and the last parts of a declarative sentence typically name things, whereas the section surrounding the verb expresses an action or a relation. To study whether these different aspects of grammatical usage affected to subjects' ability to read, we tallied the number of errors subjects made as a function of fractions of independent clauses. The clauses were divided into fifths. Thus, a clause ten words in length has two words in each fifth, a clause thirty words in length has six, and so on. Figure 3 shows the likelihood of an error as a function of parts

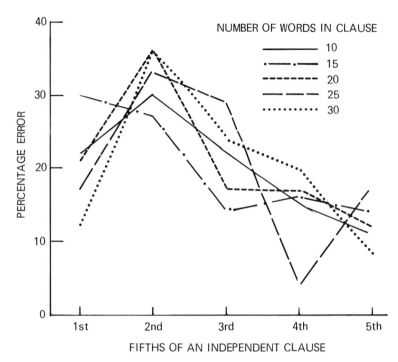

Figure 3 The percentage of errors in various parts of an independent clause.

of a clause. The maximum number of errors occurs in the second fifth of a clause for all clauses except those fifteen words long. Given the kind of gross statistical analysis this figure represents, the similarities are all the more impressive. If, in fact, the second fifth of an independent clause contains the parts dealing with verbs, the data suggest that the perception of the relations a sentence expresses is more difficult to attain than the perception of the things being related. On the other hand, the decline in the curves after the second fifth shows that the more of a grammatical structure one has grasped, the less likely he is to make an error.

By now it should be obvious that any theory that attempts to account for reading in terms of translating graphemes into phonemes, in terms of the discrimination of individual letters, or in terms of a sensitivity to the morphemic structure of single words, is hopelessly insensitive to even the simplest kinds of linguistic processing the reader engages in. I have shown this by illustrating the potent role grammar plays in reading—and grammar by its very nature involves sequences of words rather than single words. I turn now to illustrate the case with other facts.

Direct Perception of Meanings and Relations

My argument is that the skilled reader does not operate in terms of words as such. His sensitivity to the grammatical relations of the text was described above. Now I will show that he operates on the semantic or logical relations of the text he is reading, even to the point of disregarding, in a certain sense, the actual printed text, and, further, that this kind of behavior must typify the skilled reader of normal connected discourse.

Coding of Isolated Words

Imagine that words are being presented one at a time on a screen, each word for about one second. What does one see? If the words are in a foreign script one sees visual designs. If they are in a foreign language written with the Roman alphabet, the reader of English sees sequences of letters or phonetic units. What if they are in a language and script that one knows? Some people believe that then one also sees sequences of letters, or morphemic units, or some such. My argument is that a person who knows the language in which the words are being flashed sees the concepts the words represent and not just the words themselves. I shall make this point by describing two experiments with bilingual subjects.

The first experiment was performed with lists of unrelated words. If a long list of words is presented at a rate of one word per second, bright undergraduates can remember about ten words from the list. If the list is arranged so that some words are repeated within it, the likelihood of recalling some word increases with an increase in its recurrence in the list. A word presented four times, for example, is twice as likely to be recalled as another word presented twice (Waugh, 1963, 1967). The experiment I shall describe used this finding and applied it to bilingual lists of words. Here is the paradigm of the experiment:

hat	*desk*	*neige*
shoe	*desk*	*snow*

The question is with what probability will a bilingual subject recall *snow*, which translates *neige*? Will he recall it proportionately to its frequency of occurrence—equal to the average, say, of recalling *hat* and *shoe*; or will its translation affect his recall in English, so that the recall of *snow* will equal the recall of *desk*? If each word in a list were seen only as a word—as a morphemic or phonetic unit—there is no way the occurrence of *neige* could affect the recall of *snow*, or *wheat* affect the recall of *blé*, because each word and its translation look different and sound different. On the other hand, if the words are perceived and stored in memory in terms of their meaning, then presenting *neige* would affect the recall of *snow*, and presenting *wheat* would affect the recall of *blé*, because the pairs of words have very similar meanings.

In the experiment (Kolers, 1966a), French-English bilingual subjects saw long lists of words; on each list, some words appeared in French only, some in English only, and some as translated pairs. In addition all of the kinds of words were distributed haphazardly throughout a list, so that the subject never knew whether a word would be repeated or whether its translation would also appear. Nevertheless, the results showed very clearly that the recall of a word in one language was aided by presenting its translation. Using the illustration above, the probability of recalling either *neige* or *snow* was exactly equal to the probability of recalling *desk* and not to the probability of recalling *hat* or *shoe*. The conclusion seems obvious that for a person who knows them, words are perceived and remembered preferentially in terms of their meanings and not in terms of their appearances or sounds. This will now be shown in another way.

Reading Bilingual Connected Discourse

In this experiment (Kolers, 1966b), French-English bilinguals read passages such as the following:

> His horse, followed de deux bassets, faisait la terre résonner under its even tread. Des gouttes de verglas stuck to his manteau. Une violente brise was blowing. One side de l'horizon lighted up, and dans la blancheur of the early morning light, il aperçut rabbits hopping at the bord de leurs terriers.

or the following:

> Son cheval, suivi by two hounds, en marchant d'un pas égal, made resound the earth. Drops of ice se collaient à son cloak. A wind strong soufflait. Un côté of the horizon s'éclaircit; et, in the whiteness de crépuscule, he saw des lapins sautillant au edge of their burrows.

In one part of the experiment, the subjects were tested for their understanding of such bilingual passages, compared to their understanding of similar passages in French only or in English only. Our test showed that even when the time they were allowed to read the passages was always the same, the subjects were able to understand the mixed passages as well as they could unilingual ones. If the readers had had to make all of the words of a mixed passage conform to a single language before they could understand them, they would have had less time to work out the meaning of a mixed passage than of a unilingual one; and having less time, their comprehension would have been poorer. But it was not; and so we concluded that, as was shown in the preceding section, when a reader knows the words of a language, he perceives them directly in terms of their meanings.

This conclusion becomes all the more obvious when we consider another part of this experiment. There, the subjects were asked to read both unilingual and bilingual passages aloud as rapidly and as accurately as they could. In trying to do so, they made certain interesting kinds of errors, two of which are relevant to our discussion. One kind of error was a translation. For example, the reader might say, *Son cheval, suivi by deux hounds*, or *Drops of ice se collaient to his cloak*. He might say *door* when *porte* was printed, or the reverse; or *hand* for *main*; or *de sa* for *of his*; or *with* for *avec*. These translations of the word that was printed did not occur haphazardly. Most of them occurred as translations of the first word in language 2 that followed a sequence in language 1. However, others occurred as the translation of the last word in a sequence of language 1 that precede a sequence in language 2. Parenthetically, language 1 and language 2 refer equally to French and English. There was no difference in the results along these lines between Americans who knew French and native speakers of French who knew English. In both cases, the subjects were treating words in terms of their meanings rather than in terms of their appearance on the page.

In addition to translation errors, the subjects made order errors. The two passages illustrated contain distortion of normal French syntax as well as of normal English syntax (for example, *made resound the earth*). Many such syntactic anomalies occurred in the texts the subjects read, and many times the readers rectifed the disordered syntax. For example, the phrase above was read as *made the earth resound*; the phrase *in a cell dark* was read aloud as *in a dark cell*; and so on. In the greater number of cases, these departures from the printed text were not noticed by the subjects; in a similar fashion, their translations of words were also not noticed. At least, this is what the subjects said when we questioned them, and the data show that they did not often go back to correct their errors. And so again I have shown that the skilled reader of a language is not operating in terms of a passive but faithful mouthing of the text before him. He is not trying to translate graphemes into phonemes, and he is not responding especially to the morphemic structure of the words. He is not even able to see all of the words on the page, as I have shown elsewhere. Instead, he is treating words as symbols and is operating on them in terms of their meanings and their relations to other symbols.

This is probably the usual mode for the skilled reader. The skilled reader, however, is a highly sophisticated system performing a highly sophisticated act. It is a characteristic of sophistication that when the need arises, performance may proceed on less sophisticated levels, as in identifying unfamiliar words or reading proof. Thus the sophisticated practitioner of a skill has a hierarchy of options available to him. An accurate representation of any complex skill must account for the various levels at which it can be executed and for the conditions that determine any level of performance. This task cannot be performed inductively, by studying the most primitive aspects of the reader's performance and working up, because there is no principle to guide the induction. The more primitive behavior can be understood only as a part of the more sophisticated behavior. We will never come to understand reading if we concentrate our experimentation on the ability to distinguish geometric forms, or the ability to translate graphemes into phonemes, or similar tasks. Most of the experiments conducted in the last sixty years have proceeded in that way, and we are no more able to understand from them what the skilled reader is doing than we would be after another sixty.

References

Curme, G. O. *A Grammar of the English Language.* Vol. 3. *Syntax.* Boston: Heath, 1931.

Curme, G. O. *A Grammar of the English Language.* Vol. 2. *Parts of Speech and Accidence.* Boston: Heath, 1935.

Gelb, I. J. *A Study of Writing.* Rev. ed. Chicago: University of Chicago Press, 1963.

Huey, E. B. *The Psychology and Pedagogy of Reading* (1908). Cambridge, Mass.: M.I.T. Press, 1968.

Kolers, P. A. Interlingual facilitation of short-term memory. *Journal of Verbal Learning and Verbal Behavior,* 1966, *5,* 314–319. (a)

Kolers, P. A. Reading and talking bilingually. *American Journal of Psychology,* 1966, *79,* 357–376. (b)

Kolers, P. A. Reading temporally and spatially transformed text. In K. Goodman (ed.), *The Psycholinguistic Nature of the Reading Process.* Detroit: Wayne State University Press, 1968.

Kolers, P. A., & Katzman, M. T. Naming sequentially presented letters and words. *Language and Speech,* 1966, *9,* 84–95.

Kolers, P. A., & Perkins, D. N. Orientation of letters and errors in their recognition. *Perception and Psychophysics,* 1969, *5,* 265–269.

Miller, G. A. *Psychology: The Science of Mental Life.* New York: Harper & Row, 1962.

Money, J. (ed.). *Reading Disability.* Baltimore: Johns Hopkins Press, 1962.

Oppenheimer, J. R. Analogy in science. *American Psychologist,* 1956, *11,* 127–135.

Waugh, N. C. Immediate memory as a function of repetition. *Journal of Verbal Learning and Verbal Behavior,* 1963, *2,* 107–112.

Waugh, N. C. Presentation time and free recall. *Journal of Experimental Psychology,* 1967, *73,* 39–44.

5

The Independence of Letter, Word, and Meaning Identification in Reading

——with DEBORAH LOTT HOLMES

There is a wealth of experimental evidence. and common knowledge to show that what we see is determined not so much by the visual information with which the eye is confronted as by the sense that the brain imposes upon it. The eye, tool of the brain, can only look; it is the brain that sees. Paradoxically, the more information there is in the visual environment, the less we may see, because the visual system is easily overloaded. The present chapter discusses the nature of the visual system's limitations and how they can be overcome by the fluent reader (and also the beginner) through the use of meaning.

The abstract to the original publication read: "Two traditional assumptions about fluent reading are examined and rejected: that identification of letters is a necessary preliminary to word identification, and that identification of words is a prerequisite for comprehension. Memory and visual information-processing constraints preclude the prior identification of individual letters or words if comprehension is to be achieved. A feature analytic model is presented, proposing that letter identification, word identification, and the comprehension of meaning are three distinct tasks that can be performed independently on the same visual information."

Deborah Holmes is a researcher in the Social Relations Department of Harvard University. The chapter first appeared as a paper with the same title in Reading Research Quarterly, *1971, 6, 3, 394–415, and is reprinted by permission of the publishers.*

Educators have long been concerned with reading, but they have tended to focus their attention more on physiological, emotional, and environmental events which interfere with the acquisition of the skill rather than on the accomplishments of the skilled reader. "Why Johnny Can't Read" is certainly an interesting topic, but before one can examine it thoroughly one must surely ask why the great majority of children can read with a speed and efficiency which is unexplainable within most psychological theories of perception. As Ulric Neisser (1967, pp. 134–137) points out, "Unless some understanding of reading for meaning is achieved we will remain embarrassingly ignorant about questions that appear superficially easy . . . For the present, rapid reading represents an achievement as impossible in theory as it is commonplace in practice."

One reason why little emphasis has been placed on the skilled reader as opposed to the unskilled may lie in the complexity of the issue. But we feel that this disinterest has been furthered by a common and uncritical acceptance of two assumptions about the reading process: (1) That identification of individual letters is a necessary preliminary to word identification, and (2) That identification of words is a prerequisite for comprehension.

The two assumptions are frequently combined in the premise that reading involves transforming visual into spoken language: "In order to read alphabetic writing one must have an ingrained habit of producing the sounds of one's language when one sees the written marks which conventionally represent the phonemes" (Bloomfield, 1942, p. 128). "Learning to read . . . requires primarily the translation from written symbols to sound, a procedure which is the basis of the reading process" (Venezky, 1967, p. 102). "The heart of the matter [reading skill] is surely the process of decoding the written symbols to speech" (Gibson, 1970, p. 139).

A critical look at the two assumptions is particularly opportune because they appear to underlie a growing number of "systematic" and "programatic" attempts to improve reading skills through "code-cracking" instructional methods (Chall, 1967), culminating in HEW's mammoth Targeted Research and Development Program on Reading, not to mention the remarkable assertion in the *Harvard Educational Review* recently that "The problem of reading is solved" (Gattegno, 1970).

The first part of this paper is largely derived from existing theory and data related to letter and word identification, much of it discussed in more depth in Neisser (1967). But we attempt to go further in the second part of the paper by proposing that the same principles that can account for the identification of words without prior letter identification can also account for comprehension (identification of meaning) without prior identification of individual words. Just as the reader's implicit knowledge of transitional probabilities among distinctive features (visual elements) within words permits his identification of words without the prior identification of individual letters, so his implicit knowledge of additional syntactic and semantic constraints upon the same distinctive features in sequences of words permits the apprehension of their meaning without prior word identification.[1]

Assumption 1—Word Identification

The assumption that word identification can be accomplished only through prior letter identification seems often to be based on two considerations: (1) words are decomposable into letters, and (2) letter identification plays a prominent part in most methods of reading instruction. However, the first argument is obviously irrelevant since many objects are constructed by combining a number of variously shaped parts, but we do not identify the whole by discriminating the individual elements and their syntax. Moreover, the role of letter identification in reading instruction is a consequence of the assumption that letters must be identified, not a justification for it.

There is, in fact, little direct evidence that skilled readers identify letters en route to words. One might argue that letters are identified prior to words, since an anomaly is often reported when an inappropriate letter is inserted into a word, such as the *x* in *fashixn* (Pillsbury, 1897). However, awareness of anomaly in some part of a whole does not logically entail that the anomalous part was examined independently of the rest, and as Pillsbury himself pointed out, his subjects were usually not able to specify what the anomaly was. Therefore, one cannot assume that individual letters had actually been identified.

Another argument favoring the letter-by-letter view of word identification might be that readers are responsive to the transitional probabilities of letters in words, reflected in the considerable body of studies into digram

---

[1] Dictionary definitions of the words "recognize" and "identify" are tortuous, but it is clear that they are not synonymous. "Identification" involves a decision that a confronted object should be treated in the same way as a different object met before; that the two should be put into the same category, which usually has a name. There is no implication that the actual object being identified should itself have been met before. "Recognition," on the other hand, literally means that the object now confronted has been seen before, but does not necessarily entail naming. Use of the term "word recognition" seems doubly inappropriate. Experimenters rarely consider a word to be recognized unless its name can be given, and skilled readers frequently attach a name to a stimulus array that has never been met before. As a rather extreme case, is the visual stimulus *rEaDiNg* recognized or identified as the word "reading"? For further discussion of ambiguity in the use of the term *recognition* see Weiner & Cromer, 1967, pp. 625–628.

(letter pair) frequencies (Anisfeld, 1964; Baddeley, 1964; Biederman, 1966; Broadbent & Gregory, 1968; Mayzner & Tresselt, 1967). In particular, there are studies showing that nonword sequences of letters such as *vernalit* and *mossiant* are more readily perceived and memorized than sequences which are "lower approximations" to English letter structure (Miller, Bruner, & Postman, 1954). While such studies clearly indicate that it is not familiarity with the "word shape" *per se* that is the basis of word recognition, they do not prove that individual letters are identified. For example, these data are not incompatible with the view that skilled readers can move from discrimination of visual elements smaller than individual letters to "whole word (or even "whole nonword") identification without prior identification of individual letters.

Smith (1969) reported data that might be interpreted as indicating that letter identification was prior to word identification in a study that showed "whole word" recognition to be a phenomenon manifested only when an abundance of visual information is presented. By projecting 3-letter words and nonwords at below threshold levels of contrast, and gradually increasing stimulus intensity, Smith found that subjects often identified single letters before they identified a sequence "as a whole." But subjects also identified letters in words and in sequences with high transitional probabilities at lower contrasts than they identified the same letters in sequences with low transitional probabilities. This tendency occurred *even when the letter involved was the first in the sequence to be identified* (i.e. when no prior identification of another letter could account for digram frequency effects). If the identifiability of a letter varies with the identifiability of the word in which it occurs, then word identification cannot depend on preliminary letter identification. Instead, when the reader (or the experimenter) selects letters as the perceptual output, subjects in effect mediate the identification of individual letters by discriminating properties of the sequence as a whole. This finding is the direct reverse of what would be predicted by the letter-by-letter assumption.

There are a number of other sources of evidence contrary to the letter-by-letter point of view, some of which are summarized by Neisser (1967, ch. 5). For example, there is evidence that word identification is too fast for letter-by-letter analysis (Pierce & Karlin, 1957; Neisser & Beller, 1965; Neisser & Stoper, 1965). Also relevant are the demonstrations of Kolers & Katzman (1966) and Newman (1966) concerning the difficulty of word identification if letters are presented successively. In fact, reaction time to a word is scarcely longer than to a single letter (Cattell, 1885) and words can be identified in conditions under which none of their component letters are individually discriminable (Erdmann & Dodge, 1898; Smith, 1969).

Feature Analytic Model of Letter Identification

A feature analytic alternative to the letter-by-letter view, derived in part from the distinctive feature approach of Eleanor Gibson (1965), is described more fully in Smith (1971). Basically, the model regards both letter identification and word identification as processes of categorization (Bruner, 1957): a visual stimulus (or visual configuration) is identified when it is allocated to a category in a particular cognitive domain, such as to one of 26 categories in the letter domain, 10 categories in the digit domain, or an indefinite number of categories in the word domain.

While physical characteristics of a configuration may place varying degrees of constraint upon the range of categories to which it might be allocated, the selection of the domain of categories to which it is allocated, the *target domain*, and the number of alternative categories within that domain, depend largely on the prior expectation of the observer. The number of alternative categories within a domain to which a configuration might be allocated depends on alternative sources of "non-visual" information (or redundancy) available. For example, knowledge that a configuration is a vowel eliminates 20 or 21 alternatives in the letter domain.

In terms of its physical characteristics, a visual configuration is regarded as a bundle of visual features. The discrimination of any feature potentially reduces uncertainty by eliminating alternatives within the target domain. However, visual features can be distinctive only with reference to a particular categorical domain (that is, a distinctive feature for the letter domain must reduce uncertainty by at least one of the 26 alternatives). Obviously, not all features are distinctive all the time; a feature that distinguishes between *h* and *b* may not distinguish between *h* and *n*.[2]

For each bundle of features representing a familiar visual configuration, the observer has a corresponding "feature list." In any identification task, the input from feature analyzers about the configuration is compared with the feature lists within a cognitive target domain. Furthermore, within each feature list there may be a number of criterial sets, or patterns of feature specifications, each of which is sufficient for the allocation of a particular configuration to that category.

At a rough level of approximation, each feature may be regarded as a *bit* of information (that is, it reduces uncertainty by a half), with N features or bits of information eliminating all the uncertainty among 2^N equiprobable alternatives (rather less information is required if the distribution is not

---

[2] The terms "distinctive feature" and "distinguishing feature" are used unsystematically in the literature, with the former occurring more frequently probably because the word *distinctive* is more appropriate when a feature is defined as a minimal significant difference between two events. Despite the inconsistency, we shall therefore maintain the terminology that a *distinctive* feature distinguishes among alternatives.

equiprobable). The uncertainty among 26 alternatives of the letter domain is 4.7 bits if each letter is regarded as equiprobable, and 4.03 bits if the distributional redundancy of English is considered (Shannon, 1951). Because many letters have alternative forms, e.g. capitals and italics, we shall make the minimal assumption that the uncertainty of a letter in isolation or in a random sequence is between 5 and 6 bits, that is, that five or six features are required to identify it.

It is not suggested, however, that a letter configuration consists of only six features. Featural redundancy in individual letters is evidenced by the fact that letter configurations remain identifiable with much of their structure eliminated. Gibson (1965), for example, has suggested 12 possible minimal pairs of feature distinctions for capital letters.

Five or six binary features are theoretically sufficient to distinguish among the alternative letters, although each configuration may in fact contain potentially 10 or 12 features (that is, there are 10 or 12 analyzers capable of detecting unique features of the configuration). Then some (but not necessarily all) combinations of five to six features out of the possible 12 may suffice to eliminate all alternatives but one, and will constitute what may be termed a criterial set of features. Furthermore, as the number of alternative categories within a target domain is reduced, the number of features in each criterial set may diminish. It follows that the number of visual features required to discriminate a letter in a word can decline to an average level below that for any letter in isolation. Thus a model for word identification may be constructed that does not rely on letter-by-letter analysis.

Feature Analytic Model of Word Identification

The feature analytic model for word identification is a simple extension of the letter identification model. Precisely the same feature analytic mechanism operates upon the visual configuration for words as for letters, and feature lists for words exist that are similar to those for letters. However, a domain of word categories must be distinguished independent from that for letter (and other) categories, even though much of the same feature information is common to the identification of letters and words. Responses from different categories cannot be made simultaneously to the same input information. For example, one cannot "see" a visual configuration as both a word and a sequence of letters at the same time, any more than one can simultaneously see an "ambiguous" stimulus such as ⒔ as both a letter and a number (Bruner & Minturn, 1955). At this point it is not possible to determine whether this selectivity is imposed by restricting input to one domain, or blocking possible responses (including the subjective perceptual experience) from more than one domain.

There is one critical difference between feature lists for letters and those for words. Letter feature lists have only a single dimension, i.e., a single value for every feature input, while word feature lists are conceptualized as having an additional dimension of relative location. However, the concept of "location" should not be confused with that of "letter," i.e., the letter-by-letter assumption is not part of the model. In fact, "location" need not correspond exactly with "letter position" since confusions can occur in which features from one letter position are combined with features from another (Huey, 1908, p. 94). Instead, word identification can take place when there is insufficient information in any one location to constitute a criterial set for the letter that occupies that location; in other words, word identification can take place without sufficient information for letter identification in any location.

Validity of the Feature Analytic Model of Word Identification

The classic study by Cattell (1885), substantiated by Erdmann & Dodge (1898), showed that from a single tachistoscopic exposure a skilled reader can identify: (a) four or five unconnected letters; (b) two unconnected words; or (c) four or five words in a meaningful sequence (a phrase or short sentence). For the moment, consider just the evidence that two unconnected words, totaling perhaps ten letters, can be perceived at the same exposure level as four to five unconnected letters. A reasonable assumption is that the limit of two words is a result of visual information processing limitation rather than a limited short-term memory. The two unconnected words must be identified on the basis of the same amount of visual information as the four–five unrelated letters, namely a total of 25–30 bits, or 12–15 bits per word. In other words, there is a limit to the amount of visual information that can be processed from a single brief exposure and this limit is about 25 bits (Quastler, 1956).

There are two computations that would indicate that 15 bits of information are adequate to identify a word. The first argument is based on a simple calculation of the number of possible word categories that one might reasonably be expected to be discriminating among. Fifteen bits would be sufficient to discriminate among 2^{15} or 32,000 alternatives, which is probably a reasonable estimate of the sight vocabulary of a skilled reader. Shannon's (1951) estimate based on word frequency data was a little under 12 bits of entropy per word. By contrast, the minimum amount of information required to identify all the individual letters in a six letter word, namely 6×5 bits, would be sufficient to distinguish among 2^{30} word alternatives, a total in the order of a billion.

The alternative method of computing the average uncertainty of a word in isolation is from the average uncertainty of individual letters in short sequences of English, which are long enough to permit dependencies among letters within words to operate, but not long enough to provide syntactic or semantic cues. Shannon's (1951) "guessing game" technique requiring subjects to guess successive letters of English text provides such a method, and his own data provide an answer; over sequences of eight letters, the average uncertainty of a letter was 2.3 bits. Given an average uncertainty of, at the most, 3 bits per letter (or rather, per letter location) in words, it may be computed that a five or six letter word should be identified with only 15 bits of information, or only half the visual information that would be required to identify the individual letters of a word.

However, we should make it clear that "half the information" does not entail that half the letters in a word need be identified, nor does it mean that half the information available in every letter location is required. If half the letters of a required word must be identified, there is a problem of selectivity, that is, which letters are singled out for identification, since some will be more informative than others. It is true that initial letters appear to contain more information (in terms of sequential probabilities) and contribute more to identification (Broerse & Zwaan, 1966). But any statement about letters can be redefined as a statement about features— the first part of a word configuration may be more informative than other parts. There may be many alternative "criterial sets" of about 15 features for words, provided the features are a sampling from all the locations.

To summarize the argument so far, words can be identified with only half the featural information that would be required if prior letter identification were necessary, provided that the features sampled are taken from different locations within the configuration. The letter-by-letter view cannot hold, because the Cattell data indicate that only half the information required for letter identification is taken from every letter location in word identification. The feature analytic model explains how word identification is possible even though the letter-by-letter assumption is false. The model is also an improvement over the "whole word" theory of word identification because it offers an explanation of how words can be identified when component letters are not discriminable, while also accounting for the sensitivity of readers to anomalies within words, e.g. spelling errors (without necessarily being able to "spell"). The model also accounts for the apparent ability of readers to utilize sequential constraints within highly predictable sequences of letters, since any transitional dependencies among letters must entail transitional dependencies among features.

The feature analytic model is particularly compatible with redintegration theories of word recognition (e.g. Newbigging, 1961; Haslerud & Clark, 1957) which assume that a global percept of an entire word is constructed from the discrimination of only part of the configuration. However, we would question the over-simplified view that "features" of the stimulus are incorporated into the percept. Instead we prefer the signal detection approach (e.g. Broadbent, 1967) which proposes that the observer establishes a criterion level of "signal" information that has to be attained before a recognition decision is made. An observer can vary both the number and composition of his criterial sets, depending on the uncertainty he brings to the perceptual task. The feature analytic model provides a mechanism by which criterion levels may be established.

Chunking and Parallel Processing

An alternative interpretation of the Cattell data is that as redundancy is added to a sequence of letters, the good reader picks up bigger units (e.g. Gibson, 1966, p. 13), implying that the visual system processes more information if the stimulus can be chunked or "coded" (or "recoded"). Recall will be facilitated by chunking, which is precisely the sense in which Miller (1956) introduced the concept in his classical and frequently miscited paper on the magical number 7. But Miller did not assert that chunking prior to perception could increase the span of apprehension, and we can find no evidence of this. It is more economical to construe from Cattell's data that exactly the same amount of featural information enters the visual system whether one identifies letters or words, but that more information may be contained in the percept than is received from the stimulus, as in the case of word identification. The additional information is not picked up and processed by the visual system, but is contributed from nonvisual sources, namely knowledge of the redundancy of the language. The additional information is there because the observer can decompose his word percept into letters, not because he constructs it from letters.

Often related to a "chunking" view of visual perception is an argument that concurrent letter and word identification might be accomplished by the "parallel processing" of two or more individual letters. Such a hypothesis is sometimes proposed because response latency for word identification may be no longer than that for a single letter. The feature analytic model for word identification assumes, however, that information at the featural level is accumulated from broad areas of a configuration and processed "as a whole."

Letters are not processed independently when they are presented in groups. Sequences of letters are identified more easily (e.g. after briefer exposures, Nodine & Evans, 1969; or more accurately from a given exposure, Miller, Bruner & Postman, 1954), the more they reflect the spelling patterns of the language. If every letter in a sequence—or even just one— is more easily identified in a sequence than when standing alone, then information at the sub-letter level must be acquired and utilized during the process of identification. But if sequential and other information can be extracted "in parallel" from letter sequences at the feature level, it is superfluous to propose that letter identification take place at all.

Assumption 2—Meaning Identification

Despite the venerable history of the assumption that meaning cannot be extracted from text without prior word identification, there is no empirical evidence demonstrating its validity. One reason for the absence of a direct test of the assumption is doubtless its intuitive appeal: written text is made up of words; therefore how could comprehension occur without word identification? Similarly, one cannot argue that words are not identified at all since a reader often is able to name words that he is reading. But there is an alternative possibility that comprehension of meaning precedes word identification rather than follows it in normal skilled reading, and that any word identification that might occur is a by-product of comprehension.

Meaning and Uncertainty Reduction

Olson (1970) proposes that it is futile to talk of any "intrinsic" meaning of a word or sentence, and that a meaning can be defined only in terms of the alternative possibilities that it eliminates. In other words, meaning is related to the reduction of uncertainty, and must be defined pragmatically with respect to a perceiver. Meaning and comprehension may be regarded as reciprocal terms: meaning as the input to an information-processing decision-making system and comprehension as the output. In other words, "meaning" and "information" are synonymous, as are "comprehension" and "uncertainty reduction."

The operational definition of comprehension as uncertainty reduction permits us to avoid the difficulty of discussing meaning in terms of "words." It is possible to get a relative estimate of how much meaning has been abstracted from a sequence of words without having to specify what that meaning is. For example, a certain amount of information is required to identify a word and a reader who requires less visual information to name a word in a meaningful sequence than in a random sequence must acquire the rest of the required information from the semantic redundancy present.[3] Thus, in the Tulving & Gold (1963) study, the degree to which visual recognition

---

[3] We are aware that some of the sequential constraint in a sequence of words may often be syntactic was well as semantic, but the syntactic component is subordinate in normal language (Treisman, 1965) as well as difficult to disentangle. It is convenient to subsume syntactic and semantic information in the terms meaning and comprehension.

thresholds were lowered for words in sentences may be taken as a relative index of the amount of meaning abstracted from context.

Feature Analytic Model of Meaning Identification

We suggest the term *meaning identification* to embrace both comprehension and the utilization of semantic redundancy in sequences of words because the process by which such information is extracted from text by the skilled reader may be regarded as essentially no different from the process by which he identifies letters or words. Featural information from the visual array is analyzed and allocated to reduce uncertainty in: (a) the domain of letter categories, for letter identification (b) the domain of word categories, for word identification or (c) the domain of cognitive structure, for meaning identification.

Obviously it cannot be asserted that the domain of meaning to which visual information is applied in meaning identification is a domain of categories in the same way that sets of letters or of words constitute domains. Rather, comprehension may be conceptualized as either a permanent or temporary reorganization of cognitive structures or the rearrangement of feature specifications of semantic feature lists. It is also not easy to identify the mechanisms by which meaning identification reduces the set of word categories (or reduces the size and increases the number of criterial sets for a number of categories in the word domain) to produce the lowered information threshold for words in sentences. However, reluctance to speculate on the topography and dynamics of the meaning domain does not invalidate the model. We are attempting to describe a view of reading which asserts, *inter alia*, that meaning identification is generally a prior operation to word identification because it reduces word uncertainty and therefore permits word identification on minimal visual information.

The Relation between Word Identification and Meaning Identification

There is no doubt that a meaningful context facilitates the identification of words. That is, less visual information is required to identify a word if semantic (and syntactic) constraints are placed upon it from the context, (for example, Tulving & Gold, 1963). A word is identified at a lower threshold level when it is in a highly probable context than in a less probable one (Morton, 1964). Speakers and announcers customarily scan a text "for meaning" before attempting to read it aloud, at least in part because the surface structure of sentences is not marked for intonation (Chomsky & Halle, 1968). Meaningful material can be read up to twice as fast as unrelated sequences of words (Pierce & Karlin, 1957). "Eye-voice" studies (Tinker, 1958; Levin & Kaplan, 1968; Geyer, 1968) show that the eye is consistently between three and five words (about one second) ahead of the voice in normal reading, suggesting an advance sampling for meaning.

There is, moreover, considerable evidence that readers read for "meaning" rather than word identification. Over 60 years ago, Huey (1908, pp. 111–112) noted that "by whatever cues the recognition (of words) may be set off, it is certainly a recognition of word wholes, except when even these recognition units are subsumed under the recognition of a still larger unit." Elsewhere Huey summarizes his own research and that of Cattell: "It was found that when sentences or words were exposed, they were either grasped as wholes or else scarcely any of the words or letters were read" (1908, p. 72). Furthermore, many of the errors that skilled and beginning readers make are visual rather than semantic (Goodman, 1965; Weber, 1968); for example, the word *said* is more likely to be misread in context as "told" (a visual but not semantic error) than as its shapemate "sand" (visually relatively accurate but semantically anomalous). The psycholinguistic evidence is that we remember sentences for their meaning rather than for their specific words (Mehler, 1963), and the classic study of Bartlett (1932) showed that meanings rather than words are retained in long-term memory. Slobin (1965) demonstrated that children's repetitions of spoken sentences reproduce meaning rather than the precise words or sentence structure. Kolers (1968) reports that bilinguals who read texts which switch every few words between one language and another frequently make transposition errors in which they "read the right word in the wrong language"; in other tests where lists of words in two languages are read, readers frequently remember the word's meaning but not the language it was in. Cohen (1970) reports that it takes no longer to search through English text for words in a particular semantic category (e.g. "any flower") than for a specific phoneme or letter, indicating that readers can look for "semantic" features without first identifying particular words. Marshall and Newcombe (1966) have even found a brain-injured man who identified isolated words for meaning rather than name, e.g. reading *ill* as "sick," *city* as "town," *ancient* as "historic."

Let us examine more specifically the classic study of Cattell (1885). We have already calculated (see page 56) from several different sources of data that about 25–30 bits of information would be required to identify either the four to five unconnected letters or the two *unconnected* words which fill the span of apprehension of a single brief exposure. That four to five connected words can be identified in a single brief exposure indicates that word identification can occur on the basis of only about six or seven bits of information per word, which in turn entails that semantic constraints from the sequence as a whole are taken into account in order to reduce the uncertainty of each word. In other words, meaning identification precedes word identification.

Seven bits of information are obviously not enough to identify a word without any contextual cues since they suffice to distinguish among only 128 equiprobable alternatives ($2^7 = 128$). However, Shannon (1951) and Garner (1962, ch. 7) report several studies showing that the uncertainty of a word in text is about eight bits or less, while that of a letter in text is little more than one bit, i.e. little more than an average of one bit of information per letter location is theoretically sufficient to identify a word in text compared with perhaps three bits per letter location for unrelated words and five bits for unconnected letters. In other words, constraints in the structure of words make 50 per cent of the visual information redundant, and constraints in the structure of phrases and sentences make 75 per cent of the visual information redundant (ignoring featural redundancy in the actual structure of letters).

We are not suggesting that the uncertainty of a word is literally between one and two bits for each letter; this would imply that three-letter words might be identified with less total information than a single letter, and that a ten-letter word would require twice as much information as a five-letter word, whereas, in fact, long words are slightly easier to identify than short words (Howes & Solomon, 1951). Instead we are asserting that the average uncertainty of a whole word in text is about seven bits. The finding that long words are easier to identify fits the paradigm, since if only a criterial set of a limited number of features is required to discriminate a word, more criterial sets should be available in a long word than a short one.

"Decoding to Sound"

There are several counter arguments to the assertion in our introductory quotations that "reading is decoding from written symbol to sound." Written symbols do not decode to sound in any reasonably predictable fashion, and speech itself requires complex decoding into meaning (Chomsky and Halle, 1968; C. Chomsky, 1970*). The task of comprehension must begin, rather than end, if the written text is decoded into sound.

The preceding argument is also relevant to the notion that subvocalization aids comprehension. Carroll (1964, p. 338) has written:

"The activity of reading can . . . be analyzed into two processes: (a) on the basis of the written message, the construction or reconstruction of a spoken message or of some internal representation of it; and (b) the comprehension of messages so constructed. It is therefore of the greatest importance to consider these processes separately, even though typically they occur virtually simultaneously."

But if the two processes occur simultaneously, what is the point of constructing a spoken version? Because silent reading can take place at very high rates and without detectable subvocal activity, Carroll also suggests that the "internal representation" of the spoken message might be abbreviated or fragmentary. It is again dubious what the value of such an internal representation might be. We do not normally hear abbreviated or fragmentary speech, and it is implausible that we could construct it "internally" without first comprehending the passage. It is of interest that no one has succeeded in making any satisfactory analysis of such reading simply by asking the reader to vocalize his "partial reading" of the text. We have never found any evidence that anyone listens to his own (sub)vocalizations in order to comprehend what he is reading. Many readers subvocalize, at times, even in a fragmentary way, although we believe this phenomenon is not as common as it appears. However, it is not logically necessary that the reader is listening to himself subvocalize, or that if he is listening he is comprehending what he is hearing: Hardyck, Petrinovich, & Ellsworth (1966) have demonstrated that subvocalization can be suppressed without disturbing speed or comprehension.

Information-Processing Limitations on Word Identification and Meaning Identification

There are other reasons for suggesting that a skilled reader could not first identify words and comprehend what he is reading. First of all, there is a limit to the number of fixations that any reader can make to pick up visual information. Even the fastest reader is limited to about four fixations a second, which is the rate achieved by fourth graders (Taylor, Frackenpohl, & Pettee, 1960). What distinguishes the skilled reader from the novice is how much he can read in a single glance; it is not (as is frequently supposed) the amount of visual information that he can pack into a single fixation, but the amount of nonvisual information with which he can leaven the featural input and make it go the farthest. Haith, Morrison, and Holmes are currently obtaining evidence that as long as the amount of information is low, five-year-olds can pick it up as far away from the fovea as adults. It is significant that the response of the skilled reader to material which is unfamiliar or opaque is precisely that of the tyro with "easy" material—his "span of apprehension" decreases as he is reduced to word identification, or even letter identification, rather than meaning identification. "Tunnel vision" (Mackworth, 1965) in reading is not so much that the visual system is overloaded as that the visual information cannot be supplemented by the use of redundancy.

There is an interesting discrepancy among the parameters of reading. Although visual information sufficient for the identification of four words may be available in a single fixation, and four fixations a second may be made, the skilled reader cannot identify words (that is, read unlearned material aloud) at the rate of 16 words per second (almost 1000 words a minute) but instead at barely a quarter that rate (a limit which is not set by the rate at which words can be articulated). The paradox can be resolved in the following way: although four to five words can be identified from the visual information in a single fixation, their processing ("identification") is not accomplished immediately but requires about a second to complete (Geyer, 1968; J. Mackworth, 1963). Therefore normal reading aloud proceeds at the rate of about four words per second rather than 16. Why then should the reader make four fixations per second if he spends an entire second processing the information in only one fixation? An explanation might be that he does not identify words in isolation, but makes the optimum use of all the available redundancy, i.e., he is always looking four words ahead, as Geyer suggests.

This limit of a four-word lead time would again appear to be set by constraints within the visual system, rather than by the structure of the language. Miller, Bruner, & Postman (1954) showed that third and fourth order approximations to English (that is, those in which the sequential constraints extended across three or four words) were identified just as easily as English text, although of course they did not read like English text. Miller *et al.* hypothesized that perhaps three to four words was the limit to which significant sequential constraints extended in English, but we suggest it is more probable that three to four words is the limit that the normal reader can look ahead, that is, that his "working store" will not accommodate more than four to five words at any time, and that all reading aloud in effect becomes a matter of processing third or fourth order approximations to English.

Based on the preceding computation, the reader who identifies four to five words per second with three to four fixations per second is reading at an optimal rate, determined by the limited capacity of his visual information processing system. Such a reader is in fact identifying the words he reads (reducing his uncertainty) with a mix of one part visual information to three parts nonvisual information. If he is not able to dilute the visual information to such an extent, that is, if he has to rely more on visual information and less on his knowledge of redundancy, then he is going to read slower. Material which is read slowly is much more difficult to comprehend. The exact dimensions of this problem have never been examined, but they are obviously related to the limitation that information in the four to five items in short-term memory must be put into long-term memory in as comprehensive a chunk as possible, because the latter can accept only one chunk every three to five seconds (Simon, 1969). A four-second chunk for a 200 w.p.m. reader contains the "meaning" from about 13 words. We have no way of telling whether 13 is a good average number of words from which a distilled meaning can be stored in one chunk, but it is probably far more efficient than the four to five words that a reader whose rate is only 80 w.p.m. could store. In other words, unless the reader reads fast enough, that is, around 200 w.p.m. or more, he is not going to comprehend what he is reading simply because his memory system will not be able to retain, organize, and store the fragmentary information in any efficient way. This is the situation of any reader who does not read fast enough, who relies too much on visual information: he will have very little comprehension of what he reads.

Many skilled readers can scan for meaning much faster than 1000 words per minute—a speed four times faster than the rate at which individual words can be identified. Yet the common "explanation" that the speed reader only reads "one word in four" cannot hold. A simple test will show that a passage in which three words out of four are erased is completely unintelligible. Far more efficient (and feasible) would be a system that instead of identifying one word in four would sample meaning information from most words.

Conclusion

We evaded at the beginning of this paper the problem of defining "reading," a term resisting frontal attack as much as the words "comprehension" and "meaning," which themselves must be part of any definition of reading. Instead we have discussed three skills which at least are part of the repertoire of the skilled reader—the ability to identify letters, words, and meanings. Operationally we have defined meaning identification as the reduction of uncertainty. And although we have been unable to give a direct estimate of how much uncertainty has been reduced (for example by the identification of a word or the comprehension of some text) we have indicated how at least a relative measure of information acquisition (uncertainty reduction) might be obtained—by measuring the reduction in the amount of visual (featural) information required to identify a component letter or word. We have shown that there are two orthogonal methods of estimating how much redundancy is created by the fact that letters are organized into words and words may be combined into meaningful sequences: (a) Shannon's guessing game, and (b) Cattell's brief exposure. These two methods show quite independently that half of the uncertainty in a string of letters can be eliminated (by the accomplished reader) if the letters are formed into words, and that half as much uncertainty again can be removed if the words are linked in a meaningful sequence. We have shown what a number of students of reading have recently suggested (e.g. Goodman, 1965; Weiner & Cromer, 1967) and what Kolers (1968) has made implicit: reading is not primarily visual.

We can now pull the threads of the argument together. We have asserted not just that the fluent reader *can* make use of the meaning of what he reads in order to identify words but that he *must* do so in normal reading. If word identification preceded meaning identification in oral reading then the reader would not understand what he was reading. The almost limitless range of faster silent reading could not be accomplished with comprehension at all if word identification were essential. Text can be comprehended only if it is read for meaning in the first place; reading to identify words is both unnecessary and inefficient.

References

Anisfeld, M. A comment on "The role of grapheme-phoneme correspondence in the perception of words." *American Journal of Psychology*, 1964, *77*, 320–321.

Baddeley, A. D. Sequential dependencies among letters and the learning of nonsense syllables. Paper presented at the meeting of the Experimental Psychological Society, London, England, 1964.

Bartlett, F. S. *Remembering.* Cambridge, England: Cambridge University Press, 1932.

Biederman, G. B. Supplementary report: the recognition of tachistoscopically-presented five-letter words as a function of digram frequency. *Journal of Verbal Learning and Verbal Behavior*, 1966, *5*, 208–209.

Bloomfield, L. Linguistics and reading. *Elementary English*, 1942, *19*, 125–130; 183–186.

Broadbent, D. E. The word-frequency effect and response bias. *Psychological Review*, 1967, *74*, 1–15.

Broadbent, D. E., & Gregory, M. Visual perception of words differing in letter digram frequency. *Journal of Verbal Learning and Verbal Behavior*, 1968, *7*, 569–571.

Broerse, A. C., & Zwaan, E. M. The information value of initial letters in the identification of words. *Journal of Verbal Learning and Verbal Behavior*, 1966, *5*, 441–446.

Bruner, J. S. On perceptual readiness. *Psychological Review*, 1957, *64*, 123–152.

Bruner, J. S., & Minturn, A. L. Perceptual identification and perceptual organization. *Journal of General Psychology*, 1955, *53*, 21–28.

Carroll, J. B. The analysis of reading instruction: perspectives from psychology and linguistics. In *Theories of Learning and Instruction.* Yearbook 1963, Part I. National Society for the Study of Education. Chicago: University of Chicago Press, 1964, 336–353.

Cattell, J. McK. Ueber die Zeit der Erkennung und Benennung von Schriftzeichen, Bildern und Farben. *Philosophische Studien*, 1885, *2*, 635–650. Translated and reprinted in James McKeen Cattell, *Man of Science, 1860–1944.* Lancaster, Penn.: Science Press, 1947, 1.

Chall, J. *Learning To Read: The Great Debate.* New York: McGraw Hill, 1967.

Chomsky, C. Reading, writing and phonology. *Harvard Educational Review*, 1970, *40*, 2, 287–309.

Chomsky, N., & Halle, M. *The Sound Pattern of English.* New York: Harper & Row, 1968.

Cohen, G. Search times for combinations of visual, phonemic and semantic targets in reading prose. *Perception and Psychophysics*, 1970, *8*, 5B, 370–372.

Erdmann, B., & Dodge, R. *Psychologische Untersuchungen ueber das Lesen.* Hall: Niemeyer, 1898.

Garner, W. R. *Uncertainty and Structure as Psychological Concepts.* New York: Wiley, 1962.

Gattegno, C. The problem of reading is solved. *Harvard Educational Review*, 1970, *40*, 2, 283–286.

Geyer, J. J. Perceptual systems in reading: the prediction of a temporal eye-voice span. In Smith, H. K. (Ed.), *Perception and Reading.* Newark, Delaware: International Reading Association, 1968.

Gibson, E. J. Learning to read. *Science*, 1965, *148*, 1066–1072.

Gibson, E. J. Perceptual learning in educational situations. Paper presented at symposium on "Research approaches to the learning of school subjects," University of California at Berkeley, 1966.

Gibson, E. J. The ontogeny of reading. *American Psychologist*, 1970, *25*, 2, 136–143.

Goodman, K. S. A linguistic study of cues and miscues in reading. *Elementary English*, 1965, *42*, 639–643.

Hardyck, C. D., Petrinovich, L. F., & Ellsworth, D. W. Feedback of speech muscle activity during silent reading: rapid extinction. *Science*, 1966, *154*, 1467–1468.

Haslerud, G. M., & Clark, R. E. On the redintegrative perception of words. *American Journal of Psychology*, 1957, *70*, 97–101.

Howes, D. H., & Solomon, R. L. Visual duration threshold as a function of word-probability. *Journal of Experimental Psychology*, 1951, *41*, 401–410.

Huey, E. B. *The Psychology and Pedagogy of Reading.* New York: Macmillan, 1908, and Cambridge, Mass.: M.I.T. Press, 1968.

Kolers, P. A. Reading is only incidentally visual. In Goodman, K. S., & Fleming, J. T. (Eds.). *Psycholinguistics and the Teaching of Reading.* Newark, Delaware: International Reading Association, 1968.

Kolers, P. A., & Katzman, M. T. Naming sequentially-presented letters and words. *Language and Speech*, 1966, *9*, 84–95.

Levin, H., & Kaplan, E. The eye-voice span within active and passive sentences. *Language and Speech*, 1968, *11*, 251–258.

Mackworth, J. F. The duration of the visual image. *Canadian Journal of Psychology*, 1963, *17*, 62–81.

Mackworth, N. H. Visual noise causes tunnel vision. *Psychonomic Science*, 1965, *3*, 67–68.

Marshall, J. C., & Newcombe, F. Syntactic and semantic errors in paralexia. *Neuropsychologia*, 1966, *4*, 169–176.

Mayzner, M. S., & Tresselt, M. E. Individual differences in stored digram frequencies and the immediate recall of letter and number strings. *Psychonomic Science*, 1967, *7*, 359–360.

Mehler, J. Some effects of grammatical transformation on the recall of English sentences. *Journal of Verbal Learning and Verbal Behavior*, 1963, *2*, 346–351.

Miller, G. A. The magical number seven, plus or minus two: some limits on our capacity for processing information. *Psychological Review*, 1956, *63*, 81–97.

Miller, G. A., Bruner, J. S., & Postman, L. Familiarity of letter sequences and tachistoscopic identification. *Journal of General Psychology*, 1954, *50*, 129–139.

Morton, J. The effects of context on the· visual duration threshold for words. *British Journal of Psychology*, 1964, *55*, 165–180.

Neisser, U. *Cognitive Psychology*. New York: Appleton-Century-Crofts, 1967.

Neisser, U., & Beller, H. K. Searching through word lists. *British Journal of Psychology*, 1965, *56*, 349–358.

Neisser, U., & Stoper, A. Redirecting the search process. *British Journal of Psychology*, 1965, *56*, 359–368.

Newbigging, P. L. The perceptual redintegration of frequent and infrequent words. *Canadian Journal of Psychology*, 1961, *15*, 123–132.

Newman, E. B. Speed of reading when the span of letters is restricted. *American Journal of Psychology*, 1966, *79*, 272–278.

Nodine, C. F., & Evans, J. D. Eye movements of prereaders to pseudowords containing letters of high and low confusability. *Perception and Psychophysics*, 1961, *6*, 39–41.

Olson, D. R. Language and thought: aspects of a cognitive theory of semantics. *Psychological Review*, 1970, *77*, 4, 257–273.

Pierce, J. R., & Karlin, J. E. Reading rates and the information rate of a human channel. *Bell Systems Technical Journal*, 1957, *36*, 497–516.

Pillsbury, W. B. A study in apperception. *American Journal of Psychology*, 1897, *8*, 315–393.

Quastler, H. Studies of human channel capacity. In Quastler, H. (Ed.). *Three Survey Papers*. Urbana, Ill.: Control Systems Laboratory, University of Illinois, 1956, 13–33.

Shannon, C. E. Prediction and entropy of printed English. *Bell Systems Technical Journal*, 1951, *30*, 50–64.

Simon, H. A. *The Sciences of the Artificial*. Cambridge, Mass.: M.I.T. Press, 1969.

Slobin, D. I. The role of imitation in early language learning. Paper presented at a symposium on "Interaction of thinking and language in development" at the biennial meeting of the Society for Research in Child Development, Minneapolis, Minnesota, March, 1965.

Smith, F., The use of featural dependencies across letters in the visual identification of words. *Journal of Verbal Learning and Verbal Behavior*, 1969, *8*, 215–218.

Smith, F. *Understanding Reading*. New York: Holt, Rinehart and Winston, 1971.

Taylor, S. E., Frackenpohl, H., & Pettee, J. L. Grade level norms for the components of the fundamental reading skill. Huntington, New York: Educational Development Laboratories Bulletin, 1960, *3*.

Tinker, M. A. Recent studies of eye-movements in reading. *Psychological Bulletin*, 1958, *55*, 215–231.

Treisman, A. M. Verbal responses and contextual constraints in language. *Journal of Verbal Learning and Verbal Behavior*, 1965, *4*, 118–128.

Tulving, E., & Gold, C. Stimulus information and contextual information as determinants of tachistoscopic recognition of words. *Journal of Experimental Psychology*, 1963, *66*, 319–327.

Venezky, R. L. English orthography: its graphical structure and its relation to sound. *Reading Research Quarterly*, 1967, *2*, 75–106.

Weber, R. M. The study of oral reading errors: a survey of the literature. *Reading Research Quarterly*, 1968, *4*, 96–119.

Weiner, M., & Cromer, W. Reading and reading difficulty: a conceptual analysis. *Harvard Educational Review*, 1967, *37*, 620–643.

6

Decoding:
The Great Fallacy

The third theme of this book is that reading is not decoding to spoken language. This chapter sets out the major arguments against the decoding hypothesis, and considers alternative methods by which word identification can be achieved, and generally is.

The belief that reading involves decoding, or transforming, or reconverting, written symbols into spoken language is as old as the alphabet (Mathews, 1966). The belief underlies practically all approaches to reading instruction, from the "Why Johnny Can't Read" type of polemic on behalf of phonics to the current vogue for characterizing reading as a "decoding skill". I shall argue that sound, if it is produced at all, comes only after the comprehension of meaning in reading.

At its strongest, what I shall call the "decoding hypothesis" asserts that written language can be comprehended only when converted into actual or implicit speech to which the reader listens—a procedure as impossible in practice as it is untenable in theory. Such a view is not even a valid description of what readers can be observed to do. Yet the decoding hypothesis is so widespread in the literature that I hesitate to single out particular authors for specific citation. But I would note that the hypothesis is particularly conspicuous among contemporary model-makers, whose "information-processing" flowcharts for reading frequently begin with a visual input of alphabetic characters and end with an output of phonemes in some kind of auditory store. In other words, it is taken for granted that reading is accomplished when spoken language is reconstituted through "spelling-to-sound" correspondence rules of varying degrees of fidelity. If these assumptions are unfounded, then the decoding hypothesis bears no more relation to reality than the speculations of early anatomists that the liver was the organ of the intellect.

On the other hand, weak versions of the decoding hypothesis, such as the half-hearted compromise that while perhaps not every word is translated to sound, all the important words are, are even less viable. A last-ditch defence for the decoding hypothesis is that even if it cannot be proven that adults do it, surely children must. How else could beginning readers identify words that they have never seen before? But I shall show that decoding to sound is with good reason the last resort of a child confronted by an unfamiliar word. "Decoding skills" are used only to a very limited extent, and then primarily because a good deal of instructional effort is expended on impressing such methods upon children.

The Comprehension of Language

Frequently underlying the decoding hypothesis is a gross over-simplification that appears to assume that spoken language is comprehended directly and instantaneously, therefore the conversion of written language into speech is sufficient to ensure its immediate understanding. But as Goodman (1971) points out, spoken language is itself a "code" that requires to be broken if meaning is to be apprehended. Miller, in Chapter 2, demonstrates clearly that there is no simple correspondence between the sounds of language (at the surface structure level) and their meaning (deep or underlying structure). Extracting the meaning of an utterance— getting from surface structure to deep structure—involves complex syntactic and semantic decisions; in other words, the listener uses knowledge of his language and of the world. Without the contribution of this knowledge and the associated process of moving between surface and deep structure, speech just cannot be understood. It is generally not possible to determine even the sounds of language without reference to syntax and semantics— this is one of the reasons that we find it so difficult to isolate individual sounds, let alone identify individual word boundaries, when listening to a language with which we are not familiar.

The Nature of Written Language

Written language is not speech written down; I must dispose of that possibility first of all. Writing is a visual form of language (not the only one), and speech is an acoustic form of language (the only obvious one if we restrict the term language to systems in which there is a syntax, that is where meaning can be changed by modifying either the form or the order of elements). Both writing and speech are at the surface level of language, related by hierarchical systems of rules to underlying deep structures. Whether they should be called the same language depends on how broadly the word "language" is defined. Whatever the definition, however, writing and speech stand at an equivalent level to each other, and not in any hierarchical relationship. Only historically and in the chronological development of (most) individuals can speech be said to be prior to writing.

Nevertheless, although the speech and writing systems of English may share the same underlying lexicon and syntax, it is clear that we draw on these resources differently. At the level of discourse, the level at which we construct sentences and string them together, it must be clear that we are not writing down speech. Speech written down, as all know who have tried to read the written transcripts of quite intelligible talks, is a poor substitute for a paper that will be read. But material written to be read—for example the present chapter—just does not sound right if delivered aloud.

There are, moreover, distinct differences between speech and writing at the surface level. We differentiate many words in writing that we do not differentiate in speech (homophones)—for example, most of the words in the following sentence are "wrong" in writing but not when read aloud:

The none tolled hymn she had scene a pare of bear feat inn hour rheum.

It is easy to detect the improperly spelled words in the previous sentence, clear evidence that we get their meaning from their visual properties, not their sound. If we attached meaning to words only through their sound, there would be no basis for asserting that any of the words were wrong.

Less often, we differentiate words in speech that we do not differentiate in writing. Compare *He sang in a beautiful bass although he could not read music. . . .* and *He read the notice that fishing for bass was permitted. . . .* In each of the previous two sentences the words *read* and *bass* were pronounced differently but spelled the same (homographs). How could we produce the sounds correctly unless we selected them on the basis of meaning?

Furthermore, much of the meaning of spoken language is carried by the intonation, which is not directly represented in writing. (It is a fallacy to assume that punctuation indicates intonation. Most punctuation comes too late to signal anything about how the sentence should be read. Instead, intonation is signalled by meaning—once you know the meaning of a sentence you know how to articulate it.)

It is not a fact that written language is a reliable representation of the sounds of spoken language, even at the word level. The principle of relating spelling to sound is dropped in two quite frequent kinds of circumstance: (a) when it would interfere with the principle that words that are related should look alike, for example the similarity in spelling but dissimilarity in pronunciation of such word pairs as *medicine-medical, nation-national, bombing-bombard, sign-signature, extreme-extremity* and (b) when it would interfere with the principle that words which are not related should look different, as in the "none tolled hymn" example just given, which explains why there are relatively few words that look alike despite the large number of words that sound alike in our language. The alphabetic principle is sometimes contravened simply for the visual convenience of the reader, for example words like *women* and *wonder* are spelled with an *o* instead of an *i* or *u* because the thickets of up and down strokes in letter sequences like *wim* . . . , *wun* . . . would be difficult to read (Jespersen, 1909–1949).

In some languages the relation between written and spoken forms is far more tenuous than in English. In Chinese, for example, the written language is largely ideographic and can be read quite independently of the reader's spoken language. In fact reader and writer may speak quite different spoken languages, but because Chinese writing is ideographic they can communicate through writing when they cannot communicate through sound. The situation is precisely analogous to the way in which unilingual speakers of English or French may share a common understanding of such numerical and mathematical ideographs as $2 + 2 = 4$, but not of "two and two are four" or "deux et deux font quatre".

Meaning and Sound

Meaning Is Independent of Sound

All written languages can be translated into spoken language. But it is not necessary for any written language to be translated into speech in order for the language to be understood by a reader. Instead it can be argued that written language must be understood before an acceptable (that is, comprehensible to a listener) translation into spoken language can be produced. I shall consider at a later point the relatively rare exception when a reader might try to identify a visually unfamiliar word through the intermediary of his spoken language vocabulary, for example the name of a person or geographical location which is already known acoustically but not visually. But ability to generate approximate or even recognizable sounds for individual words is a long way removed from reading aloud with an accuracy and intonation adequate for comprehension—from the sounds thus produced—by either the reader or a second party.

With ideographic writing systems, like Chinese, it is quite clear that "decoding to sound", if this takes place at all, is dependent upon the prior apprehension of meaning. But precisely the same situation obtains with alphabetic writing systems. The process of "decoding" from written language to spoken language is essentially no different from that of translating from one language to another. Translation from English to French, for example, whether the written or the spoken forms of the two languages are involved, must be mediated through meaning. No other "code-breaking" system is available. Word-for-word transliteration is a completely inadequate substitute, as anyone knows who has tried to "read" a paper—or even a sentence—in an unknown language with the help of a dictionary, or who has been involved in the massively complicated enterprise of machine translation. The task of a conference interpreter translating from English to French is easily specified: he listens to the surface structure of the English, extracts deep structure and generates an appropriate French surface structure for that meaning. Similarly, in translating from written English to written French, the only possible bridge is meaning. Meaning is essentially all that the original English and the French translation have in common.

By the same token, meaning can be extracted from written words—from the visual code—without any reference to the fact, quite coincidental to reading, that the written code of English bears some indirect or imperfect relation to the sound system of the language.

The frequent suggestion that our written language should be easier to read simply because it is alphabetic is fallacious; there is no evidence for either the assertion or the argument. We identify all the other appurtenances of our visual world directly, without the mediation of naming, for example we immediately recognize a cow, or a picture of a cow—we do not first associate the object or picture with the name "cow" which we then utter aloud or subvocally in order to hear ourselves say the word and identify the referent. Such a suggestion would indeed be absurd, because obviously we must identify the object or picture before we can utter the name. How then can it be possible to utter the name in order to get the meaning? Yet despite the abundant evidence that we can remember the names of thousands of visual objects and their pictorial representations, it is still asserted that the alphabet is the only means by which we can remember the names or meanings of written words.

Sometimes this belief in the superiority of the alphabet is based on confusion about the process of remembering. Morris Halle, one of the most seminal thinkers in the relationship between sound and meaning in spoken language (e.g., Chomsky & Halle, 1968), makes an elementary psychological slip when he observes that "since the strokes (in Chinese ideographs) are arbitrary symbols the writer's or reader's task is equivalent to that of a person trying to remember [several thousand] telephone numbers" Halle,

1969, p. 18). But Halle confuses recognition with recall (as well as the demands of writing compared with those of reading). Far less information is required to recognize a number, or a word, or a face, than to reproduce it. Besides, we can both recognize and recall many thousands of words in our spoken language vocabulary, and recognize many thousands of different faces and animals and plants and objects in our visual world. Why should this fantastic memorizing capacity suddenly run out in the case of reading?

It is surely no more difficult for a person to remember that or

the printed word *house* is called "house" than that  (or an actual

house) is called "house." Unfortunately, we tend to believe that the alphabetic form *house* is read in an exclusive manner, simply because it is composed of letters.

Meaning Facilitates Reading

There is substantial experimental evidence that meaning in the form of semantic and syntactic constraints is employed by readers to minimize the amount of visual information required to identify words occurring in meaningful and predictable sequences (see Chapter 5). Such experiments typically demonstrate that words are identified faster, or from briefer exposures, or in conditions of greater stimulus impoverishment, when they occur in a meaningful context than when they occur alone or in less predictable contexts. In short, the more a reader can contribute "nonvisual information" from his prior knowledge of the probabilities of words (and meanings) in language, the less visual information he requires in order to read, whether he is attempting to identify letters, words, or entire meanings.

The notion that the underlying meaning of a set of words can be utilized to aid in the identification of the words themselves may appear bizarre and even perverse. Surely words must be identified in order for their meanings to be determined? The paradox can be resolved if two common conceptual obstacles are eliminated, one concerning meaning and the other word identification.

The difficulty with *meaning* is that we frequently have trouble conceptualizing it independently of words. But meaning is clearly something extralinguistic, something beyond words (or "underlying" words, if we adopt the convention that the meaningful interpretation of sentences or utterances takes place at a "deeper" level of language). Words are eminently convenient—although not unique—vehicles for expressing and conveying meaning, but in the ultimate analysis we cannot point to one particular set of words and say that they *are* a particular meaning. The meaning transcends the actual words. The phrases *John gave a ring to Jane* and *Jane received a ring from John* may have the same underlying meaning, but it would be futile to persist with the question of which phrase was the actual meaning, or what the meaning was that the two phrases conveyed.

Many semantic and philosophical snares can be avoided if we regard "meaning", as far as the process of reading is concerned, as "information", and "comprehension" as the "reduction of the reader's uncertainty". Such a juxtaposition of words may appear trivial, but it enables us to plug the term "meaning" into the whole powerful conceptual (and metric) apparatus of information theory. In information theoretic terms, information is transmitted when uncertainty is reduced, uncertainty in turn being defined with respect to the number of alternative decisions among which the receiver of information must select (and some complications that I shall ignore concerning the relative probability of each alternative decision). For example, the statement *Queen Elizabeth I died in 1603* may be less informative to you than to me because you already know that Queen Elizabeth died in the seventeenth century while I am unsure whether she died in the 1600s or the 1500s. I had more uncertainty than you in the first place, therefore I received more information than you.

This conceptualization of information as uncertainty reduction has considerable psychological relevance because it has been shown in a variety of ways that the amount of perceptual information required to identify a particular object or event is directly related to the size of the set of alternatives from which the object or event is taken, that is, to our uncertainty. More visual information—a longer look, or a clearer representation—is required to identify a letter or word when it might be any one of 20 alternatives than when it is just one of two.

All our conventional tests of language comprehension are based on the implicit assumption that meaning if acquired will be reflected in the reduction of uncertainty. If we ask a reader who killed Cock Robin, or the great white whale, or John F. Kennedy, we expect a reduction of variability in the answer that he might give if he has understood a relevant text that he has been reading (and we would not credit him with having acquired any meaning if we know that he knew the answer already, that is, he had no prior uncertainty).

Now if the effect of acquiring meaning from a sentence is defined as the reduction of the reader's uncertainty, then we can argue that any uncertainty reduction that takes place as a consequence of reading a sentence must reflect the acquisition of information, or meaning, from that sentence. If we require less visual information to identify a word in a meaningful or predictable sequence than to identify the same word in a random order or a less predictable sequence, then our uncertainty about the identity of the word must have been reduced by some information from the sequence as a whole—by the information that I have been calling meaning.

The kind of argument that I have been using may appear counterintuitive for a second reason: We are habituated to the notion that *word identification* is an all-or-none affair—either you see a word or you don't. But it is not the case that a fixed amount of visual information is required to identify words; the amount of visual information required depends on the uncertainty of the reader, that is, on the amount of nonvisual information that he can contribute. If you don't have enough visual information to identify a word in isolation, you might have enough visual information to identify it in context, just as a letter which is so vague that we could never identify it standing alone may be easily identifiable when it occurs in a word. We identify a letter or a word not when we have accumulated a fixed amount of visual information, but when we make the subconscious perceptual decision that we have enough information. And the amount of information that we require is inversely related to the degree of our uncertainty— to the number of alternatives that we want to eliminate.

Meaning Is Required To Produce Sound

The example of translation has been used to show that meaning is something independent of the sounds of language. The same example also demonstrates how meaning can be used to produce sound. An interpreter could not produce the appropriate sounds of French unless he first comprehended the meaning underlying the English sounds. It can similarly be shown that written English could scarcely be read aloud (or subvocalized silently) unless the meaning of the passage is first extracted.

Individual written words do not carry any information about how they should be articulated. A "list" of words such as *minute on permit print read should the the we* cannot be read with anything but what is called "list intonation", which is quite different from the intonation the same words get when put together in the sequence *We should read the minute print on the permit.* Before you can utter a sentence, you must know what it means. Only the meaning of the entire sequence will tell you the syntactic role of the individual words, which for some words is essential for any decision about intonation. The written word *permit* could have been pronounced quite differently, depending on whether it was perceived as a noun (PERmit) or verb (perMIT). *Read* has two quite different pronunciations (/reed/ or /red/) depending on tense, and so has *minute*, depending on its meaning and syntactic form, none of which could be determined until the meaning of the sentence as a whole was worked out. How could meaning ever be comprehended if the words must first be correctly articulated?

There Is No Time To Produce Sounds without Meaning

Suppose reading was indeed a matter of decoding the written symbols to sound, and that "reading ahead" of the sound for meaning did not take place. Such a form of reading would be physically impossible. Individual letters cannot be identified faster than four or five a second, because the visual system just will not process information any faster, as Kolers demonstrates in Chapter 4. In addition, short-term memory will not hold more than four or five letters at a time, so that by the time the end of the word has been reached, the beginning has been forgotten. But we must exclude letter by letter identification of words in any case. If we labored through words a letter at a time we could not read any faster than 60 words a minute.

But it has been argued in Chapter 5 (Smith & Holmes, 1971) that even the most skilled readers can identify no more than a couple of unrelated words a second. (Words are "unrelated" when they cannot be meaningfully associated with each other, which is precisely the situation that obtains when a person reads "a word at a time" rather than for meaning.) Reading in this manner would completely overwhelm our working memory (short-term memory), which has its own limitations and is confounded rather than helped if speech is slowed to 100 words a minute. In any case, anyone reading with comprehension can read faster than two words a second, so he must be doing something other than translating writing to sound before extracting meaning, which is the assertion of the decoding hypothesis.

Instead, normal reading aloud involves reading ahead, reading from groups of words, in order to acquire meaning. Turn out the light or close the book while a proficient reader is reading and he will continue to utter four or five words, even though he has been deprived of visual information (Levin and Kaplan, 1968). This "eye-voice span" of four or five words (which equals four or five fixations) is the extent to which the eye is ahead of the voice; it indicates the distance ahead that the reader is sampling before committing himself to the actual utterance of a word. We need information over an average span of about four or five words in front (and also four or five words behind) if we are to read a word aloud comprehensibly and with comprehension.

Decoding to Sound Is Not the Natural Way To Read

I have argued that meaning can be extracted from sequences of written words independently of their sounds, and that in fact meaning must be comprehended if sounds are to be appropriately produced. It remains to be shown that this is in fact the way proficient readers do read, and to demonstrate that—and explain how—children learning to read appear to know instinctively that reading involves reading for meaning, not reading to identify individual words.

Fluent readers rarely read word for word, even when reading aloud. Professional speakers and newsreaders make frequent "errors" at the word level, but these misreadings are unimportant because meaning is retained. If you are reading so that listeners will comprehend you, it is far more important that you comprehend yourself what you are reading than that you identify every word correctly. Usually only actors, singers, and poetry readers attempt word-perfect reading, and such an accomplishment always demands rehearsal—the apprehension of meaning on a prior run-through or the use of a coach.

But if you are not reading word for word, you are obviously not reading by decoding to sound. The decoding point of view requires a word by word model of reading, and any evidence that readers do not read word for word is evidence against the decoding hypothesis.

It is sometimes argued that decoding to sound must take place at least when the reader meets a word that he cannot identify on sight. Such an objection overlooks the redundancy of language. Decoding to sound is the last resort of any reader. Instead the fluent reader ignores the occasional word that is not in his sight vocabulary. He takes advantage of the fact that one word in five can be completely eliminated from most English text (Shannon 1951), with scarcely any effect on its overall comprehensibility. One of the tricks in learning to read a foreign language is to minimize reliance on the dictionary and to skip over those words that cannot be immediately identified.

By the same token, only a small amount of information is required from *any* word, provided the reader is reading for meaning rather than to identify words; that is the secret of speed reading. Speed reading does not, as often thought, involve reading just one word in four, or one in ten; such a reduction would make nonsense of any text despite the redundancy of English. Instead the speed reader reads by utilizing just a fourth or a tenth of the information available from every word, diluting a minimum of visual information with a maximum of uncertainty-reducing redundancy.

Even when the fluent reader comes across an unfamiliar word that he must identify, for example because he is reading aloud, or because he believes the word is one that is in his spoken language vocabulary, he still does not decode into sound in order to acquire meaning. Rather he makes use of meaning in order to discover the sound. In such a situation a reader will first of all guess—he will make use of syntactic and semantic redundancy to reduce his uncertainty about the word. Further strategies available to both fluent and beginning readers are considered in Chapter 10. Minimal use can be made of the system of spelling-sound correspondences in English because it is not very reliable, as I show in Chapter 7.

In short, a fluent reader knows that "reading" is reading for meaning, not reading to identify or sound out individual words, even though few readers have been taught this explicitly. I use the word "knows" advisedly, since many children seem to share the same insight as soon as they begin to learn to read.

Goodman and his associates (see Chapter 14; Burke & Goodman, 1970; Weber, 1969) have shown that while more proficient beginning readers do not tend to make fewer errors than other children, they make errors (Goodman calls them "miscues") of a different kind. The errors of less proficient readers typically reflect a good deal of the graphic information in the written text (for example, "saw" for "was", "butter" for "batter") but may make little sense in the context of the passage as a whole. More accomplished readers tend to make errors that may appear quite gross visually—omitting, substituting or rearranging entire sequences of words— but that nonetheless retain the underlying meaning of the passage read. They do not stop to sound out or even identify individual words.

Furthermore there is a significant difference in the manner in which the two extreme types of beginning reader react to errors that are anomalous with respect to the sense of the passage they are reading. The less proficient reader either corrects an error immediately—because he has adopted the cautious and inefficient habit of double checking every word that he reads —or he reads on regardless of whether his word-identification errors make sense. He is not monitoring himself for meaning. The more skilled reader on the other hand is most unlikely to correct errors until he reaches a point where a mistake in meaning becomes obvious. At that point a child who is reading for meaning will, like the fluent mature reader, check back to see what has gone wrong.

The fact that many children appear to know that "reading for meaning" is the natural way to read does not require any metaphysical or biological explanation. Children will tend to regard the process of reading literally as a meaningful pursuit simply because children are adept at looking for and discovering sense in every aspect of their lives. Children are insufficiently cynical about the motives and habits of adults to imagine that they would engage in, and try to teach, an activity as meaningless as the serial identification of lists of unconnected words. But in addition there is a potent physiological imperative for children to read for meaning because it is impossible to read word for word unless meaning is identified first of all. Confronted with the task of reading children implicitly know from the burden placed on their visual systems that they have a choice between apprehending underlying meaning and the laborious and meaningless labelling of individual words. The better readers are those who, perhaps despite instructional insistence to the contrary, follow their instinct that reading is a process that is supposed to make sense.

The Relevance of Subvocalization

It is sometimes conceded that "reading for meaning" may be the practice when the material being read is easily comprehended, but that vocalization or subvocalization is necessary when the reader runs into difficulty.

In part this objection is based on the observation that many fluent readers tend to subvocalize when confronted with unfamiliar material, and that subvocalization, or inadequately repressed lip movements, are frequently observable in less proficient readers.

There is a logical flaw in arguments based on the proposition that anything we do habitually, or in times of stress, must therefore be necessary and efficacious. Such an argument is of course simply a description of superstition. The fact that we tend to subvocalize only when our reading slows down—there is no evidence that we slow down our reading to subvocalize—suggests nothing more than a regression to classroom-induced behavior. Subvocalization is often regarded as a handicap to efficient reading and can be suppressed without the slightest detriment to comprehension (Hardyck, Petrinovich, and Ellsworth, 1966).

It is quite fallacious to assume that "meaning" that is not available during unvocalized silent reading will suddenly appear when words are read aloud, or subvocalized. Where is this surplus meaning to come from? Nonsense is nonsense, whether subvocalized or not. If a reader can extract sufficient meaning from text to read aloud (or subvocalize) in an intelligible way, then he has extracted sufficient meaning to dispense with vocalization or subvocalization altogether.

An occasional variant of the subvocalization fallacy is that children should read aloud because they are "ear minded" and can extract meaning more readily from speech than from writing. But such an observation properly applies only to the speech of others; a child unable to read well enough to comprehend has no way of reading aloud intelligibly. He cannot be expected to understand himself reading aloud something that he does not understand sufficiently well to read in the first place.

Conclusion

If we accept the difference between the two levels of language, that is, between a deep structure of underlying meaning and the physical representation of surface structure, then the conventional model of reading that can be depicted like this:

| surface structure of writing | $\rightarrow$ | surface structure of spoken language |

is obviously oversimplified. At the very least comprehension must involve

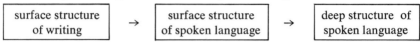

But as I have shown, it is not possible to go from the surface structure of written language to the surface structure of speech without meaning, without the deep structure of written language:

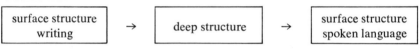

However since the two deep structures are the same, there is no point in extracting meaning twice; the deep structure is common to both the written and spoken forms. For reading aloud the following representation is sufficient:

and for reading silently the final stage can be removed completely:

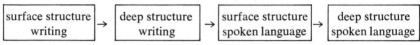

In such a conceptualization, there is no room to hypothesize decoding to sound at all.

References

Burke, Carolyn L., & Goodman, Kenneth S. When a child reads: a psycholinguistic analysis. *Elementary English*, 1970, 121–129.

Chomsky, Noam, & Halle, Morris. *The Sound Pattern of English*. New York: Harper & Row, 1968.

Goodman, Kenneth S. Decoding, from code to what? *Journal of Reading*, 1971, *14*, 7, 445–462.

Halle, Morris. Some thoughts on spelling. In Goodman, K. S., & Fleming, J. T. *Psycholinguistics and the Teaching of Reading*. Newark, Delaware; International Reading Association, 1969.

Hardyck, C. D., Petrinovich, L. F., & Ellsworth, D. W. Feedback of speech muscle activity during silent reading: rapid extinction. *Science*, 1966, *154*, 1467–1468.

Jespersen, Otto H. *A Modern English Grammar on Historical Principles*. Heidelberg: C. Winter, 1909–1949.

Levin, Harry, & Kaplan, Eleanor. The eye-voice span within active and passive sentences. *Language and Speech*, 1968, *11*, 251–258.

Mathews, Mitford M. *Learning To Read: Historically Considered*. Chicago: University of Chicago Press, 1966.

Miller, George A. Some preliminaries to psycholinguistics. *American Psychologist*, 1965, *20*, 15–20.

Shannon, Claude E. Prediction and entropy of printed English. *Bell Systems Technical Journal*, 1957, *36*, 497–516.

Smith, Frank. *Understanding Reading*. New York: Holt, Rinehart and Winston, 1971.

Smith, Frank, & Holmes, Deborah Lott. The independence of letter, word and meaning identification in reading. *Reading Research Quarterly*, 1971, *6*, 3, 394–415.

Weber, Rose-Marie. The study of oral reading errors; a survey of the literature. *Reading Research Quarterly*, 1968, *4*, 96–119.

7

The Efficiency of Phonics

Part of the argument against the decoding hypothesis is that the system of spelling-to-sound (or grapheme-phoneme) correspondences of English is far too complex and unreliable to be used as a tool for identifying unrecognized words, especially by beginning readers. This chapter examines the complexity of spelling-to-sound correspondences in English.

It is taken from Chapter 12 of Understanding Reading, © *1971 by Holt, Rinehart and Winston, Inc., and reprinted by permission of the publishers.*

The aim of phonics instruction is to provide rules that will "predict" how a word will sound from the way it is spelled. The value of phonics would appear to depend on how many rules are required to establish correspondences between the letters and sounds of English, or to what extent our phonemes can be predicted by the rules of phonics. But by now it is probably no surprise that any question related to language involving a simple "how many" leads to a very complicated and unsatisfactory evasion of an answer. Phonics is no exception.

Everything is wrong about the question. The first problem concerns our expectations about rules. If we expect a rule to mean a regularity that has no exceptions, then we shall have a difficult task finding any rules in phonics

84

at all. Here is a phonic rule that would appear to have impeccable ante-cedents: final *e* following a single consonant indicates that the preceding vowel should be long, as in *hat* and *hate*, or *hop* and *hope*. And here is an instant exception: *axe* has a single consonant but a short /a/ (while *ache*, which has a double consonant, takes a long /a/). We have the choice of admitting that our traditional rule is not impervious to exceptions, or else we have to make a rule for the exceptions. One explanation that might be offered is that *x* is really a double consonant, *ks* (and that *ch* is really a single consonant, *k*). But then we are in the rather peculiar position of changing the notion of what constitutes a single letter simply because we have a rule that does not fit all cases. If we start to say that the definition of what constitutes a letter depends on the pronunciation of a word, how can we say that the pronunciation of a word can be predicted from its letters? Besides, what can we say about the silent *e* at the end of *have* or *love*, which is put there only because there is a convention that English words may not end with a naked *v*? Or the *e* at the end of *house*, which is to indicate that the word is not a plural?

Having made the point that phonic rules will have exceptions, the next problem is to decide what constitutes an exception. Some exceptions occur so frequently and regularly that they would appear to be rules in their own right. In fact it is quite arbitrary how anyone decides to draw the line be-tween rules and exceptions. We have a choice of saying that the sounds of written English can be predicted by relatively few rules, although there will be quite a lot of exceptions, or by a large number of rules with rela-tively few exceptions. In fact, if we care to say that some rules have only one application, for example that *acht* is pronounced /ot/ as in "yacht", then we can describe English completely in terms of rules simply because we have legislated exceptions completely out of existence.

If the concept of a rule seems somewhat arbitrary, the notion of what constitutes a letter is even more idiosyncratic. It is true that in one sense there can be no doubt about what a letter is—it is one of the 26 characters in the alphabet—but any attempt to construct rules of spelling-sound corre-spondence is doomed from the start if we restrict our terms of reference to individual letters. To start with, there are only 26 letters to represent about 46 phonemes, so some of them at least must do double duty. We shall find, of course, that many letters stand for more than one phoneme, while many phonemes are represented by more than one letter. However, many sounds are not represented by single letters at all—*th*, *ch*, *ou*, *ue*, for example—so that we have to consider some combinations of letters as really representing quite distinct spelling units—rather as if *th* were a letter in its own right. It has been asserted, with the help of a computer analysis of over 20,000 words, that there are 52 "major spelling units" in English, 32 for consonants and 20 for vowels, effectively doubling the size of the "alphabet".[1]

The addition of all these extra spelling units, however, does not seem to make the structure of the English writing system very much more orderly. Some of the original letters of the alphabet are quite superfluous. There is nothing that *c* or *q* or *x* can do that could not be done by the other consonants. And many of the additional spelling units that are recognized simply duplicate the work of single letters, such as *ph* for *f*, and *dg* for *j*, and, similarly, there are compound vowels whose effect is the same as the silent final *e*, like *ea* in *meat* compared with *mete*. Some combinations have a special value only when they occur in particular parts of a word—*gh* may be pronounced as *f* (or as nothing) at the end of a word (*rough, through*) but is pronounced just like a single *g* at the beginning (*ghost* and *gold, ghastly* and *garden*). Often letters have only a relational function, sacrificing any sound of their own in order to indicate how another letter should be sounded. An obvious example is the silent *e*, another is the *u* that distinguishes the *g* in *guest* from the *g* in *gem*.

So for our basic question of phonics, what we are really asking is how many arbitrarily defined rules can account for an indeterminate number of correspondences between an indefinite set of spelling units and an uncertain number of phonemes (the total and quality of which may vary from person to person).

Some aspects of spelling are simply unpredictable, certainly to a reader with a limited knowledge of word derivations, no matter how one tries to define a spelling unit. An example of a completely unpredictable spelling to sound correspondence is *th*, which is pronounced in one way at the beginning of words like *this, than, that, those, them, then, these* but in another way at the beginning of *think, thank, thatch, thong, theme*, and so on. There is only one way to tell whether *th* should be pronounced as in /this/ or as in /think/, and that is to remember every instance. On the other hand, in many dialects there is no difference between the sounds *w* and *wh*, so that in some cases it can be the spelling that is not predictable, not the sound. (As always, you can even find exceptions to exceptions if you look for them—for example, the word *who*.)

Almost all our very common words are exceptions—*of* requires a rule of its own for the pronunciation of *f*.

The game of finding exceptions is too easy to play. I shall give only one more example to illustrate the kind of difficulty one must run into in trying to construct—or teach—reliable rules of phonic correspondence. How are

---

[1] R. L. Venezky, English orthography: its graphical structure and its relation to sound, *Reading Research Quarterly, 2* (1967), 75–106. See also Ruth H. Weir and R. L. Venezky, Spelling-to-sound patterns, in Goodman, K. S., *The Psycholinguistic Nature of the Reading Process*. Detroit: Wayne State University Press, 1968.

the letters *ho* pronounced, when they occur at the beginning of a word? Just to start you on the way to counting all the alternatives, here are a few examples: *hot, hoot, hook, hour, honest, house, hope, honey, hoist.*

Of course, there are rules (or are some of them merely exceptions?) that can account for many of the pronunciations of ho. *But there is one very significant implication in all the examples that applies to almost all English words—in order to apply phonic rules,* words would have to be read from right to left. *The way in which the reader pronounces* ho *depends on what comes after it, and the same applies to the* p *in* ph, *the* a *in* ate, *the* k *in* knot, *the* t *in* -tion. *The exceptions are very very few, like* asp, *which is pronounced differently if preceded by a* w, *and* f, *pronounced* /v/ *only if preceded by* o. *The fact that "sound dependencies" in words run from right to left is an obvious difficulty for a beginning reader trying to sound out a word from left to right, or for a theorist who wants to maintain that words are identified on a left-to-right letter-by-letter basis.*

In summary, English is not a highly predictable language as far as its spelling and sound relationships are concerned. Just how much can be done to predict the pronunciation of a relatively small number of common words with a finite number of rules we shall see in a moment. But before we conclude the catalogue of complications and exceptions, two points should be reiterated. The first point is that phonic rules must be considered as probabilistic, as guides to the way words might be pronounced, and that there is rarely any indication of when a rule does or does not apply. In other words, it is often impossible to know for certain which phonic rules apply. The rule that specifies how to pronounce *ph* in *telephone* falls down in the face of *haphazard*, or *shepherd*, or *cuphook*. The rule for *oe* in *doe* and *woe* will not work for *shoe*. The probability of being wrong if you do not know the word at all is very high. Even if individual rules were likely to be right three times out of four, there would still be less than one chance in three of identifying even a short four-phoneme word without at least one error. The second point is that English phonics tends to look deceptively simple when you know how words are pronounced; the problem for the beginning reader trying to use phonics is not just the number of rules he must remember, but that he also has to have some knowledge of when they apply and what are the exceptions. The only way to distinguish the pronunciation of *sh* in *bishop* and *mishap*, or *th* in *father* and *fathead*, is to be able to read the entire word in the first place.

One systematic attempt has been made to construct a workable set of phonic rules for English.[2] The effort has had modest aims—to see how far

---

[2] Betty Berdiansky, B. Cronnell, and J. Koehler, *Spelling-Sound Relations and Primary Form–Class Descriptions for Speech-Comprehension Vocabularies of 6–9-Year-Olds.* Southwest Regional Laboratory for Educational Research and Development, Technical Report, no. 15, 1969.

one could go in establishing a set of correspondence rules for the 6092 one- and two-syllable words among 9000 different words in the comprehension vocabularies of six- to nine-year-old children. The words were all taken from books to which the children were normally exposed—they were the words that the children knew and ought to be able to identify if they were to be able to read the material with which they were confronted at school.

The researchers who analyzed the 6092 words found rather more than the 52 "major spelling units" to which I have already referred—in fact, they identified 69 "grapheme units" which had to be separately distinguished in their rules. A group of letters was called a "grapheme unit", just like a single letter, whenever its relationship to a sound (or sounds) could not be accounted for by any rule for single letters. Grapheme units included pairs of consonants such as *ch*, *th*; pairs of vowels such as *ea*, *oy*; and letters that commonly function together, such as *ck* and *qu*, as well as double consonants like *bb* and *tt*, all of which require some separate phonic explanation. The number of grapheme units should not surprise us—the previously mentioned 52 "major units" were not intended to represent the only spelling units that could occur, but only the most frequent ones. As we shall see, there were other grapheme units that could not be accounted for in terms of general rules.

An arbitrary decision was made about what would constitute a rule—it would have to account for a spelling-sound correspondence occurring in at least ten different words. Any distinctive spelling-sound correspondence— and any grapheme unit—that did not occur in at least ten words was considered an "exception". Actually, the researchers made several exceptions among the exceptions—they wanted their rules to account for as many of their words as possible, and so they let several cases through the net when it seemed to them more appropriate to account for a grapheme unit with a rule rather than to stigmatize it as an exception.

The researchers discovered that their 6000 words involved 211 distinct spelling-sound "correspondences"—this does not mean that 211 different sounds were represented, but that the phonemes that did occur were represented by a total of 211 different spellings (obviously, some of the grapheme units were related to more than one sound). The results are summarized in Table 1. Eighty-three of the correspondences involved consonant grapheme units, and 128 involved vowel grapheme units, including no fewer than 79 that were associated with the six "primary" single-letter vowels, *a*, *e*, *i*, *o*, *u*, *y*. In other words, there was a total of 79 different ways in which the single vowels could be pronounced. Of the 211 correspondences, 45 were clusters of exceptions, about half involving vowels and half consonants. The exclusion of 45 correspondences from the "rules" meant that nearly ten percent of the 6092 words had to be regarded as "exceptions".

The pronunciation of the remaining words was accounted for by a grand

Table 1 Spelling-Sound Correspondences among 6092 One- and Two-Syllable Words in the Vocabularies of Nine-Year-Old Children

	Consonants	Primary Vowels	Secondary Vowels	Total
Spelling-sound correspondences	83	79	49	211
"Rules"	60	73	33	166
"Exceptions"	23	6	16	45
Grapheme units in rules	44	6	19	69

total of 166 rules! Sixty of these rules were concerned with the pronunciation of consonants (which are generally thought to have fairly "regular" pronunciations) and 106 with single or complex vowels.

The research that has just been described is important in a number of ways for understanding reading and the teaching of reading. Some of the conclusions that can be drawn are far-reaching in their implications. The first is very simply that phonics is complicated. Without saying anything at all about whether it is desirable to teach young children a knowledge of phonics, we now have an idea of the magnitude of the endeavor. We now know that if we really expect to give a child a mastery of phonics, then we are not talking about a dozen or so rules. We are talking about 166 rules, which will still not account for hundreds of the words that a child might expect to meet in his early reading.

It is obvious that the most that can be expected from phonics is that it will provide a *clue* to the sound (or "name") of a configuration being examined. Phonics can provide only approximations. Even if a reader did happen to know the 79 rules that are required to account for the pronunciation of the six vowels, he would still have no sure way of telling which rule applied—or even that he was not dealing with an exception. However, we should not make the situation seem more complex than it really is; it ought to be added that a reader is rarely in absolute doubt about what a word might be. Just as many letter combinations do not occur in the written language, so many sound combinations do not occur in speech. Many of the phonics rules might be excluded in particular instances because they would lead to a sound combination that is not a word. And we do not need to have all available sound cues to identify a word, any more than we need all possible visual cues to read it. There is still the possibility, however, that not all alternatives can be eliminated by phonic rules.

A more serious problem perhaps is the possibility that reliance on phonic methods will involve a reader in so much delay that his short-term memory will be overloaded and he will lose the sense of what he is reading. Particularly relevant is the possibility that a tendency to rely exclusively on the rules will create a handicap for the beginning reader whose biggest problem is to acquire speed. Use of the redundancy that exists within groups of words may be far more efficacious in identifying a particular word than dealing with the word as if it were standing in isolation.

There is still one question that has not been touched. An answer has been provided to the question of how efficient phonics might be—that a fairly complex rule system would be required to account for the pronunciation of 90 percent of quite common words, and that at best it would only operate probabilistically; there is no way of guaranteeing that a word will be correctly identified by phonics alone. The question that cannot yet be answered concerns the *effectiveness* of phonics: is the limited degree of efficiency that might be attained worth acquiring? Other factors have to be taken into account related to the *cost* of trying to learn and use a phonic system. Our working memories do not have an infinite capacity and reading is not a task that can be accomplished at too leisurely a pace. Other sources of information exist for finding out what a word in context might be, especially if the word is in the spoken vocabulary of the reader.

8

Reading, Writing, and Phonology

——CAROL CHOMSKY

The orthography of English has been poor-mouthed for centuries. Confronted by the evidence that the sounds of words cannot be predicted directly from their spelling, many "reformers" have refused to change their views about the nature of reading, and instead have long sought to modify the alphabet, or the spelling system, or both.

One of the most important contributions of psycholinguistics to reading, still widely unknown and little appreciated, is a radical reconsideration of the function and efficiency of English spelling. According to some authorities, English is blest with the best of all possible orthographies. They argue that English spelling is not an inadequate system for representing sounds, but rather a highly efficient system for representing meanings. In fact, there might even seem to be greater consistency and reason in the spelling of words than in their sounds.

Two distinguished proponents of this new approach to spelling are Noam Chomsky and Morris Halle, who argue for the existence of an underlying abstract level of word representation in a very technical work cited in this chapter. Carol Chomsky elaborates upon aspects of Chomsky and Halle's work most relevant to reading, and puts the result into somewhat plainer language. The abstract to the original article says that she "discusses the relation of conventional English orthography to the sound structure of the language, showing that this relation is much closer than is ordinarily assumed. She points out that many of the non-phonetic aspects of English spelling are motivated rather than arbitrary, in that they correspond to a level of representation within the phonological system of the language which is deeper than the phonetic level".

91

The argument is based on the notion that every speaker of language possesses an internalized set of rules, or a grammar, *that he uses to put words together in order to express meaning in speech. This internalized grammar includes a* lexicon *which lists information concerning the pronunciation (the "phonetic representation"), syntactic function, and meaning of words, and how they are related to each other. Carol Chomsky refers to the representation of every word in this internal lexicon as its "abstract underlying form", and conceptualizes that each form has a "lexical spelling" which shows its relation to other words.*

It is important that the concept of lexical spelling should not be interpreted literally. For example, when the author argues that reading involves the reconstruction from spelling of the "abstract lexical spelling of words", she is not implying that reading is a matter of decoding from one spelling system to another. What she is saying (according to my interpretation) is that readers "interpret" written words according to an underlying system in which words are specified and related according to their meaning rather than their sound.

Dr. Chomsky is a scholar at the Radcliffe Institute and a research associate at the Harvard Graduate School of Education. The chapter is taken from a paper with the same title in Harvard Educational Review, *1970, 40, 2, 287–309, reprinted by permission of the author and publishers.*

The inconsistencies of English spelling are often a source of regret to the reading teacher and to those concerned with reading in general. Because English spelling is frequently not phonetic, because of the large number of words which are lacking in grapheme-phoneme correspondence, it is often concluded that the orthography is irregular and a relatively poor system for representing the spoken language. While it is true that English spelling in many instances is deficient as a phonetic transcription of the spoken language, it does not necessarily follow that it is therefore a poor system of representation. This paper discusses a far more positive view of English orthography which has emerged from recent work in phonological theory within the framework of transformational grammar.

In *The Sound Pattern of English*[1] Chomsky and Halle demonstrate a variety of ways in which the relation of conventional English orthography to the sound structure of the language is much closer than is ordinarily assumed. Simply stated, the conventional spelling of words corresponds more closely to an underlying abstract level of representation within the sound system of the language that it does to the surface phonetic form that

[1] N. Chomsky and M. Halle, *The Sound Pattern of English* (New York: Harper & Row, 1968).

the words assume in the spoken language. Phonological theory, as presented in *The Sound Pattern of English*, incorporates such an abstract level of representation of words and describes the general rules by which these abstract underlying forms are converted into particular phonetic realizations. English spelling corresponds fairly well to these abstract underlying forms rather than to their phonetic realizations. When viewed in its correspondence to this underlying form, English spelling does not appear as arbitrary or irregular as purely phonetic criteria might indicate. Indeed, from this viewpoint, conventional orthography is seen in its essentials as a "near optimal system for representing the spoken language."[2] In this paper I will attempt to clarify this notion of abstract underlying form, to show its place and function within a grammar of English, and to explain its relation to the spoken language. . . .

The motivation for postulating an abstract form of words which underlies their phonetic form is roughly as follows. One aspect of writing a grammar for a language is deciding how words are to be represented in the grammar's dictionary, or lexicon. This essentially means deciding on a spelling for each word, what I will call "lexical spelling." One way, obviously, would be to proceed according to pronunciation and use a phonetic transcription, or the type of broad phonetic transcription that is often termed a phonemic transcription. (Those who regret the frequent lack of grapheme-phoneme correspondence in English spelling seem to be looking for just this in orthography.)

At first glance, this phonetic approach would seem to be the simplest and certainly the most direct way of proceeding. However, the attempt to incorporate into the grammar a spelling system so closely tied to the pronunciation of English immediately runs into trouble. There are numerous reasons why. Let me give one example here. In English, words undergo pronunciation shifts when suffixes are added to them: e.g., the [ɛy]—[æ] alternation in *nation-national*, *nature-natural*, *sane-sanity*. These pairs of words, because of the vowel alternation, would have to receive two spellings each in a "phonemic" lexicon, each member of the pair constituting a separate lexical item. That is, one spelling would be needed with [ɛy] for the word in isolation: *nation*, and another with [æ] for the stem to which certain suffixes are added: *nation*, *-al*, *-ality*, *-alistic*, etc.

Now these [ɛy]—[æ] alternations, as it happens, are not isolated cases or irregular occurrences. This type of vowel alternation is very common in English and takes place under specifiable conditions of great generality and wide applicability. It is in fact an integral feature of the phonological

---

[2] N. Chomsky, "Phonology and Reading," in *Basic Studies in Reading*, edited by Levin and Williams (New York: Basic Books, 1970).

system of the language which speakers of English have internalized and which they use automatically in producing and understanding utterances. For we find that the same principles which govern the [ɛy]—[æ] alternation cited govern also other vowel alternations, such as the [ɪy]—[ɛ] alternation in extr*e*me-extr*e*mity, conv*e*ne-conv*e*ntion, the [ɑy]—[ɪ] alternation in exped*i*te-exped*i*tious, w*i*de-w*i*dth, and the [o]—[ɑ] alternation in ph*o*ne-ph*o*nic, comp*o*se-comp*o*site.

Word pairs such as these, though phonetically different, are recognized by speakers of the language as variant forms of the same word. It is revealing, therefore, when designing the grammar's lexicon, to postulate just one lexical spelling for the vowel, and then to state the general principles which apply to this one shared vowel to produce the two different vowels actually present in the pronunciation of the words. The lexical spelling thus acquires the character of an abstract representation, from which the actual phonetic realizations are predictable according to general rules of pronunciation.

This dual feature, of abstract spelling and rules for converting to pronunciation, is a highly desirable feature of a grammar. Among other things, it retains in the lexical spelling similarities which are real in the language. *Nation* and *national* are not different words in the sense that *nation* and *notion* are different words. They are different forms of the same word. For the lexical spelling to capture this sameness, in spite of surface phonetic differences, is highly desirable. Of course this sameness is exactly what is captured by conventional English orthography in the examples above, where the alternations presented are the familiar long-short vowel alternations. From this viewpoint, this divergence of the conventional orthography from phonetic transcription appears well motivated. It offers the advantage of expressing an underlying reality of the language which is masked by surface phonetic features.

In order to clarify the role of the lexical spelling of words within a transformational grammar, let me indicate what place this abstract entity occupies in the grammar. I have said that the lexical spelling is the way words are spelled in the grammar's lexicon. The other components of the grammar that concern us here are the syntactic component and the phonological component. The syntactic component consists of phrase structure rules and transformational rules. Its output is, among other things, a sentence whose syntactic structure is indicated (see diagram below), in which the words are represented in their lexical spelling, just as they come from the lexicon. It is this string of words, together with information about their syntactic structure, that serves as input to the phonological component. The phonological component in its turn is a complex system of phonological rules that apply to this string and convert it into a phonetic representation. This sequence may be diagrammed thus:

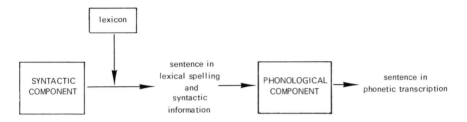

The sentence "We established telegraphic communication," for example, would assume the following forms in the above sequence of operations:

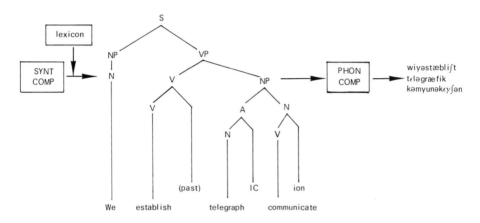

The phonological component contains rules that operate on the lexical spellings, taking into account their syntactic environments, in order to produce a phonetic representation. These are rules that place stress where it belongs, that introduce phonetic effects such as palatalization, velar softening, spirantization, voicing, diphthongization, vowel reduction, vowel shift, laxing and tensing of vowels, and so on. In short, all the rules that make up the phonological system of the language. Their role is to operate on abstract lexical representations within their syntactic context in order to produce the phonetic forms that actually occur in speech.

In producing and interpreting speech, a speaker of the language constantly operates with rules such as these. Certainly he has no conscious knowledge of them any more than he has conscious knowledge of the syntactic rules which enable him to produce and understand sentence structures in his language. In the course of acquiring his language he has internalized the rules of its phonological system, and as a mature speaker he operates in accordance with them both in speaking and in comprehending the spoken language.

Among the interesting decisions that have to be made when designing the grammar is the question of what information properly belongs in the lexical spelling and what should be introduced by the phonological rules. The necessary phonetic output could be achieved with a number of different distributions of information and operations within the grammar. In general, the principle adhered to is that phonetic variation is not indicated in the lexical spelling when it is predictable by general rule. All such predictable phonetic information is left to the phonological rules. As an example, consider the long-short vowel alternations discussed above: *nation-national, wide-width, phone-phonic,* etc. It is sufficient to use only the long vowel in the lexicon, and to leave it to the phonological rules to shorten this vowel automatically in the presence of certain suffixes. Although the vowel shift could theoretically be introduced either in the lexicon or by the phonological rules, it is preferable to introduce it by phonological rule, as mentioned, for the double reason of expressing the underlying sameness of the vowel, and generality of the feature of vowel shift within the language.

Consider also the common items of words such as *courage/courage-ous,* or *anxi-ous/anxi-ety,* or *photograph/photograph-y/photograph-ic.* Although the phonetic variations are considerable, they are perfectly automatic, and the lexical spellings can ignore them. They will be introduced by the phonological component. Of course, the conventional orthography ignores them as well. These are good examples of cases where the conventional orthography, by corresponding to lexical spelling rather than phonetic representation, permits immediate direct identification of the lexical item in question, without requiring the reader to abstract away from irrelevant phonetic detail. Conventional orthography has itself abstracted away from the phonetic details, and presents the lexical item directly, as it were.

Now it is a feature of English that it has a rich system of phonetic variations which function very much like the vowel alternations discussed. That is, English has many kinds of surface phonetic variations which need not, and preferably ought not, be represented in the lexical spelling of words. They are wholly predictable within the phonological system of the language, and are therefore best introduced within the grammar by means of automatic phonological rules. As with vowel alternation, these other variations obscure an underlying sameness which the lexical spelling is able to capture. And as with vowel alternations, these surface phonetic variations are not reflected in the conventional orthography.

Consider, for example, the extensive system of consonant alternations in English which are surface phonetic variations only. These phonetic variants are expressed neither in the lexical spellings of words in the grammar, nor in the conventional orthography. Such consonant alternations are surprisingly common. Some examples are:

PHONETIC VARIANTS	SAMPLE WORD PAIRS
[k] — [s]	medi*c*ate—medi*c*ine
	criti*c*al—criti*c*ize
	romanti*c*—romanti*cize*
[g] — [dʒ]	sa*g*acity—sa*g*e
	prodi*g*al—prodi*g*ious
[d] — [dʒ]	gra*d*e—gra*d*ual
	mo*d*e—mo*d*ular
[t] — [ʃ]	residen*t*—residen*t*ial
	expedi*t*e—expedi*t*ious
[t] — [tʃ]	fac*t*—fac*t*ual
	ques*t*—ques*t*ion
	righ*t*—righ*t*eous
[z] — [ʒ]	revi*s*e—revi*s*ion
[s] — [z]	*s*ign—re*s*ign
	gymna*s*tics—gymna*s*ium

All of these phonetic variations are automatic and predictable within the phonological system of the language. They need not be represented in the lexical spelling of the words, and indeed, underlying similarities which are real in the language would be lost in the grammar if these differences were to be represented on the lexical level. And the same is true of the conventional orthography. By being "unphonetic" in all of these cases, by not exhibiting grapheme-phoneme correspondence, the orthography is able to reflect significant regularities which exist at a deeper level of the sound system of the language, thus making efficient reading easier.

Two other such surface phonetic variations of English, in addition to vowel alternations and consonant alternations, are the interrelated features of stress placement and vowel reduction. Again, these two features are not reflected in the lexical spelling of words because they operate predictably according to rule. The orthography also fails to record them. Surprising as it may seem, the placement of primary stress and the varying degrees of lesser stress in English works largely according to phonological rule, given the lexical spellings of words and information about the syntactic structures in which they appear. Less surprising is the fact that vowel reduction, the pronunciation of certain vowels as a neutral schwa [ə] in unstressed positions, takes place according to rule.

Take, for example, the word *télegraph*. It is stressed on the first syllable. In *telegráphic*, primary stress shifts to the third syllable, and in *telégraphy*, to the second syllable. Since this is a regular variation which many lexical items undergo, and not an unusual feature of this particular word, none of this need be expressed on a lexical level, nor is it expressed in the conventional orthography. It is left to the phonological component of the grammar to introduce these variations.

Consider also the phenomenon of vowel reduction in this same word. The above forms assume the following phonetic shape in speech:

(a) telegraph   [té lə græf]
(b) telegraphic   [tɛ lə gréf]-ic
(c) telegraphy   [tə lɛ́ grəf]-y

In (a) and (b) the second vowel is reduced; in (c), the first and third vowels. The predictable nature of these variations is discussed by Chomsky and Halle in the following passage from *The Sound Pattern of English*.[3]

It is quite obvious . . . that this phonetic variation (of stress shift and vowel reduction in the three forms of *telegraph*) is not fortuitous—it is not of the same type as the variation between *I* and *we*, which depends on specific assignment of the latter to the category of plurality. Given the grammar of English, if we delete specific reference to the item *we*, there is no way to predict the phonetic form of the plural variant of *I*. On the other hand, the rules for English grammar certainly do suffice to determine the phonetic variation of *telegraph* without specific mention of this lexical item, just as they suffice to predict the regular variation between *cat* and *cats* without specifically mentioning the plural form. It is quite obvious that English grammar is complicated by the fortuitous variation between *I* and *we* but not by the totally predictable variation between *cat* and *cats*. Similarly, the grammar would be more complicated if *telegraph* did *not* undergo precisely the variation in (a)–(c); if, for example, it had one phonetic form in all contexts, or if it had the form (a) in the context -ic, (b) in the context -y, and (c) in isolation.

Once again, surface phonetic variations which are automatic and which obscure similarities in lexical items are not represented at the lexical level (or in the orthography), but are introduced by the phonological component of the grammar.

I have referred several times to the abstract nature of the lexical spellings in the grammar. Now that a number of examples has been given, this abstract character of the lexical level becomes clearer. In the lexical spelling, many predictable phonetic features of the spoken language are suppressed, e.g., vowel alternations, consonant alternations, schwa, stress, and others that I have not gone into. The lexical spelling, and the conventional orthography which corresponds so closely to it, abstract away from these variations in pronunciation and represent deeper similarities that have a semantic function in the language. The lexical items are, after all, the meaning-

---

[3] Chomsky and Halle, *op. cit.*, pp. 11–12.

bearing items in the language. Lexical spellings represent the meaning-bearing items directly, without introducing phonetic detail irrelevant to their identification. Thus on the lexical level and in the orthography, words that *are* the same *look* the same. In phonetic transcription they look different. In reading, one is very likely aided by this feature of the conventional orthography. It permits reading to occur with more efficiency. That is, the spelling system leads the reader directly to the meaning-bearing items that he needs to identify, without requiring that he abstract away from superficial and irrelevant phonetic detail. In speech, on the other hand, one operates on both the abstract and the phonetic levels, with the phonological rules mediating between the two.

It seems also that this abstract lexical level is highly resistant to historical change, and remains the same over long periods of time. Pronunciation shifts that occur as a language changes over time appear to be the result of changes in phonological rules rather than changes in the lexical spellings themselves. For this reason a stable orthography remains effective over time in spite of changes in the way a language is pronounced. And it appears that a wide range of dialect differences also stem from adjustments of phonological rules rather than differences in lexical spellings. This would explain why conventional English orthography is a reasonably adequate system of representation for both British and American English, and the vast range of English dialects that exist within each country and around the world.

Given that lexical spellings differ from phonetic representations in the numerous ways just illustrated, the question naturally arises what implications this may have for speakers of the language and their internal organization of its sound system. Are these abstract lexical representations that are postulated by the linguist merely convenient fictions that the linguist manufactures for the purposes of his grammar, or do they have a psychological reality for the language user? In other words, is the claim that the orthography corresponds to something real in the linguistic knowledge of the reader based on anything that the reader can honestly be said to know?

It seems to me that in a very real sense the lexical level of representation and the corresponding aspects of English orthography do have a psychological reality for the language user. I realize that this assertion will be troublesome to many readers, so let me be very specific about what I mean. I spoke above of the "common item" of words such as *anxi-ous/anxi-ety*, and *courage/courage-ous*. Pairs such as *critic-al/critic-ize, revis-e/revis-ion, illustrat-e/illustrat-ive* also contain common items. There is little question that speakers recognize these words as related. But clearly what is common to these pairs is not their *surface* form, their phonetic representation, for they are pronounced differently:

anxi - ous : [ǽŋkʃ]
anxi - ety : [æŋgzáy]
courage : [kʌ́rədʒ]
courage - ous : [kəréydʒ]
critic - al : [krítɪk]
critic - ize : [krítɪs]
revis - e : [riváy̆z]
revis - ion : [rivíʒ]
illustrat - e : [íləstrɛyt]
illustrat - ive : [ɪlʌ́strət]

What is common to them, as was shown earlier, is their *underlying* form, their lexical spelling, which the orthography corresponds to quite closely. To say that this form has psychological reality is to say only that this common item is recognized by the language user *as a common item*, and that its different phonetic realizations are regular within the sound system of the language. The variations in the pairs listed above are not idiosyncratic within the grammar, as is for example the variation between *woman* and *women*, but take place according to general phonological rule. These variations are automatic and do not complicate the grammar in any way. Indeed they would complicate the grammar if they did *not* occur precisely the way they do.

To look at it another way, one might consider, for example, the status of the [k]-[s] alternation in *kill/sill* as compared to *medicate/medicine*. The difference in status can readily become clear to one who knows the language. In *kill/sill* the phonetic change from [k] to [s] creates a new lexical item. It is both a phonetic and a lexical change. But in *medicate/medicine* it is a phonetic change only. The lexical item remains the same, as does the lexical spelling and the orthography. A speaker who is not aware of this differing status of the two [k]-[s] alternations can have the difference brought to the level of awareness without difficulty, because it reflects a fact about his language that he uses continually, and that is far more general than this one example. In order to become aware of this fact he does not need to be taught, as a foreigner learning English would, but merely to have it brought to his attention.

The implications of this view of English orthography with regard to reading are several. First, it implies that what the mature reader seeks and recognizes when he reads is not what are commonly called grapheme-phoneme correspondences, but rather the correspondence of written symbol to the abstract lexical spelling of words. Letters represent segments in lexical spelling, not sounds. It is the phonological rule system of the language, which the reader commands, that relates the lexical segments to sounds in a systematic fashion.

Stated somewhat differently, the mature reader does not proceed on the assumption that the orthography is phonetically valid, but rather interprets the written symbols according to lexical spellings. His task is facilitated by the fact that the orthography closely corresponds to this lexical representation. He does not need to abstract away from unnecessary phonetic detail to reconstruct this lexical representation as would be required if the English spelling system were phonetically based. What he needs to identify are the lexical items, the meaning-bearing items, and these are quite readily accessible to him from the lexically based orthography.

It is highly likely that the child, however, in the beginning stages of reading, does assume that the orthography is in some sense "regular" with respect to pronunciation. In order to progress to more complex stages of reading, the child must abandon this early hypothesis, and come eventually to interpret written symbols as corresponding to more abstract lexical spellings. Normally he is able to make this transition unaided as he matures and gains experience both with the sound structure of his language and with reading. It may be, however, that the difficulty encountered by some poor readers is related to the fact that they have not made this crucial transition. This question should be amenable to study. If it appears that this is indeed a factor for some poor readers, then a second related question can be raised, namely how to encourage this progress in children who have not achieved it on their own.

Most methods of teaching reading have little or nothing to offer with respect to this shift in emphasis from a phonetic to a lexical interrelation of the spelling system. Beginning reading instruction that deals analytically with letters and sounds, whether it is based on phonics, the linguistic method, or any other method, tends to treat phonetically accurate spellings as regular in the language, and phonetic inaccuracies as irregular. Children translate spellings into sounds by means of letter-sound correspondences or spelling patterns without ever being expected to apply their knowledge of the phonological system of English to the task. They learn to decode written English much as a foreigner would who knows nothing of English phonology. The child thus gains the impression that spelling is meant to be a direct representation of the pronounced form of words. No provision is made at any point for having him revise this notion in favor of a more realistic view of spelling regularity based on word relationships and underlying lexical similarities. It would seem wise to take this view of regularity into account in dealing with reading beyond the introductory stages. At some point emphasis ought to be shifted away from the phonetic aspects of spelling to a consideration of the underlying lexical properties of the orthographic system. Crucial to this shift in emphasis is the expectation that the child will rely more and more heavily on phonological processing as he learns to decode written English more efficiently. . . .

It is of interest to realize that the child, when he learns to read, is not being introduced to a system of representation that is inconsistent with the language that he speaks. It is simply that the orthography bears an *indirect* rather than a direct relation to his pronunciation. The direct correlation is to lexical spelling, a level of linguistic processing that is beneath the surface, related to pronunciation by regular phonological rules that are part of the child's normal linguistic equipment. This correspondence can be diagrammed as follows:

$$\text{LETTERS} = \begin{array}{c} \text{segments in} \\ \text{lexical spelling} \end{array} \xleftarrow{\;\; \text{phonological rules} \;\;} \rightarrow \text{PRONUNCIATION}$$

Letters correspond to segments in lexical spelling, which in turn are related to pronunciation through the medium of the phonological rules. The correspondence is to something real in the child's linguistic system that he is equipped to handle. It is because it is one step removed from his pronunciation that it is not superficially apparent.

To make this point clearer, consider the role that knowing the language plays for an adult in reading English aloud. The written form *photograph*, for example, is convertible into a particular phonetic configuration, with primary stress on the first syllable, lesser stress on the third syllable, second syllable unstressed, reduced second vowel, and full vowel quality expressed by the first and third vowel. The adult speaker of English is able to utilize elementary letter-sound correspondences to recognize the basic morphological components of the word, *foto-græf*, and then to superimpose all the above phonetic information on these components *because he knows the language* and can apply its phonological rule system. Add the written suffix *-y* to this form, *photography*, and the phonetic information which he superimposes is radically different: primary stress on second syllable, first and third syllables unstressed, reduced first and third vowels, full vowel quality of second vowel. He converts to different phonetic configurations in the two cases *because of phonological knowledge which he brings to the reading situation, not because of anything that is explicit in the orthography.* He does not have to be told how to apply stress and change vowel quality in these forms because he already knows.

On the other hand, a foreigner who knows no English but has learned the elementary letter-sound correspondences of the English alphabet will be unable to do this. Knowing nothing of the language, such a foreigner finds himself in a very different position when he tries to pronounce these two words. Lacking the necessary information about English phonology, he will read phonetically, and pronounce *photograph* alike in both contexts. What the foreigner lacks is just what the child already possesses, a knowledge of the phonological rules of English that relate underlying representations to sound. To be sure the child (or adult) has no awareness of this knowledge, and would be hard pressed to bring it to the level of awareness. But of course there is no need to do so. It works automatically and enables English speakers to manage well with the orthography that in a sense tells them what they need to know and leaves the rest to them.

The ability of the child to interpret the orthography directly at the lexical level should increase naturally as his phonological competence increases and as he becomes more familiar with the relations expressed by the spellings of words. The full phonological system of English depends heavily on a learned stratum of vocabulary including Latinate forms and a network of affixes which account for a large portion of surface phonetic variations. As the maturing child comes to control these forms in the spoken language he internalizes both their underlying representations and the phonological rules which relate the latter to pronunciations. This process of internalization depends in part on recognizing the relevant similarities in words which are pronounced differently. It is no doubt facilitated in many cases by an awareness of how words are spelled. Thus the underlying system which the child has constructed from evidence provided by the spoken language and which contributes to his ability to interpret the written language may itself be improved by his increased familiarity with the written language.

Another aspect of progress in reading relates to the freedom that the reader has given the lexical nature of the orthography, to avoid phonological processing as he reads. Earlier I pointed out an advantage of the lexically based orthography: the reader does not have to abstract away from unnecessary phonetic detail to reconstruct the lexical representation of words. It is also true that he does not have to carry out the inverse activity. He does not have to construct phonetic forms from the underlying lexical forms presented by the orthography. Silent reading may take place primarily at the lexical level, without requiring the experienced reader to convert to the surface phonetic level. If he wishes to convert to phonetic representation, as for example in reading aloud, he does so through the automatic application of the phonological rules of the language. But this phonological processing may be minimal in rapid silent reading. Indeed, it may be that part of learning to read rapidly and well is learning to dispense with the application of phonological rules. Experienced readers probably engage in varying degrees of phonological processing depending on the type of material they are reading and the reading speed they employ at any given time. But they have learned how to dispense with a good deal of the phonological processing when they wish to. Less skilled readers may not have acquired this ability. Children probably do pronounce to themselves while they are still inexperienced at reading, and only later begin to be able to relinquish this phonological processing. It is likely that with increasing experience they gradually come to exploit the lexical nature of the orthography more and more effectively. Certainly there would seem to be no need to deal with words at the surface phonetic level, given an orthography that directly represents the underlying form of words. Children's reading, therefore, ought to improve as the amount of phonological processing that they engage in decreases.

9

American Children with Reading Problems Can Easily Learn To Read English Represented by Chinese Characters

——PAUL ROZIN, SUSAN PORITSKY, RAINA SOTSKY

A large part of the extensive research literature on reading is primarily concerned with the effect of different methods of instruction, and is therefore not directly relevant to this book. Many psychological and linguistic studies are of considerable relevance, but individually they do little to illuminate the broader picture, and so they are represented in the lists of references rather than in their entirety.

But I find the article that forms the basis of the present chapter irresistible. The basic idea was beautifully simple: to take a group of children who were experiencing difficulty in learning to read English by conventional methods, and teach them to read a limited amount of Chinese. In the words of the original abstract: "With 2.5 to 5.5 hours of tutoring, eight second-grade inner-city school children with clear reading disability were taught to read English material written as 30 different Chinese characters. This accomplishment eliminates certain general interpretations of dyslexia, for example, as a visual-auditory memory deficit. The success of this program can be attributed to the novelty of the Chinese orthography and to the fact that Chinese characters map into speech at the level of words rather than of phonemes".

The implications of the paper for an understanding of the reading process are obvious: Readers do not use (and do not need to use) the alphabetic principle or decoding to sound in order to learn or identify words. Equally obvious, I think, are some debatable points about the article. It is not entirely clear what the researchers were primarily studying—the effect of a different writing system, or of a different instructional approach, or of motivation. Nor do some of the conclusions seem to follow logically from the data. Many readers will probably ask why the authors conclude that since whole "word" instruction appeared more effective than phonics for their subjects, an emphasis on syllables might be the best way to teach reading.

Paul Rozin is a member of the psychology department of the University of Pennsylvania, where his collaborators were students. Their article appeared originally in Science, *1971, 171, 1264–1267, and is reprinted by permission of the authors and publishers. Some immediate reactions to the paper—quite different from the psycholinguistic approach of this book—will be found together with a rejoinder on behalf of the authors in the correspondence pages of* Science, *1971, 173, 190–191.*

American urban school systems are experiencing great difficulties in teaching reading. In many major cities, average reading performance is a few grades behind national norms; many children never learn to read adequately. This enormous problem undoubtedly has many causes (*1*), including (i) our failure to understand the reading process and thus to design a most effective method for teaching it; (ii) difficulty in motivating and engaging children, particularly those in inner-city schools, in activities related to reading; (iii) the possibility that some perceptual (*2*) or cognitive abilities necessary for reading are not well or equally developed in all 6-year-olds; and (iv) dialect differences between teachers (or texts) and students (*3*).

In attempts to teach second graders with reading backwardness in a Philadelphia inner-city school, one of us (P.R.), in collaboration with H. Savin, found two characteristic problems. One was clearly motivational: the children had had difficulty in the past with reading and seemed to be deliberately and actively uninvolved in reading or anything that they considered to be reading.The children's interest was easy to engage, but not in reading. Second, the children seemed to have particular difficulty in giving phonological interpretations in response to visually presented letters; that is, they could not, at least overtly, recognize such letters as representing components of their own or others' speech. Thus, they had difficulty (i) in identifying words by initial or final sounds and (ii) in combining a sequence of letters into a known English word (what is often called "blending"). Many of the children did not know all the alphabetic symbol–sound correspondences, which was surprising since they seemed to have excellent memories and could be taught arbitrary new symbols rather quickly.

If we assume that this "phonetic mapping" inability and inadequate motivation are two fundamental causes of reading disability in this inner-city population, then it should be possible to teach such children to read a simplified version of the Chinese logographic system, with interpretation into English. Such material would obviously be new to the children and thus might provide adequate motivation. The phonetic mapping inability would also be circumvented, because Chinese characters map into language at the morphemic (word) level rather than at the phonemic level. We emphasize that the purpose of this experiment was not to devise a new curriculum for reading but to highlight specific problem areas for future research and enrichment programs.

Nine black children in the second semester of the second grade in an inner-city Philadelphia school were randomly selected from the class list of one second-grade homeroom class (*4*), with the restriction that no child have a reading level higher than level 3 (middle first grade) according to the system in use in the Philadelphia school system (*5*). The nine children selected were individually tested for reading skills by the experimenters. The basic criterion for acceptance in the experiment was that the child be unable to read a series of six simple consonant-vowel-consonant trigrams (PIP, ZIF, WAT, LAG, REN, GUB) and be unable to read reliably a set of rhyming words (CAT, FAT, MAT, SAT) after being given the pronunciation for AT. Eight of the nine children were unable to handle this material adequately. They were usually unable to guess even the initial sound of the unfamiliar trigrams. The child who showed some competence at these tasks was not continued in the experiment.

Tutoring sessions were held in supply closets or small rooms with minimum furnishings. Individual sessions lasting from 20 minutes to 1 hour were held during the afternoon school hours approximately two or three times a week. The tutoring took place from March through June 1970 and involved a total of 14 to 25 sessions, or 8 to 14 hours per child (see Table 1). Each child dealt with only one of the three experimenters throughout the entire period, and tutoring was always on a one-to-one basis.

The tutoring sessions were informal; an initial session or two was devoted to getting to know the child and gauging his reading ability. A tutoring session was generally made up of four components:

1. Gaining rapport. A small portion of the time was spent in talking informally with the child or in playing games with him.
2. Tutoring in normal English reading. This consisted of practicing letter-sound relationships, "blending" sounds, and reading primer and pre-primer material. It occupied about one-third of the total tutoring time.
3. Intelligence testing. The Wechsler Intelligence Scale for Children was administered to each child during the course of the experiment. No more than three subtests were given in any one session.
4. Chinese tutoring. The material to be taught consisted of 30 Chinese characters. They were read directly in their actual English translation. Chinese was never spoken. The symbols were read from left to right in the customary pattern of English orthography. The characters were selected primarily for their ability to fit together to form a wide variety of

English sentences (Figure 1). The sentences used could be read and understood by a native Chinese (6). An additional criterion was the avoidance of characters of great visual complexity or high similarity to already selected symbols.

The set of actual characters selected, with their English equivalents, is presented in Figure 1. For convenience in instruction, the set was divided into six subsets, to be presented in sequence. The subsets were planned to allow formation of many English sentences from the very beginning.

For the first unit, symbols of minimum visual complexity were selected from a full set of 30. At the beginning of the experiment these symbols (Xerox copies from an introductory Chinese reader) were pasted on 1-inch (2.54-cm squares) of cardboard and were arranged in different sequences. In later stages, pages with written material (similar to the test page in Figure 2) were also used (7). The children were introduced to a few symbols at a time, were given a few rote-memorization trials, and were then presented with a sequence of characters that could be translated into simple English sentences. They were encouraged to make up sentences of their own. In the tutoring sessions, the children were corrected when they mis-read a word, unless they offered a word that was semantically equivalent, such as little instead of small. Since the Chinese orthography maps directly into the meaningful units, synonyms constitute correct responses. Of course, the fact that these children have quite different pronunciations for some of these words in their dialect was ignored. When children had particular difficulty in learning particular words, additional practice was given. Occasionally, when a child had consistent difficulty with a pair of symbols, we asked him to describe the differences between them or pointed out what we considered distinctive differences between them.

When a child seemed to have mastered the materials in one stage, one new symbol from the next stage was introduced, and a set of test sentences was constructed, each sentence containing the new symbol. This procedure guaranteed that the representation of the test sentences in Chinese orthography had not been seen before by the child. Tests were administered after each of the first five stages (8). Each of the tests included, at least once, every character taught up to that point. As a result of this constraint, plus the absence of articles and the use of the new symbol in each sentence, some of the resultant sentences were not "well formed." We attempted to administer the tests at the beginning of a session, but, when that was not possible, the test was preceded by at least 10 minutes of non-Chinese material. No prompting was given, and the performance was recorded word for word. When we were convinced that a child had mastered a stage, by virtue of his performance on a test, material from the next stage was introduced.

Stage	Noun	Verb	Adjective	Other
I	母 Mother 刀 Knife	見 See 有 Has	大 Big	
II	書 Book 父 Father 人 Man		一 One 二 Two 小 Small	
III	家 House	買 Buy	白 White	跟 And
IV	你 You	說 Say	紅 Red	
V	車 Car 魚 Fish	要 Want	好 Good	
VI	他 He 口 Mouth	用 Use 給 Give	這 This	不 Not (don't)
Final test	哥哥 Brother		黑 Black	

Figure 1 Order of presentation of Chinese symbols.

Figure 2 Final test. Sentences including all symbols. The sentences read: "Father buys black car. This man doesn't (not) see black house and two knives. Brother says mother uses white book. You want one big fish and black house. He says 'brother has small mouth.' Good brother doesn't (not) give man red car." Eight subjects made a mean of three errors on this 40-item test. The four timed subjects took a mean of 1 minute and 40 seconds to complete this task.

For a final evaluation of performance, the children were presented with a set of sentences (Figure 2) that incorporated all of the 30 symbols taught. Each sentence included one of the two new symbols (Figure 1, bottom line) introduced after completion of stage VI. In addition, the children read aloud three short stories, which were made up from the 30 symbols but did not include all of them. In all cases, no cues or corrections were provided. The time required to complete the sentences and to complete each story was measured, and the experimenters made a written transcription of what the children said. Errors were then tabulated. After each story, the children were asked a few questions about the "plot" but were not allowed to refer back to the story to answer these questions (9). In three cases, the final readings were tape-recorded.

The basic results are presented in Table 1. Unfortunately, relatively little progress was made in reading the English alphabet. In no cases were there any major improvements in this area, although in most some improvement in letter-sound correspondences or word formation was obvious (Table 1). The improvement in reading level was probably due primarily to the regular classroom instruction.

In contrast, the tutoring with Chinese characters progressed rapidly and was quite successful. Children who had failed to master the English alphabet sounds in over 1½ years of schooling immediately understood the basic demands of the task and were able to read stage I sentences in the first 5 or 10 minutes of exposure to Chinese. As a measure of early progress, the performance on the stage II test (8) is presented in Table 1. In an average of 52 minutes of Chinese tutoring, the children were able to read the new material in the stage II test with few or no errors (Table 1). In an average of about 4 hours of Chinese tutoring, they were able to negotiate the final sentences and one story with relatively few errors and some comprehension (Table 1). Performance on two additional stories was comparable to that indicated for the mother-car story (9) (Table 1). On the total of three stories, there were 50 errors (137 characters in the three stories for eight children, or 1096 items). The comprehension score was 22.5 correct answers out of 48 questions.

Five children were retested on the mother-car story and the sentences in Figure 2 after 24 to 33 days had elapsed since the termination of the experiment (10). Two of the children seemed to have forgotten about half of the characters, but the remaining three made relatively few mistakes (a total of 36 out of 240 items).

In the early stages of tutoring, a number of children had difficulty in arranging the individually mounted characters to form sentences presented orally, even though they knew the correspondences of the appropriate symbols and words. This difficulty disappeared as tutoring progressed. After completion of the final tests, five children were asked to use the characters

Table 1 Summary of Results. The Test for Stage II Contained a Total of 21 Characters (12 Different Characters). The Final Test Sentences Contained 40 Items. The Mother-Car Story (9) Contained 40 Items. The IQ Is the Score on the Wechsler Intelligence Scale for Children.

| Subjects | | Tutoring | | Stage II | | Final Sentences | | Mother-Car-Story | | | | Reading Level (5) | |
SEX	AGE (YEARS: MONTHS)	TOTAL (HOURS: MINUTES)	CHINESE (HOURS: MINUTES)	TIME (MINUTES: SECONDS)	ER-RORS (NO.)	TIME (MINUTES: SECONDS)	ER-RORS (NO.)	TIME (MINUTES: SECONDS)	ER-RORS (NO.)	COMPRE-HENSION	IQ	BEFORE	AFTER
M	7:11	10:03	4:28	0:36	1	2:08	6	2:42	5	1/3	83	1	2
M	7: 9	14:10	4:42	0:54	0	1:43	0	2:07	6	1.5/3	85	2	2
M	7:11	11:00	5:24	1:15	0		4	0:56	4	3/3	80	2	3
F	7:11	10:42	5:00	1:05	0		4	1:06	3	1/3	82	3	3
M	8: 0	11:51	4:06	0:34	2	1:50	6		4	2/3	96	2	3
M	8: 8	8:30	3:30	0:40	0		2	1:00	0	2/3	80	2	3
M	8: 2	8:26	2:35	1:00	0	1:00	1	1:30	1	3/3	96	2	2
F	7: 5	9:10	2:36	0:50	2		1	2:40	0	3/3	107	3	4

to form and rearrange sentences. Their performance on this test was excellent. In problems involving a single substitution, addition, or deletion, but no rearrangement (for instance, change "mother *sees* white car" to "mother *has* white car"), of which there were five examples, all of the five children tested averaged between 6 and 7 seconds to complete the task; they proceeded systematically and without error to find and insert a new element, or to remove or exchange an old element. The most complex task of this type involved two additional characters and some rearrangement (change "father sees mother" to "father and mother see car"). Four of the five children negotiated this problem in less than 1 minute.

The material in stage VI, with the notable exception of "mouth," seemed the most difficult. Some of the children began to get a little bored with the Chinese as they ran into some difficulty in stages V or VI. In a few cases, particular confusions ("see" and "say" in one case, for example) became partially "fixated." A certain amount of confusion resulting from visual similarity between certain symbols (for instance "say" and "and," or "give" and "red") was apparent.

In spite of these problems, all of the children read the Chinese materials adequately. Comprehension was clearly only partial, but it should be emphasized that we made little attempt in the tutoring to stress this aspect of the task.

In a total of about 4 hours we taught children to read English represented by Chinese characters that were in many ways more complex than normal English orthography. Yet these same children had failed to acquire the basics of English reading in almost 2 years of schooling. The private tutoring situation cannot account for the success with Chinese, since we also tutored these children privately in English orthography. Furthermore, in our experience of traditional tutoring with standard orthography and procedures, there is no marked improvement over equivalent time periods. We suggest that the main value of this demonstration is to highlight the factors that *cannot* be used to account for the reading backwardness of these children and the many like them in the Philadelphia and other school systems. There was clearly no problem with learning to associate more than 26 complicated and arbitrary visual symbols with certain sounds (words). Furthermore, there was no difficulty in ordering these sounds or symbols so that they could be read in a systematic pattern. Much of this ability, of course, such as the left-to-right reading habit, had already been acquired by the children in their minimum learning of English reading in school.

What, then, accounts for the large difference between the performance in Chinese and that in English? One factor may be increased motivation produced by the novelty of the Chinese material. Another factor is intrinsic to the nature of Chinese orthography, which does not map into the sound system altogether, in contrast to our alphabet, which maps (at least in large part) into the level of phonemes. What is the critical feature of the difference between the Chinese logographic and the English alphabetic system which leads to reading difficulty? It could be the complete absence of sound mapping in Chinese; it could be the particular properties of the phoneme, rather than sound mapping per se; or it could be the irregularities of the grapheme to phoneme mapping in English.

We suspect that the phonemic representation contributes most heavily to reading difficulty. We and many others have found that children with reading backwardness have difficulty in "constructing" words from these isolated sounds. There is further evidence both from speech output (articulation) and input (perception) that the alphabetic unit or phoneme is unnatural or at least highly abstract (*11*).

If our suspicions are correct, then some unit intermediate between the morpheme and the phoneme—for example, the syllable—might be more suitable as a vehicle for introducing reading. An efficient orthography must satisfy only two requirements. It must be easy to learn and it must be productive in the sense that, after mastery, new words can be read without learning new symbols. Hence, the ultimate unworkability of the whole word method (*12*). The syllabary may meet these requirements (*13*). It has the advantage of pronounceableness (many phonemes cannot be pronounced in isolation) but still maintains its productivity or open-endedness. It may therefore be a good step on the road toward learning to read alphabetic writing (*14*).

References and Notes

1. J. Money, *The Disabled Reader* (Johns Hopkins Press, Baltimore, 1966); A. J. Harris, *How To Increase Reading Ability* (McKay, New York, ed. 3, 1970).

2. P. Katz and M. Deutsch, in *The Disadvantaged Child*, M. Deutsch and associates, Eds. (Basic Books, New York, 1967), p. 233.

3. J. C. Baratz and R. W. Shuy, *Teaching Black Children To Read* (Center for Applied Linguistics, Washington, D.C., 1969).

4. Because homeroom classes were not graded by school performance, we can take the children selected to be representative of children with reading problems in the second grade of the school.

5. Levels 1 to 4 are intended to be completed in the first grade. Level 3 (Primer) includes learning of words by sight and "developing skill in 'attacking' new words through phonics." Level 4 (Book I) includes "developing additional skills in 'word attack' including compound words, contractions and possessives." Levels 5 and 6 are expected to be completed in the second year and involve completion of Books II-1 and II-2, respectively. The above descriptions are taken from the description of reading levels in "Progress Reports" of the Phila-

delphia public elementary schools. The books referred to in the description of levels are in the Scott-Foresman Reading Series.

6. Our familiarity with the Chinese language consists of a few hours spent reading elementary books on reading Chinese. We consulted with two fluent speakers of Chinese. Certain constructions that did not translate literally into English were avoided, and some minimal liberties were taken in creating correspondences between Chinese and English.

7. The lettering for the stories and sentences was done by a Chinese member of the staff of the Library of Oriental Studies at the University of Pennsylvania. Although the written symbols appeared to us to differ significantly in some cases from the Xerox copies of individual symbols, the children had little difficulty in generalizing from one to the other.

8. The second stage test was composed of the following sentences in Chinese orthography: "Man has house. Small mother has one house. House has two books. Big father sees one small house. House has knife." The new element introduced for this test was the item "house."

9. One of the three stories was the mother-car story, which does not include all the symbols taught. It was: "Mother wants white car. Brother wants red car. Father gives mother white car. He doesn't (not) give brother red car. Brother says he wants red car. Father says, 'You use white car.' Brother doesn't (not) want white car; he doesn't (not) use car." The eight subjects made a mean of 3 errors (total of 23 errors) on this 40-item story. Seven timed subjects read it in a mean time of 1 minute and 43 seconds. The three comprehension questions were: (i) What did brother want? (ii) What will father let brother do? (iii) Who has the white car? A correct answer on each question is worth one point. Out of a possible total of 24 points, the eight subjects achieved 16.

10. Two of the children in the 24- to 33-day retest were tested without any practice or "warm-up." The remaining three were allowed to read one set of six sentences, with corrections, before proceeding to the retest. The practice set contained each character at least once.

11. A. Liberman, F. S. Cooper, D. P. Shankweiler, M. Studdert-Kennedy, *Psychol. Rev. 74*, 431 (1967); H. Savin and T. Bever, *J. Verbal Learn. Verbal Behav. 9*, 295 (1970).

12. J. S. Chall, *Learning To Read: The Great Debate* (McGraw-Hill, New York, 1967).

13. It is interesting to note that in Japan, where the written language consists of a syllabary (a much more "natural" transcription of the language), plus logographs, there is reported to be a very low rate of illiteracy [K. Makita, *Amer. J. Orthopsychiat. 38*, 599 (1968)].

14. In a sense this experiment is simply a particularly clear demonstration of the fact that children with reading disability can learn many names of things in the visual world and can learn, to some extent, the connection between whole written words and their spoken equivalents ("look-say" method). The Chinese material may be easier because it is novel and because Chinese symbols are perhaps easier to discriminate visually than whole words written in English orthography. The point of the experiment is to highlight areas of competence and areas of specific difficulty in a type of reading disability commonly encountered in inner-city children, and to suggest new approaches to the problem.

15. Supported by NSF grant GB 8013 to one of us (P.R.). We thank the research office of the Philadelphia Board of Education and the staff of the Drew School for their cooperation; and H. Gleitman, L. Gleitman, E. Rozin, and H. Savin for their contribution to the formulation of the issues discussed and constructive comments on the manuscript.

10

Alphabetic Writing—
A Language Compromise?

It is frequently asserted that since the English language is written in alphabetic symbols, the alphabetic system must be the basis of reading. This is rather like the argument that hotel guests should pay for the telephone answering service, even if they don't make use of it, just because it is there.

Just how useful is alphabetic writing to the reader? Is it possible that the writer (or printer) is the one that the alphabet was designed for? These are the questions examined in the present chapter, and I conclude that readers may not have got the best of the bargain when writing became alphabetic. Obviously, if the alphabet has very little to do with reading—and nobody has ever really tested how little it has to do with learning to read—then the argument that reading is not decoding to spoken language is supported.

My concern now is the alphabetic principle, the system that relates the written and spoken forms of our language through correspondences between the phonology of the one and the orthography of the other. However, I do not intend to discuss in detail the alphabetic principle itself, the actual relationship between the sounds of words and their spelling. The nature of this relationship, discussed in Chapter 8, has been analyzed by Reed, Venezky, and by Chomsky, all of whom may conveniently be found in a new volume edited by Levin and Williams (1970). Instead I shall consider some of the implications for writers and readers of the fact that the English writing system *is* alphabetic.

116

Writing and reading are often thought of as mirror images of each other, as reflections from opposite angles of the same phenomenon, communication through written language. But there are radical differences between the skills and knowledge employed in reading and those employed in writing, just as there are considerable differences in the processes involved in learning to read and in learning to write. And I offer as a reasonable working hypothesis that anything tending to make writing easier will make reading more difficult, and *vice versa.* In other words, our writing system can be regarded as a compromise between the interests of the reader and the interests of the writer, each of whom benefits—at the expense of the other—by one aspect or another of this system. And in particular I want to suggest that the fact of there being any relationship at all between the written form of language and its sound may be one of the major concessions made by readers to writers.

(It is convenient for the moment to talk about readers and writers as if they are different people. Of course, most literate persons have both reading and writing skills, and a little later I shall discuss the presence—and relative independence—of the two subsets of written language skills in the same individual.)

The notion that the forms of language represent compromises between the transmitter of information and the receiver is not new, although it has been explored far more on the practical level (for example by telephone engineers) than by linguists and psychologists. However, Saporta (1955) has suggested that the sounds of words represent a compromise between speakers, who prefer minimal differences within phoneme clusters, and listeners, who prefer maximum differences. Slurred speech is easier to produce than speech in which every difference is clearly articulated, but not so easy to understand. Listening would be easier if there were no word pairs distinguished by a single feature only, such as "bet" and "pet", or "bet" and "bed", but speaking becomes more complex as additional contrasts are introduced.

In written language, ease of production seems similarly opposed to ease of discrimination. As a very obvious example, compare the scrawl of rapid writing with any script in which every letter is carefully and precisely represented—and consider the relative costs in terms of time and effort for writer and reader. Clearly, the gain for the rapid writer is at the expense of the reader. I suspect that several gains for writers were made at the expense of readers when the alphabetic principle was developed.

Alternative Writing Systems

Three broad classes of writing system can be distinguished. They are—in their usually accepted order of historical development—pictographic, ideographic, and alphabetic. In pictographic writing the visual symbol is more or less directly related to the *visual appearance* of its referent—the written word for "cow" resembles an actual cow. In alphabetic writing the visual symbol is more or less directly related to the *sound* of the name of its referent—the written word for "cow" reflects the spoken word rather than the appearance of a real cow. And in ideographic writing the visual symbol is related directly and arbitrarily to the "idea" of a cow —the symbol *means* "cow", and bears no resemblance to animals that look like cows or to words that sound like "cow".

For those languages (relatively few even today) that have developed alphabetic systems, ideographic writing appears to represent an intermediate stage of development. Kolers (1970) has recently written an interesting paper on this evolution. However, it would be rash to assume that alphabetic writing is necessarily more efficient than ideographic. For example, there is no reason to believe that it is particularly difficult to associate sounds to visual stimuli, even when these visual stimuli are not systematically related to each other or to the sounds of their names. We have all learned very early in life to relate the sound of the word "dog" to the actual visual configuration of a dog, the sound "cat" to a real visual cat (or a drawing of a cat), the sound "tree" to all manner of different visual events, and so forth. None of the objects or events for which we have names (and that accounts for most of the lexicon) represents itself to our eyes alphabetically; the relation of spoken word to object is usually quite arbitrary. In fact, spoken language might be called "ideophonic" because the sounds of words are related to the "idea" of their referent, and not at all to its appearance or (with a few exceptions) to its sound.

Anything that can be communicated by spoken language can also be expressed in ideographic writing. This becomes in effect another language, unrelated to speech, just as spoken Chinese is unrelated either to written Chinese or to spoken English. I have found no evidence that ideographic scripts of Chinese and Japanese, for example, are any more difficult to read than scripts based on the phonetic principle. In Chapter 9, Rozin, Poritsky and Sotsky demonstrated that it may be easier to teach some American children to read Chinese logographs than the same words in their usual English spelling. The difficulty of *learning to read* ideographic scripts would appear to depend largely on the extent to which the ideographic symbol has drifted away from the original pictogram (Makita, 1968) in the direction of simplification and conventionalization—which is obviously of benefit to the scribe. But while readers can cope very well with ideograms—in fact we can read as efficiently as most of us do only because we treat our written language as if it were ideographic—the alphabetic system would appear to be easier for writers, both for ease of reproduction and for consistency. It is interesting to speculate that the alphabet might not have gained its ascendency over more direct means of communicating meaning visually but for the historical accident that printing with moveable type was invented a few centuries before photographic and electronic reproduction. Even the ideographic writing systems of China and Japan appear at last to be in the process of becoming extinct—solely because of the exigencies of the typewriter and typesetting industries. How can you put thousands of different symbols on a keyboard?

Relative Difficulty for Readers and Writers

I am proposing that the alphabetic nature of our language makes quite different demands on memory and information-processing capacities, depending on whether you happen to be writing or reading. Before I become more specific about the relation of the alphabetic principle to writing and reading, it will be useful to outline some of the more fundamental asymmetries between these two activities, most of which would appear to be to the distinct advantage of the reader.

To begin with, there are the experimentally well-established facts that recognition is easier than reproduction—it is easier to recognize a face than to draw one—and that recognition memory is generally more efficient than recall—it is easier to recognize faces that have been seen before than to recall how they looked. In other words, it is not only easier to recognize a word than to write it, the form of a written word, even an ideogram, is more easily recognized by the reader than it is recalled by the writer.

There are also a number of advantages related to the fact that the reader's direction of information processing goes from the surface structure of the written symbol to the deep structure of meaning (Chomsky & Halle, 1968) while the writer must work in the opposite direction. For example, the reader can take advantage of the many forms of redundancy in language—he need not identify every word, or even every phrase— although the writer is committed to reproducing them. As a consequence, the reader is able to proceed much faster than the writer and can skip over items that he is not sure about or that he regards as relatively unimportant. It does not matter if the reader is unfamiliar with the spelling or meaning of a particular word; for a writer such a failure may be quite disabling. By the same token, the writer is forced to put into the text a good deal of redundancy that the reader probably will not look at. In "normal" 200-words-a-minute reading we are probably using barely a quarter of the visual information available on the page, a quarter of the information that the writer has to provide. In addition the reader can turn to other sources of information, such as illustrations, to reduce his uncertainty about individual words or entire meanings. Once again, the writer is constrained far more rigidly than the reader to follow the line of text.

Consistency also seems far more of a problem for the writer than for the reader—there are quite severe conventional sanctions against a writer using rough and ready spelling even in such trivial matters as writing *recieve* or *disimilar*, but I doubt whether this is because such spellings constitute grave difficulties for readers. Readers can comprehend passages without very much difficulty when as much as one letter in two is omitted (Shannon, 1951); a useful study could be done to see the extent to which they can tolerate spelling errors. We may notice when a word is spelled wrongly, but we generally know what the word is that is being misspelled.

By contrast, the writer seems to have only one basic advantage over the reader: he is assumed to know what he has said and what he will say. This should mean that the writer has much less of a working memory load than the reader as he works through a sentence, a proposition that should be easily testable but which has not to my knowledge been examined.

By and large, then, the nature of written communication would appear to be intrinsically more demanding for the writer than for the reader—which may be the reason most of us prefer reading to writing (although the preference is usually the other way around when listening and talking are compared). It might seem reasonable, therefore, that compromises would be made on precisely those points that are intrinsically more difficult for the writer, namely in the simplification of distinctive forms used in written language and the reduction of their number. It is no mean feat to acquire a repertoire of several thousands of distinctive symbols of an ideographic writing system, especially when these symbols are formalized to the extent that they are minimally different from each other. It is much easier for writers to use a system in which there are only a couple of dozen different symbols which can be combined in a variety of ways to produce many thousands of unique configurations, just as spoken language consists of a few dozen sounds which can be combined to form many thousands of different words. But the writer has also demanded some convenient way of learning how to combine the elements of written language—the alphabetic characters—although no such rules are available nor are any required for combining the phonemes in spoken words.

The solution, the alphabetic system of relating written language to sound, at least makes prediction of the written form possible in theory. However even *that* advantage was largely offset from the writer's point of view as it became necessary—a self-inflicted injury—to make spelling consistent at the expense of keeping it easily predictable. Spelling tends to remain constant although the sound pattern of language varies radically depending on time, place, and occasion.

The development of the alphabetic short cut to written word formation has not been without other costs to the writer. In addition to the concessions made to readers by the frequent deviation from strict sound-to-spelling correspondences (Chapters 6, 8), there is the problem, not always properly acknowledged, of considerable differences in the style and content of spoken and written language (for example, see Joos, 1962; Halliday, 1969). A writer must learn to do rather more than just write down language as it is spoken.

To comprehend fully the relative benefits and cost of the alphabetic principle to writer and reader, we must examine more systematically the knowledge or skills that a writer needs in order to be able to write a word correctly, and those that a reader needs in order to read it. We can then assess to what extent the match—or mismatch—of orthography to phonology is help or hindrance to the writer and to the reader.

The Reader and Word Identification

There appear to be two quite distinct kinds of strategy or method available to a reader for identifying words. The first method can be characterized as "direct"; we look at a word and recognize it from its visual configuration, just as we can look at cows and trees and horses—and individual letters—and identify them. I have termed this type of recognition, sometimes called sight recognition, *immediate word identification.* Such identification is not immediate in the sense that it occurs instantaneously—any identification process takes almost half a second or more—but because it is not *mediated* by the identification of sub-units, such as individual letters or spelling units or syllables. In effect, the word is identified as an *ideogram;* the fact that its spelling has some relationship to the sound of a word is quite irrelevant to the recognition process because the spelling is not examined. The word is identified in the same way as numerals and mathematical symbols, all of which *are* ideograms by any definition. One way of conceptualizing the process by which words are identified immediately is that cognitive *feature lists* are established specifying sets of distinctive visual features for each word, just as we might have distinctive feature lists for each letter and for all other symbols and objects that we can identify visually. Each feature list for a word would be associated with the "name" of the word; thus a word that meets the specifications of a distinctive feature list associated with the name "horse" would to read as "horse", just as an actual animal that met the specifications of the appropriate visual feature list for real animals would be called a horse. Visual feature lists for words can similarly be conceptualized as associated with a complex semantic structure that mediates the meanings of words and groups of words (Smith, 1971).

Immediate word identification implies the identification of words on the basis of visual feature relationships in the configuration as a whole and not by the synthesis of information about individual letters or letter groups.

The immediate method is the usual way in which we read words, as I pointed out in Chapter 6. It is also the method by which children identify their first words, before they are exposed to any formal instruction about how to read.

The first word a child learns to recognize, generally his name, and those that follow, are learned on this categorical basis—he establishes visual feature lists for them. He certainly does not learn to identify the configuration *John* as "John" because the letters J-O-H-N spell "John".

The question of how to distinguish one word configuration from another is the greatest problem faced by the beginning reader in learning to identify words, partly because it is usually taken for granted that children can "see" that the words *dog* and *cat* are different, in the same way that they are expected just to "see" that the letters *A* and *B* are different. Fortunately, most children have had long experience in establishing feature lists for visual categories, learning to distinguish individual people, animals, and all the other furniture and fittings of the world, without any specific instruction.

The second part of identification—learning to associate names with the visual categories—is relatively easy. Children establish hundreds of these name-category associations every year. When a child "forgets" how to read a letter or word, it is usually not because he has forgotten the name of a category, but because he has not learned how to distinguish instances of that particular category from all others. Before a child becomes involved in a formal instructional situation at school, obliging adults tell him what the names of words are, so that he can concentrate on the more complex task of establishing feature lists. But at school this vital assistance is precipitately removed—he is expected to find out for himself the names of words. And in recompense he is offered a set of phonic rules which are only marginally efficient, which if depended on would overload his memory and result in his trying to read in a most unnatural manner.

What does a child usually do when he meets a word that he cannot identify on sight? He does the same as a fluent adult reader in similar circumstances—he tries to ignore the unknown word, or else he guesses. Unless he is under the watching eye of an expectant adult he will not try to sound out an entire word a letter at a time.

I call the assortment of strategies for the identification of visually unfamiliar words *mediated word identification* because the reader has no alternative but to identify parts of words—for example individual letters or groups of letters—and to try to synthesize the whole from the parts. Research is needed to see how often, or rather how rarely, experienced readers come across words not in their sight vocabulary, and what they do about such words (if they do not ignore them altogether).

In analyzing mediated systems for word identification, it will help if we consider two distinct cases, (1) words that are already established in our spoken language vocabularies, and (2) words that are not.

There is practically no research evidence about what a reader does when he meets a word with which he is quite familiar by ear—a prime case would be words heard on radio or television, especially the names of places and people—but which he has never seen in print. I think it very unlikely that spelling to sound correspondence rules are used to any large extent to establish the association between the visual form and the meaning already associated with the acoustic representation. Instead, all available clues from context, including illustrations, are probably used to make the association to meaning directly, perhaps in conjunction with what I shall call "analogic" cues based on morphological and syntactic relationships to known words, making use of what Carol Chomsky in Chapter 8 called the lexical level of representation. The rich strategies that we have for such word identification problems are acquired quite unconsciously and are not subject to our awareness. In other words, the skill that enables us to associate for example the written word *Solzhenitsyn* when we first meet it with the sound of the word with which we are already familiar is minimally likely to be phonic—it is far more likely that we deduce the meaning or the referent nonalphabetically and go from that to the sound, rather than construct the sound in order to get access to the meaning. Once the word is identified in this mediated fashion, a visual feature list can be associated with the sound and referent already in our spoken language vocabulary, so that we can henceforth identify the word immediately, without any recourse to intermediate cues.

When our reading confronts us with a word not in our spoken vocabularies, I suspect the general strategy is to give the word only a very rough pronunciation, nothing more than a cognitive placeholder in effect. We associate the visual representation (the feature list) with an approximate meaning or reference and some kind of primitive or partial auditory label —perhaps just enough to hold the spelling in mind if we go to the dictionary or the atlas. It is not uncommon to find fluent readers with "mispronunciations" of written words, for example, the rhyming of *Penelope* with "envelope". I had to learn and rehearse a pronunciation of *Solzhenitsyn* long after I could read it; I had never bothered to try to pronounce the name when I met it in print. I still hesitate over the pronunciation of *Evelyn Waugh*, or *Ronald Wardhaugh*, although I immediately identify the names visually.

To summarize, of the two systems by which a fluent reader can identify words, the immediate or visual method, which is the one employed most of the time, has nothing to do with phonology at all. The mediated methods are only indirectly related to phonology, and then only approximately, when we want to look up a word or to ask how it is pronounced or what it means. The relationship between orthography and phonology is a last and partial resort even for mediated word identification. The strategies that we use seem far more likely to be analogic devices based on knowledge that we have acquired unconsciously, just as we have unconsciously acquired our knowledge of how to distinguish dogs from cats.

On balance, is the alphabetic principle much of an advantage for a reader?

To the fluent reader the alphabetic principle is completely irrelevant. He identifies every word (if he identifies words at all) as an ideogram. He is probably not concerned with the sound of words in the first place, and if he does read aloud or subvocalize it is because he has already identified the words, not in order to identify them. We subvocalize our mistakes.

An unfortunate consequence of the alphabetic principle for the fluent reader is the widespread conviction that because words are constructed of letters, letters must be identified in order for words to be read—a misconception that could have created havoc in written language communication if our instinctive behavior in reading was not to ignore individual letters. A second disadvantage of the alphabetic principle for the reader may be that individual letters are minimally discriminable. There is so little visual information in a letter that normally we cannot identify it at a greater distance than two feet, and even then only when it is in large print. Usually we have to peer much closer to discriminate the minimal amount of featural information put into handwriting. Yet the solution of making type larger is out of the question, both economically and visually, because our words are so much wider than they are deep. If our alphabet had a thousand characters, no word would need be more than two characters wide. Contrast the ribbon development of our alphabetic texts with two-dimensional and multidirectional ideograms and comic strips that make for more efficient use of the space on the page and the visual field of the reader. Other dramatic consequences of the linear nature of the alphabetic principle I leave to Marshall McLuhan.

It is in reading instruction that the fixation upon the alphabetic principle may have had the most severe consequences. Many educators seem to have believed that Johnny can learn to read only through the alphabetic principle. Of course, if a child is deprived of the opportunity to identify a word in any other way—by asking adults or cooperative peers, or by using devices like "talking typewriters", or by guessing—he has no alternative to phonics. This alphabetic puritanism can be so strong that phonics may become a subject in its own right, quite independent of reading for both teacher and pupil.

The Writer and Word Representation

Like the reader, the practised writer has command of a large repertoire of written word forms that he can use without reference to individual letters. And just as *immediate identification* is the fastest and most natural system for reading words, so the analogous *immediate representation* of words is the fastest and most natural way of writing them. Writers rapidly acquire the ability to write large numbers of words as units which I shall call *integrated movement sequences*. Such words can be produced much faster than if the letters are produced one at a time.

It is instructive to write a well-known series of letters for which you have no integrated movement sequence—for example the alphabet from *a* to *z*— and a series of words such as *The quick brown fox jumps over the lazy dog* in which all the letters of the alphabet are organized into integrated sequences. You will find that noticeably more time and effort is required to write (or type) the alphabet than the sentence. On the other hand, we can recite the alphabet letter-by-letter far faster than the letters of the sentence (t-h-e-q-u etc.).

Many people these days have two integrated movement systems for writing, one for handwriting and one for typewriting. These two systems would seem to be quite independent—most people are not equally fluent when writing by hand and on the typewriter. It would appear a feasible research topic to investigate whether in fact there are words that can be written immediately by hand but not on the typewriter, or vice versa, and whether some words tend to be spelled differently depending on how they are written.

Normal writing would be impossible if we had to stop and think about every letter individually, just as piano playing would be impossible if the pianist had to think about and play every arpeggio one note at a time. I choose the analogy of piano playing deliberately because it and writing are two major examples considered by Lashley (1951) in his classic paper on the serial ordering of behavior. Lashley asserts that individual movements become integrated into "generalized schemata of action which determine the sequence of specific acts". In other words, the writer or musician becomes "preprogrammed" to run off a complex motor act as a unit—as an integrated sequence that cannot be modified or broken down into its parts without considerable disruption. For example we cannot ask a skilled typist to omit the letter "e" from the word *the* or to spell it *hte* without slowing down.

Incidentally, it is quite obvious with writing as with reading that written language is related directly to meaning, not to sound. We would be just as likely to write "a none tolled hymn" as "a nun told him" if we were writing down the sound of the words.

As in the case of immediate word identification, I suspect that the development and use of integrated movement patterns for writing are both the natural objective and the ultimate achievement of the skill. A child beginning to learn to write his first word—his name, for example—begins with a number of unrelated shapes that he rapidly integrates into one continuous movement (even though there may be breaks where the pen is lifted from the page).

However, because of the additional information and effort that a writer must put into a word compared with the relatively effortless task of establishing a visual feature list, the majority of words are initially put together letter by letter, by copying from a visible model or through the intermediary of dictation or memory. In other words, some mediated form of word representation intervenes between first acquaintance with a word and an integrated movement sequence, even though readers can go directly to visual feature lists and immediate word identification without mediated processes.

When we turn to the question of the mediated systems available to the writer for discovering how to represent words for which he does not have integrated movement sequences, we find that he can get no assistance from anything that he might already know as a reader. I see no way in which one can "translate" from a visual feature list to a spelling. Such feature lists are not constructed in terms of letters and probably do not contain enough information to reproduce an entire word. The few sound-to-spelling rules that a reader might use are generally not bidirectional—the digraph *ph* is usually pronounced /f/, but it would be risky to conclude that /f/ is usually written *ph*. Instead, an independent set of sound-to-spelling rules would seem to be required by the writer (Venezky, 1967). Remembered spellings, which are an obvious basis upon which a writer might be able to produce words for which he has no integrated movement sequences, are of no utility in reading and almost certainly will not have been developed for that purpose. The preceding idea may seem surprising, but consider whether a reader ever could proceed on the following basis: "The word in front of me is spelled e-l-e-p-h-a-n-t. I know that these letters put together constitute the spelling of the word 'elephant', therefore that word must be 'elephant' ".

Instead of being able to rely on any of the systems available for reading, it would appear that the writer must develop mediated systems for writing each word until practice in writing it has established an integrated sequence. One mediated system I have already suggested, a "list" of memorized spellings of individual words. These are the words whose spellings we can vocalize immediately, letter by letter, when asked. We know that "receive" is spelled r-e-c-e-i-v-e, that "woman" is spelled w-o-m-a-n, and so forth. Luria (1970) has observed that children required to write while their mouths were open so that they could not articulate spellings made six times as many spelling errors. It should be noted that such an internalized spelling list has nothing to do with either orthography or phonology—in fact the words we remember on this letter-by-letter basis tend to be those whose spelling is relatively unpredictable by any spelling rule. Brown (1970) has shown that we spell familiar words (even when irregularly spelled) better than unfamiliar but regularly spelled words—we tend to learn and use specific spellings, or integrated movement sequences for these spellings, not rules. It sometimes happens that we have an integrated movement sequence for a word that is different from the spelling we would verbalize for it, perhaps because we have modified the spelling (rightly or wrongly) since the movement sequence was established, perhaps because we may have uncertainty about two alternative spellings. I shall give an example later.

There are also a variety of mediated strategies available to the writer for dealing with those words for which neither an integrated movement sequence nor a remembered spelling is available. One strategy is based upon a set of taught or induced "sound-to-spelling rules" which typically have extensive use, with quite indifferent success, by children. In an important paper, Read (1971) argues that children's spelling tends to reflect quite systematically the underlying phonological structure of speech, demonstrating a linguistic sophistication and auditory acuity far in excess of anything they are usually given credit for. A more efficient strategy than spelling from sound is constructing or remembering words by analogy—"telegraph" is spelled with a *ph* because that is the way "photograph" is spelled. There are in addition some purely orthographic rules that dictate whether certain letter combinations are applicable, for example the use of *y* rather than *ie* before *ing* as in *lying, dying*. The matter of position in the word is particularly important for orthographic decisions; the reason that George Bernard Shaw's invention *ghoti* could not really be pronounced "fish" is that *gh*, for example, can have an /f/ sound only at the end of a syllable, not at the beginning, a purely orthographic restriction.

Is the alphabetic principle useful for writers? There is no doubt that the physical act of reproducing a word is easier and faster when it is constructed from a set of just 26 alternative forms (excluding variants of the same letter) rather than from thousands of distinctive pictograms or ideograms. It is also far easier to maintain consistency across writers when there is a spelling that can be conventionalized. A word is easier to copy, and thus to learn, when it can be broken down into easily recognizable elements like letters. None of these advantages, however, seems to have anything to do with the reader, except as I have suggested that they probably make the discrimination of words rather more difficult. The fact that the letters of the alphabet are related to the sounds of spoken language is, I suggest, a mixed blessing, even for the writer. On the one hand there is indeed predictive power in the alphabetic principle, although far less than we often think. Phonological-orthographic correspondence would play a much greater part in both writing and reading if spelling were allowed to vary as much as pronunciation. However, the desire to maintain consistency over time and space, regardless of dialectical variations, together with the general rule that morphological and etymological relationships are usually not subordinated to considerations of sound-spelling correspondence, reduce the overall importance of the alphabetic principle to the writer. And as in the case of reading, I think a major disadvantage of the alphabetic principle is that it becomes overstressed both in theory and practice—writing tends to be seen primarily as a matter of reproducing letters, which it is not, just as reading is often mistakenly viewed as a matter of identifying them.

Sometimes the very fact that our language is alphabetic blinds us to the nature of differences in spoken language, or even to the fact that similarities or differences exist. For example, we may think we hear and observe a distinction in sound between the two words written as *rider* and *writer* when such a contrast does not exist in the speech of many people. When "rider" and "writer" are distinguished in speech the difference between the sounds /d/ and /t/ is usually described as one of voicing; to be specific, the vibration of the vocal cords for the following vowel is delayed a fraction of a second longer after /t/. However, the distinction between /d/ and /t/ at the beginning of words, such as *down* and *town*, is primarily one of aspiration, while the distinction at the end of words, as in *need* and *neat*, lies mainly in the length of the preceding vowel (Fudge, 1970). To suggest that accurate sounds can be reconstructed from the alphabetic representation is like suggesting that flour, eggs, and water can be reconstructed from cake.

The Independence of Written Language Systems

I have discussed the systems available to the reader for word identification, and those employed by the writer for word representation, as if I were talking about two different people. Of course, most of us are both reader and writer, and I can conveniently respect individual integrity by summarizing the systems I have discussed within a single diagram, Figure 1.

However, as I have already suggested, it seems clear that even within the same person the six or seven systems involved in written language are independent from each other, in the sense that they are acquired in quite distinct circumstances and can be used only indirectly to supplement each other. I cannot claim to have labored through all the possibilities, but let us consider just one illustration of how a writer/reader might call on each of these sources of knowledge in turn to assist with a problem in quite a different way.

If I am asked how to spell the word "dominant" I may turn first to my stock of remembered spellings and find an uncertain choice between

	Reading *(Word Identification)*	Writing *(Word Representation)*
Immediate	1. Visual Feature Lists	4. Integrated Movement Sequences
Mediated	2. Analogic Strategies 3. Spelling to Sound Rules	5. Spelling Lists 6. Analogic Strategies 7. Sound to Spelling Rules

Figure 1 Written Language Systems

d-o-m-i-n-a-n-t and *d-o-m-i-n-e-n-t*. Since the actual sound of the word does not offer sufficient evidence for me to choose between the alternatives I might try to write them, and if I have an integrated movement sequence for the word I might well produce the correct representation first time. If I do not have an integrated sequence (a "motor memory") for the word, I could apply analogic or sound-to-spelling strategies for producing something. In any event, I can check on the written outcome by referring it to my visual feature list—looking to see if the construction is acceptable according to immediate word identification. This examination is a frequent but limited method of checking spelling; if the word "looks right" I know it at once, although if it "looks wrong" I often cannot say why. Finally, I might "play back" an acoustic or subvocalized reconstruction of my spelling to see if it "sounds right", or compare it visually with related or analogous words.

Conclusion

I can now return to the question I asked at the beginning of this chapter: In what way is the relationship between phonology and orthography related to writing and reading? I have very little further to say on this question, except that it should perhaps be reformulated as: In what ways is the relationship between phonology and orthography involved with the different systems employed in writing and in reading? I have made my main point if the question now seems much more complex then it did when I started.

Briefly, I think that the connections between written language and speech matter far less than is often assumed, especially those between phonology and orthography. The sound-spelling relationship has practically nothing to do with immediate writing and immediate reading, except to the extent that the alphabetic characters make production easier and discrimination more difficult. The alphabetic principle has rather more relevance to some mediated writing and reading systems, but the relationship is complex and by no means always advantageous. The mere fact that sound-spelling correspondences exist does not necessarily entail that they are of critical importance in either writing or reading.

References

Brown, H. D. Categories of spelling difficulty in speakers of English as a first and second language. *Journal of Verbal Learning & Verbal Behavior*, 1970, *9*, 232–236.

Chomsky, Carol. Reading, writing, and phonology. *Harvard Educational Review*, May, 1970, *40*, 2, 287–309.

Chomsky, N., & Halle, M. *The Sound Pattern of English*. New York: Harper & Row, 1968.

Fudge, E. C. Phonology. In Lyons, John (ed.) *New Horizons in Linguistics*. Harmondsworth, Middlesex: Penguin, 1970.

Halliday, M. A. Relevant models of language. *Educational Review*, 1969, *22*, 1, 26–37.

Joos, M. *The Five Clocks*. The Hague: Mouton, 1962.

Kolers, P. Some formal characteristics of pictograms. *American Scientist*, 1969, *57*, 3, 348–363.

Lashley, K. S. The problem of serial order in behavior. In Jeffress, L. A. (ed.), *Cerebral Mechanisms in Behavior*, New York: Wiley, 1951, pp. 112–136.

Levin, H., and Williams, Joanna P. (eds.), *Basic Studies on Reading*. New York: Basic Books, 1970.

Luria, A. R. The functional organization of the brain. *Scientific American*, 1970, *222*, 3, 66–78.

Makita, K. The rarity of reading disability in Japanese children. *American Journal of Orthopsychiatry*, 1968, *38*, 4, 599–614.

Read, C. Pre-school children's knowledge of English phonology. *Harvard Educational Review*, 1971, *41*, 1, 1–34.

Rozin, P., Poritsky, Susan, & Sotsky, Raina. American children with reading problems can easily learn to read English represented by Chinese characters. *Science*, 1971, *171*, 1264–1267.

Saporta, S. Frequency of consonant clusters. *Language*, 1955, *31*, 23–30.

Shannon, C. E. Prediction and entropy of printed English. *Bell Systems Technical Journal*, 1951, *30*, 50–64.

Smith, F. *Understanding Reading*. New York: Holt, Rinehart and Winston, 1971.

Venezky, R. L. English orthography: its graphical structure and its relation to sound. *Reading Research Quarterly*, 1967, *2*, 3, 75–105.

11

Illiteracy in the Ghetto

———JANE W. TORREY

We broach now a topic with considerable political and social implica-
tions as well as educational and theoretical interest—the effect of dialect
on reading. An extensive literature is accumulating both on the nature
and the consequences of differences between the language of the child
and the language of the teacher. A number of other questions are deeply
involved, such as the basic understanding of the child (and teacher),
various motivational factors, and person-to-person or intergroup differ-
ences that the language differences merely reflect.

If, as Chomsky asserts (Chapter 8), the English spelling system is
optimal for all dialects, then difficulty experienced by speakers of some
dialects in learning to read must be attributable to some other factor
than the way in which they talk. Jane Torrey contends that it is cross-
cultural variations in the social functions and significance of language,
rather than minor structural differences, that create barriers to teaching
and learning. She calls for cultural and linguistic pluralism not only in
grade school, but throughout educational and occupational systems.

Dr. Torrey is a professor of psychology at Connecticut College.
Her paper appeared first in Harvard Educational Review, *1970, 40, 2, 253–*
259, and is reprinted by permission of the author and publishers.

For those learning to read, the implications of dialect differences
can affect two quite different aspects of language. First, the differences
between the Afro-American and standard dialects—in their phonological,

grammatical, and semantic structures—might lead to confusion and mis-understanding, complicating the already difficult reading process. Second, the cultural and personal functions of language and language differences might affect the social relations between a child and his school in such a way as to block effective learning. It is the thesis of this paper that the functional aspects of language have more serious implications for illiteracy than the structural ones. These functional aspects are closely connected with the conditions of life that keep people out of schools and the conditions of schools that keep people from learning to read in spite of ostensible efforts to teach them.

Although standard English serves as the medium of instruction in reading and other subjects and is the only dialect accepted as "correct" in the dominant society, the deviations of many black children from the standard forms cannot be regarded as errors. These so-called "errors" actually con-form to discernible grammatical rules, different from those of the standard language, but no less systematic. Furthermore, the patterns of black children's grammar that strike the standard English speaking teacher as incomplete, illogical, or linguistically retarded actually conform closely to rules of adult language spoken in the ghetto environment. The following quotes from children in Harlem illustrate patterns that have been inter-preted as showing that such children are "poorly languaged."

> *We at Jane house.*
> *Jane makin' me a cow.*
> *It look like you don' brush your teeth.*

While these sentences may appear incomplete or incorrect to standard speakers, the rules of Afro-American English permit the deletion of the words "is" and "are" in many contexts. The possessive "s" is also optional and the third person singular of present tense verbs has no distinctive "s" ending. All of these seemingly careless omissions are in fact quite consistent grammatical usages, which are increasingly being interpreted as differences in dialect rather than as deficiencies of language development (Labov, 1969).

On the surface it might seem that structural differences between dialects would be important considerations in teaching speakers of Afro-American to read. Since all or nearly all of the reading materials they meet are in standard English, their situation would be something like that of Spanish-speaking children trying to learn to read English before they could speak it very well. Since the Afro-American phonology involves reduction or dele-tion of many terminal consonants and modification of the pattern of standard vowel differentiation, there would seem to be special obstacles for the black child in learning phoneme-grapheme correspondences. Many con-sonants correspond to no audible sounds in his speech, and different vowel letters are used for sounds that are the same to him.

However, the difference in phonology between standard English and black English is not directly relevant to reading. All children who learn to read English have to break a fairly complex code of sound-spelling relationships. The fact that the correspondences are different for speakers of Afro-American does not in itself prove that they are more difficult than for standard speakers.

I have reported elsewhere (Torrey, 1969a*) on a five-year-old self-taught reader who could both recognize and spell correctly words that he did not pronounce in a way comprehensible to a speaker of standard English. His Afro-American sound system had no discernible effect on his reading or writing even though he had discovered how to read and write for himself without any instruction or guidance. Similarly children in England or Boston have no particular trouble in learning words that end in "r" despite the fact that they hardly ever realize these "r's" as such in their speech. These considerations make it seem doubtful that instruction in standard English pronunciation would have any material effect on the ability of black children to learn how to read.

Grammatical differences between the two dialects might also be expected to create problems. However, if we examine specific grammatical differences, we find very few that are likely to lead to misunderstanding. For example, the third person singular present tense verb inflection of standard English, missing in Afro-American, is regarded as one of the most serious problems because it results in many "errors of subject-verb agreement" in black children's writing. However, it is very difficult to find sentences in standard English that could actually be misunderstood because of failure to attend to this inflection. Number is nearly always signaled by a noun inflection also, so that the verb inflection is entirely redundant. It is possible, but quite difficult, to invent sentences where meaning is dependent upon the verb ending alone. "The deer runs" would be a case, since only the "s" of "runs" tells how many deer. However, there are few such nouns in English. People normally tend to the noun as a signal of number, and even speakers of standard English have some trouble using a verb ending as a clue.

There is empirical evidence to suggest that a speaker who uses Afro-American forms often understands the standard forms perfectly well. Labov (Labov, *et al.*, 1968) asked teen-age boys to repeat sentences that were presented orally. These boys commonly "translated" some standard forms into Afro-American as though they were not aware of any difference. For example, "I asked Alvin if he knows how to play basketball" was rendered as "I ax Alvin do he know how to play basketball." The latter form has the same meaning as the original, showing that the speaker understood the standard version even though he was unable to produce it himself. My own research (Torrey, 1969b) has shown that many second-graders in the same area where Labov's subjects lived make this same translation. However, they read the standard forms aloud without changing them.

Another dialect difference is in the possessive inflection. Black children would often say "That's Peter doggie," when the doggie belongs to Peter. Usually this omission produces no ambiguity, but in the few situations where it does, the children in the second grade seemed to understand the distinctive meaning of the "s." I asked them to choose between two pictures representing "The man teacher" (a man standing before a class) and "The man's teacher" (a woman teaching with a man in the class). Many could select the latter picture for "The man's teacher" and name the two pictures correctly in standard English even though they themselves did not spontaneously use the possessive "s" in conversation. The same was true with other dialect differences for these children.

From the above evidence it seems unlikely that the failure of many urban children to progress in reading is primarily due to structural differences between their dialect and school English. A passive understanding of standard dialect should suffice for purposes of learning to read, even if a given child never learns to use the standard forms in speech.

Turning from the structural properties of language to its functions, we can roughly distinguish two classes of functions, the intellectual and the social. The intellectual functions include communicating information between people as well as using language as a tool of thought within an individual. It has been supposed by Bernstein (1961) and others that some dialects spoken by members of lower socio-economic classes are intrinsically less adequate for educational purposes than middle-class dialects. However, there has been very little specification of the forms in the substandard dialects that might be inappropriate for intellectual expression and very little evidence that substandard speakers differ from standard speakers in the quality or subtlety of their thought. If there is such a difference favoring standard grammar, the burden of proof is upon those who maintain it exists. Such proof has yet to be presented. Labov (1969) argues cogently that clear expression, logical thought, and artistic subtlety are as characteristic of "lower-class" language as of academese, perhaps more so. In the absence of convincing evidence that any intellectual differences are inherent in language, I would argue that we should look at the social functions of language for possible explanations of the failure of urban schools to teach all black children to read.

Groups and societies could not exist without languages to link their members together. The language of a group is also the medium of its culture, an integral part of its characteristic style of expression and thought. Language and mannerisms of speech are not just passively adopted from the social milieu. People use them as means of expressing themselves and signifying their membership in a community. Language also signals to other people whether a person is likely to become a friend, what his attitudes are, and what his social status is.

Speakers of different dialects belong to different subgroups in the larger society, and they usually can identify each other by language alone. Some dialects, such as those associated with regions, may carry no particular status or evaluative significance. Others belong to subgroups of recognized high or low status. The characteristic culture, manners, style, and language of the black American have been intimately associated in the minds of black and white alike with his historical status. White America has made it necessary for a black man to divest himself of these cultural traits including dialect in order to change his status or find a secure place in the dominant white society. The schools have regarded it as their prime obligation to stamp out all possible manifestations of black culture and language, assuming that only when that was accomplished could an individual reap the benefits of his education and ability. To the extent they believed that imposing white language and manners was necessary for social advancement, teachers have accepted the acculturating function that was assigned to schools in the handling of foreign immigrants.

My thesis is that the main impact of Afro-American dialect on education has not been its structural differences from standard English, nor its relative intrinsic usefulness as a medium of thought, but its function as a low-status stigma and its association with a rejected culture. The attitudes of teachers toward this dialect and of dialect speakers towards the teachers' language have affected the social relationships of children with the schools in such a way as to make education of many children almost impossible. Black children of rural southern background have entered the urban schools to find that nearly everything they said was branded as "wrong." In order to be "right" they had to adopt forms that seemed alien even when they were able to learn how to use them. Their own spontaneous products were punished and treated as worthless, including the only language they knew really well. Because of this, they were almost forced to regard themselves and their society as bad, ugly, or even sinful.

Children in the lower grades commonly accept a teacher as a kind of substitute mother. Teachers make use of this attitude in motivating and teaching. However, no such mother-child relationship can be established with someone who cannot accept the other person and his ways as legitimate. The black child is more likely to become alienated from the teacher and from the culture the teacher represents, including reading, than he is to conform to strange and unfriendly ways. The differences in language and culture become a basis of hostility and rejection of the whole educational process. Indeed, one might speculate that the evolution of an elaborate secret language among blacks has been essential to their survival—that the highly symbolic, metaphorical references used by blacks constitute a defense against the alien culture.

The relationship between black child and white-dominated school parallels the pattern of racial polarization in society and is being increasingly incorporated into the larger struggle. This is not to say that all the black-white division in society and school can be attributed to linguistic differences alone. Illiteracy that occurs in urban America today is not a direct result of language differences, but language is one of the cultural differences that have played a key role in the failure of schools to reach black children.

In other words, one could not claim that schools are imposing an alien language, because there is adequate evidence that the structural differences are minor. But within the social context, minor differences in structure can take on enough symbolic importance to be construed by black children and teachers alike as alien and therefore threatening. Changing the attitudes of teachers toward black English and the attitudes of black children toward standard English will not in itself solve the problem of urban education, but it will almost certainly have to be part of any considerable improvement in school effectiveness. Consideration of the personal and social functions of language is vitally important for deciding when, how, and in what spirit to introduce second dialect learning.

The idea that Afro-American English is a legitimate "language" in its own right has many possible implications for education. The initial response of many educators has been that efforts to teach standard English might make use of the new techniques of foreign language teaching. However, several basic implications should be considered first. One is that the teaching of standard English should not have the purpose of "stamping out" the native dialect. Standard English would be a second language, or rather, a second dialect, to be available alongside the native one for special purposes such as school and contact with the standard-speaking community. People would still use Afro-American English in their own community and the school would not have to stigmatize it any more than it should condemn the use of Spanish.

Other basic questions raised by this view of Afro-American include, first, whether a command of the standard language is really necessary for educational purposes at all; second, whether in higher education and in the society at large there should be a more flexible interpretation of "correctness" in spoken and written English; and, finally, whether the Afro-American language and the culture associated with it are not in themselves worthy objects of study in the school curriculum. Should not the grammar of Afro-American be taught just as the grammar of Spanish should for Spanish-speaking children? Should not the folklore and style of that medium be given the same respect as other forms of folk art?

It would be unrealistic to talk of changing the attitudes of grade school teachers toward linguistic variation without at the same time proposing other changes in the whole educational and occupational systems. It would be dishonest to raise children in an atmosphere of cultural and linguistic tolerance in the early grades if they found at higher levels of school and in the job market that their own language was regarded as inferior and that only the traditional literature and science were treated as worthwhile knowledge. The academic world in general must broaden its cultural base beyond those subjects, methods, and media that have been traditional in schools and universities, or else they will continue to discriminate in fact against the "other" cultures and languages of the nation. We should stop asking schools and colleges to be the instruments of melting down our cultural variety and originality, as the Spanish conquerors melted down the metallurgical arts of the Incas into square gold bars of value on the Euro-American market. LeRoi Jones looked around the city and saw a lot of "square gray buildings" built by "square grays." Many of those buildings were schools turning out illiterates because they could not adjust to all the different shapes of their task. Our traditional cultural and linguistic imperialism has been self-defeating not only because it has failed to acculturate its more divergent elements, but also because it has prevented our nation as a whole from appreciating the true richness of its diverse heritage.

References

Bernstein, B. Social structure, language and learning. *Educational Research*, 1961, *3*, 163–176.

Labov, W. The logic of non-standard English. *Georgetown Monograph Series on Languages and Linguistics*, Monograph No. 22, 1969.

Labov, W., Cohen, P., Robins, C., and Lewis, J. *A Study of the Non-Standard English of Negro and Puerto Rican Speakers in New York City*. Final Report, Cooperative Research Project No. 3288, Office of Education, Washington, D.C., 1968.

Torrey, J. W. Learning to read without a teacher: a case study. *Elementary English*, 1969, *46*, 550–556. (a)

Torrey, J. W. Teaching standard English to speakers of other dialects. Paper prepared for the Second International Congress of Applied Linguistics, September, 1969. (b)

12

The Learner
and His Language

There is no specific faculty of reading in the human brain, and there is no exclusive trick or essence in the process of reading that requires a child to do something he has never done before. Obviously, reading is a visual activity, but making sense of the visual world, learning to discriminate and utilize significant visual differences, is something all schoolchildren have been doing for years. This argument is developed further in Chapter 16. The pseudo-explanation that children require special visual (or auditory) discrimination skills for reading is a red herring. Children may not have discovered what are the cues they should be looking or listening for, but they are capable of looking and listening.

Reading, as several of the preceding chapters have emphasized, is also a language activity, and a child expected to learn to read who has a deficient comprehension of spoken language obviously has a problem, but the problem is not one of reading. Almost all children beginning reading instruction have learned to speak, which means that they have already demonstrated the ability to learn language skills. It is with the ability to learn spoken language that this chapter is concerned.

I do not wish to hammer at implications for reading instruction at this point, but I think the chapter does invite comparisons between the kind of information available to a child learning to talk and the information available to him when he is expected to learn to read. Although we tend to look on the positive side in education, concerning ourselves with the amount of information given to a child, our efforts can go for nothing if the information is irrelevant to him or in a form that he cannot use. Some classroom schedules and instructional routines are so inflexible

138

and unresponsive to pupils' needs that they are little more than a systematic deprivation of information.

A slightly modified version of the present chapter is published under the same title in Language and Learning To Read, *edited by R. E. Hodges and E. H. Rudorf (Boston: Houghton Mifflin, 1972), and is reprinted by permission of the editors and publishers.*

Language, as several chapters of this volume have asserted, is a two-level system. In the case of spoken language, the two levels of the system are related to sound and meaning, and the task of the language learner is to construct a set of rules that will enable him to translate from one to the other. Many linguists refer to the two levels of language as surface and deep structure, with syntax, or grammar, as the set of rules that permits the language user to operate between the two.

Similarly, the task of the beginning reader is to construct a set of rules that will enable him to translate the surface structure of written language—represented by the visual symbols on the page—into meaning. To a considerable extent these rules for reading will include rules that the beginning reader has already acquired in his mastery of the spoken form of language, although other rules are specifically related to the visual aspects of written text. The purpose of the present chapter is to discuss briefly the degree to which the beginning reader has already mastered the syntax of spoken language, and more importantly to consider the means by which this mastery is acquired.

The attention to the first question, the beginning reader's competence in spoken language, will be relatively brief because to all intents and purposes, the process of spoken language learning may be considered to be complete by the time a child's attention is turned to reading. But the question of *how* this competence in spoken language is acquired, of the kinds of information and learning experiences that a child requires in order to acquire a grammar, warrants consideration in a little more detail. An understanding of the manner in which a child develops spoken language skills provides a clue to the kind of information that a child requires in order to learn a complex skill such as reading, and indicates the strategies that he is likely to employ. Acquaintance with the manner in which spoken language is learned also reminds us of the remarkable intellectual potential of a child in his first few years of life, at an age when he is often considered the least attentive and tractable. At such an age practically every child constructs and verifies a set of rules that summarize the relationships and regularities underlying language, even though adults are far from any understanding of what these relationships and regularities are, let alone how to impart them through formal instruction.

Linguists still cannot describe fully the system that is language. The problem is not paucity of data—there is no shortage of language in the world—but rather that there is an inadequacy of theories of language, an inability to construct valid and testable hypotheses for the rules that relate deep and surface structure. There is as yet no theoretical basis that will permit the construction of computer programs to translate from one language to another, or even to distinguish grammatical from ungrammatical sentences in one language, with anything like the facility of a human.

Of course, it would be absurd to suggest that linguists are not able to distinguish a grammatical sentence from an ungrammatical one; they are in the frustrating but not uncommon position of being unable to explain how they do something which they are in fact able to do very well. Fortunately it is not necessary for a child to be told what the rules of language are in order to acquire them, and few people have the impression that they know enough about spoken language even to attempt to teach a child to talk. This is not the case with reading, of course. And because children often learn to read at the time when a parent or teacher is engaged in the behavior we call instructing, there is a widespread belief that the rules a child develops in order to read must be the rules an adult has verbalized. But the fact that a child demonstrates some desirable behavior after exposure to a particular kind of instruction does not logically entail that he has acquired a particular kind of rule. The instructional situation may quite coincidentally provide the child with the information that he needs in order to develop and test unverbalized rules of his own. There can be no other explanation for the fact that so many children learn to speak and to read in such a variety of instructional environments.

The Nature of Child Language

The language competence of the beginning reader can be summarized very succinctly. Although linguists have been unable to provide anything like a complete description of the rules of grammar, the great majority of children develop a set for themselves within the space of about two years. (Relevant references are cited in the Further Readings.) At the age of about 18 months a child produces his first two-word sentence, and by three-and-a-half years he appears to have mastered all the important rules of his language. Of course, a child of four does not speak like an adult—his vocabulary is not as rich and his memory is more limited—but he has acquired the competence to produce and comprehend all the possible forms of sentence construction found in adult speech.

First-language learning proceeds in an extremely rapid, smooth, and predictable sequence, indicating that a child is predisposed biologically both to use *and to learn* language. Because of this innate ability, and the fact that all the world's languages have many basic similarities, the view has been developed that the task confronting the newborn infant is not so much to learn what language is as to discover the idiosyncratic aspects of the particular language spoken in his own community. The child is born ready to start speaking a unique language—which adults denigrate with the name of baby talk—and progressively modifies this language until it comes closer and closer to that spoken by his parents. Some linguists and psychologists use the metaphor that the child learning to talk is "testing hypotheses", literally conducting linguistic experiments, to discover specifically what kind of language is talked around him.

Other sources of evidence support the view that the essential skills of language learning are innate; they concern the idiosyncratic nature of child language and the fact that its progressive refinement into adult language follows an orderly sequence. Thorough analyses of the verbal productions of infants have shown that the language they speak is neither a miniature or deformed version of adult language, nor a random throwing-together of words. Very little language learning is attributable to imitation, because very few of the constructions that children utter are arrangements of words that they could possibly have heard their parents utter. In fact one of the most difficult things to ask a child to do is to imitate either a sound or a phrase that he has not already spontaneously produced for himself. Children change their ways to conform to adult language, but they do this by starting with a language of their own, not by starting from nothing. Their language is always systematic.

The Process of Language Development

The baby who starts to babble at the age of three months does not build up from silence to the sounds of his own language; he starts with all possible language sounds and gradually eliminates those not used by the people around him. For those of us who are not skilled polyglots, the only time that we find it physically possible to utter sounds that are not in our native language is when we are babes in arms.

During the first few years of life children find no particular difficulty in learning *any* language. They are not born more ready to speak one than another. At three months it is impossible to distinguish the babbling of a Chinese child from that of a Dutch child or an American. At the age of six months, however, this is not the case. A six-month-old baby may not be able to speak a word of his native tongue, but he is "babbling" in French or German or English. There is experimental evidence that the "native language" of a six-month-old child can be identified from a tape recording of his babbling. The baby is demonstrating that he has acquired rules for the sounds that are produced around him. But it would be an oversimplification to say that he has learned these sounds by imitating his parents. The baby acquires them the way a sculptor "acquires" a statue—by disposing of surplus material that he originally had available for use if required.

By the age of one year, many children are speaking single words: *drink, mama, bye-bye*. Are they imitating their parents when they produce these words? Again the answer is that the elements are the result of successive approximation, and not imitation in the sense that the child is aping an adult model. For one thing, many child words are quite unique—the child could not possibly have heard his parent saying them (unless the parent was imitating the child, which is not an infrequent grown-up pastime). Further, the child uses these first words in quite a different manner from the way in which adults use them. While adults put words together in accordance with a grammar, one-year-old children do not. Instead, infants use single words to express entire sentences (holophrases is the technical term)—an economy not generally practised by grownups. Underlying the single words of the holophrastic stage may be quite complex meanings; *drink*, for example, might mean anything from "Bring me a drink" or "Look at that drink" to "I did not want that drink and I have just thrown it all over the floor".

Contrary to popular parental belief, the child is not learning words and then finding meanings for them. Instead he is acquiring or inventing words, which may or may not have a close relation to adult language, to meet his own particular requirements and represent quite complex deep structures.

By eighteen months, many children have developed a powerful grammatical rule. At this age they are producing two- or three-word phrases, like *allgone milk* or *see baby* or *want big truck*. Two aspects of this development are significant: first, these short sentences are certainly not imitated from parents (how many adults would say *allgone milk* or *want big truck*?), and second, the constructions are not random. The child, who may have a vocabulary of two or three hundred words by this time, does not put his words together arbitrarily in his first sentences—he has a system, a rule. *This rule is developed by children for their own use, for it does not occur in adult language.*

The condition for the first rule is that all words of the vocabulary are ordered into one of two classes, which some researchers call Pivot and Open. The Pivot class is relatively small and "closed"—new words are not added very frequently—while the Open class, relatively large, is the class to which most new words are added.

The first rule can be represented like this:

$$S \rightarrow (P) + O + (O)$$
$$P \rightarrow \text{allgone, see, my} \ldots$$
$$O \rightarrow \text{milk, baby, big, truck} \ldots$$

and interpreted as follows:

A sentence S can be formed by an Open class word O optionally preceded by a Pivot class word (P) and optionally followed by another Open class word (O). Among the sentences that can be produced are *allgone big truck*, *see milk*, *my baby* but not *big truck allgone*, *milk see* or *baby my*.

The words in each class vary of course from child to child, and a word that originates in one child's Pivot class may be in another child's Open. But all children appear to go through the same first-rule stage although no children are explicitly taught it. The development of the rule is one of the universals of language development in children.

From the first coarse-grained Pivot-Open class distinction, children go on to make successive differentiations within each class, progressively making their language more complex and gradually bringing it closer and closer to that spoken by adults. All the time a child is speaking a rule-governed language of his own; at no time does he just throw words together randomly, and at no time can he be said to be slavishly imitating an adult model. Those rules which are productive in the construction or comprehension of sentences in adult language are retained, the others the child progressively modifies.

Sometimes it is very clear that a child is not imitating. One very revealing example of the manner in which children discover rules rather than copy examples lies in the highly predictable sequence in which almost all children utter *incorrect* forms of very common verbs after they have apparently learned the correct forms. The phenomenon occurs among "strong" verbs like *come, go,* and *drink* which occur frequently in the language and which have irregular past tense forms such as *came, went,* and *drank*. Frequently a child produces these past tense constructions correctly until he discovers the +*ed* rule for the "regular" inflection *walk-walked, climb-climbed, laugh-laughed*. As a demonstration that he has learned the past tense rule, the child suddenly begins to lose the correct forms *came, went, drank* and to overgeneralize the +*ed* rule and say *comed, goed, drinked*. These are obviously not forms that the child has heard his parents or anyone else utter; he is trying out a new rule, and does not use it correctly until he gets the information that certain words like *come, go* and *drink* are exceptions.

In fact it can be shown that imitation of adult speech is one of the hardest tasks that can be set. If an adult tells a child at the Pivot-Open class stage to say *"the milk is all gone"*, the child will reply "allgone milk" or whatever construction has the same meaning according to his own rules.

How Language Is Learned

The task of the child is to find out the underlying rules of grammar—to uncover the system that underlies the surface of every utterance and relates sound and meaning. He never "just repeats" a sentence that he hears an adult utter; what would be the point of that? Nor does he try to learn by rote the sentences that adults produce; that would also be pointless, because almost every sentence we hear and use is novel. The child needs to learn to produce and understand all the potential sentences of his language, that is to say, to learn the rules by which the sentences of his language are produced. And of course, that is something no adult even attempts to teach a child. The child in effect performs a detection task— he hears a sentence and tries to determine a possible rule by which it could be produced. Then he tests whether the rule is correct, by using it to produce a few sample sentences and seeing whether they are acceptable as sentences of the language.

In this light, the responsibility of adults becomes rather clear, although it is quite different from the role traditionally attributed to them. Basically, adults supply the child with two types of information which may be termed *general* and *specific*. They capitalize on the child's implicit knowledge of the way to learn by keeping him exposed to plenty of adult language. This is the *general information* that a child requires. The adult who does not help his child is the one who tries to speak only "baby talk".

Specific information is best given to a child only when he needs it. The child does not want, and cannot use, little snippets of information thrown at him arbitrarily in a formal learning situation. Instead, he needs feedback to tell him whether he is observing the significant differences of his language in a particular situation. The simplest way to provide feedback at the right time is perhaps to regard every utterance made by a child as having a double function, the first being the expression of a need or feeling, and the second the test of a rule.

If the preceding discussion makes the task of the adult sound too vague, there is one simple rule of thumb: A child wants information about a grammatical rule when he uses it. Many parents follow this rule unknowingly when they engage in the game which has received the technical name of "expansions". In this transaction, parents take a sample of child speech and expand it into adult form. For example when the child says *want milk*; the parent "expands" the statement into *You want some milk, do you?* or *May I have a glass of milk, please?* An adult expanding child language is providing a specific adult-language surface structure for a deep structure that the child already has in his mind. It is not simply a matter of "correcting", but of giving information so that the child can verify a rule that he has just applied, at a time when he can relate it to the appropriate deep structure.

General Comments

There are several aspects of learning to speak and learning to read that are common to many cognitive tasks. One common aspect is that learning cognitive skills is far more complex than we conventionally believe. But the child is able to overcome instructional deficiencies because his learning competencies are far richer than we usually give him credit for.

To take a non-linguistic example, consider the situation when a child is "taught" to tell the difference between cats and dogs. This type of task, involving the determination of "significant differences" of particular categories of objects or events, is something that a child is very good at accomplishing and an adult very poor at explaining. We never *tell* a child what are the differences between cats and dogs, in fact it is doubtful whether most adults could verbalize a foolproof set of rules. Instead we let the child see many instances of cats and dogs, and of objects which are not cats and dogs (this is all *general information*), and leave it to him to work out what the significant differences must be. In order to learn what it is about cats that makes them cats, the child needs to examine positive and negative examples. It is no use exposing him just to cats and saying each time, "This is a cat"—the result may well be that he thinks all four-legged animals are cats. Instead he needs to see dogs, horses, cows, and so forth, and to be told that these are *not* cats. Only by being shown what the alternatives are will he get any clue about what a cat is.

Having been shown what the alternatives are, a child will draw his own conclusions, which he will test by seeing if he can use the terms "cat" and "dog" in a manner concordant with the way adults use them. The child does not go to an adult and say, "Kindly give me a set of rules to commit to memory that will permit me infallibly to distinguish a cat or dog whenever I meet one". Again, what adult could oblige him? Instead the child tests his hypotheses, plays his hunches, by using the words "cat" and "dog" and looking for the *specific information* of feedback. It does not matter if he calls an occasional Pekinese a cat or a Siamese a dog, provided he is given the appropriate feedback about whether he should modify his rules. The sure way of preventing a child from discovering what are the distinguishing characteristics of cats and dogs would be to discourage him from using these terms on any occasion that he might be "wrong".

I have come to a critical point in this chapter. The time when specific information is most useful to a child is when he is making a response *which could be wrong*. He has got to make some kind of response, to put some kind of rule into practice, otherwise he can never receive feedback. He will not learn by sitting and listening or looking—the brain does not assimilate information in that way. But there is no value in making a response if the child waits for those occasions when he knows he must be right. In that case, he is merely exhibiting rules that he has already confirmed. Instead the child must test hypotheses that he has not yet confirmed, which means that there must be a probability that his response will be "wrong" by adult standards. He will only learn adult language if he is encouraged to use his child language, and receives the necessary feedback.

We do not usually punish young children for not speaking like adults, and the parents who encourage their children to be articulate are generally rewarded by the ease with which the baby talk is discarded. Similarly, we are usually not inclined to get emotionally unsettled when a child has trouble distinguishing cows from horses. The situation in reading is rather different; we are far more prone to talk of mistakes and errors, and far less tolerant of the child who is hypothesis-testing. A major insight to be gained from the study of spoken language development is that we cannot expect a child to learn simply on the basis of the rules that adults try to feed to him.

13

Learning To Read without a Teacher: A Case Study

—JANE W. TORREY

This chapter is the story of John, middle child in a black family of five, son of a trucker and a hospital maid, living in subsidized housing in a crowded southern city. According to most predictions, John should have reading problems all through his school career. But John is one of the thousands of children who somehow learn to read in much the same way that millions of children learn to speak—before they arrive at school, without the help of a teacher, and without very much in the way of obvious instruction from parents or other adults. Like many other precocious readers, John taught himself to read with the aid of labels and television.

John was not disconcerted because English spelling was not perfectly consistent with his pronunciation. He "asked the right questions" about the relations between language and print, and he read for meaning, not words. In short, John appears to have known (implicitly) at the age of four much of what has been asserted in the previous chapters of this book. Jane Torrey addresses herself to the question of what happened to John that enabled him to learn to read with such facility. An equally valid question asks what happens to many other children that makes learning to read so difficult.

Dr. Torrey's paper was published first in Elementary English, *1969, 46, 550–556, and is reprinted by permission of the author and publishers.*

Most children are taught to read after they are in school, but a certain number have some reading skill already when they enter first grade. Dolores Durkin (1966) reports that about one per cent of approximately 5000 children who entered the Oakland, California public school system in 1958 were able to read as many as 18 out of 37 words in her simple test. Since reading is a language skill, it is reasonable to suppose that children who read earlier than usual do so because of especially high language ability or especially appropriate exposure to language. When children fail to learn reading, it seems reasonable to look for lower verbal ability or lack of appropriate exposure to language. Thus, the reading problems of slum children are commonly attributed to a lack of knowledge of language, and it is suggested that if they were given special training that would make their articulation, vocabulary, or grammatical patterns more like those of middle class children; they would be able to compete also in reading.

In view of the explanations that suggest themselves both for early reading and for reading problems in disadvantaged children, it is worthwhile to examine a case of one child of average general and verbal ability according to tests, whose language deviates from standard English both in articulation and in grammar, but who has nevertheless mastered very early and without much help the difficult art of reading.

Background

I had the opportunity to spend three hours a week for four months with a five-year-old child whom I will call John. John had entered kindergarten in a Negro school in a large southern city at the age of four years ten months. His teacher discovered that he could both read and write and that he was not interested in doing much else. The school asked me to "tutor" him, that is, to observe his reading in detail and help him put his skills to good use. These sessions took place in the living room of his home, so I was able to observe his background and environment in some detail.

John's father had approximately eight years and his mother about ten years in the Negro schools of southern cities. The father drives a truck while the mother works as a maid in a hospital. With five children, their combined income is low enough for them to qualify for subsidized housing. They suffer from those "disadvantages" that go with limited education in poor school systems plus all those others that go with having a dark skin. Although these are real deprivations, the family has the same kinds of desires and ambitions as most middle-class Americans for a home of their own and good education for their children. They seem to be making the best use of their resources toward these ends. Theirs is not a case of hard-core poverty with the hopelessness and disorganization that sometimes go with it.

John is the third of five children. At the time I was seeing him, they ranged from less than a year to eleven years. The older sister and brother had begun their education in a school that had recently gone from all white to all Negro and in the process had become badly over-crowded and full of severely deprived children. Their reading was average for the school, which meant a year or more behind national norms. By the time John entered kindergarten, the family had moved into the area of a much newer and less crowded but still virtually all Negro school. (Later John entered first grade in an integrated school.) John seemed to be on good terms with his siblings, and they all seemed happy and well cared for, either by their mother or grandmother. The home, a new three-bedroom garden apartment, was well kept and had the normal equipment such as washing machine, TV, Hi-Fi and so forth. The children had toys and books.

History

John's mother reported that he had not begun talking especially early, but that he had been able to read almost from the time he could talk. She said no one had read to him or taught him to read. At five he read better than his older brother and sister and was occasionally able to tell his father a word. His mother once said that he must have received the gift directly from God (perhaps along with the gift of tongues). The only plausible earthly source of instruction she was able to mention was television commercials. She reported that when he was younger, he had known all the commercials by heart and recited them as they appeared on the screen. She said she could never get his attention until the commercial was over. My own check on television showed that an average of about 40 words per hour are simultaneously shown and pronounced. On children's programs a higher proportion of these words are labels on cans and boxes. John's grandmother reported that her earliest evidence of his reading knowledge came when he read labels of cans in the kitchen.

Durkin's survey studies of early reading provide a background for comparing John with other early readers. In many respects he is quite typical of this unusual group. Of her sample of 49 early readers only seven came from professional or upper middle-class homes, the rest being like John, from lower middle-class or lower. John also resembled many early readers in that he took the initiative in learning rather than having the skill taught to him at someone else's behest. Like most early readers he took a great interest in identifying words and numbers he saw. Like them, he enjoyed writing and spent much time printing words and numbers. John's earliest reading material, TV commercials and can labels, is quite typical. His social life is also similar to many others in that he was something of a loner, a Mama's boy. He had good relations with adults but lacked enough aggressiveness to be happy and hold his own with other children. He got along well with his own brothers and sisters, being particularly fond of his brother who is two years older. However, he probably did not have the benefit of his older siblings' help in reading, since he read better than either one. His mother reported that he read stories to his brother at night, stories his brother could not read for himself. He took great pride in reading and in showing off that he knew better than his brother. Durkin reports that high competitiveness is typical of early readers.

The principal difference between John's case and the others is the absence of any report of his receiving help. His mother insisted, even under cross-examination, that he had learned by himself. All reports of his reading from her or from his grandmother were simple accounts of their surprised discovery of something he already could do. His grandmother had been unprepared for his spelling and reading can labels and written TV notices. His mother had been worried about damage he might do to the library books his sister brought home. She said she often took them away from him and did not know he could read them until one day he read aloud to visitors all of what she described as a "third grade library book."

Although John's mother's reports of his reading were all cases simply of his showing off what he knew, it is quite possible that she gave him help without realizing that she was doing it. For example, in getting him to demonstrate how he could do arithmetic, she told him the answer when he guessed wrong. She and others may have done this kind of thing with words, too. She did report his playing bingo and concentration with some teen-age relatives. He could have been told numbers and words by them.

The one known source of instruction remains television commercials. It has already been mentioned that John watched and memorized them. Commercials are frequently repeated, so that whatever a child fails to learn in one showing can be drilled ad nauseam in subsequent days and weeks. Commercials are designed to get attention, so they are usually loud, lively and simple. Memorizing of short sentences is facilitated by catchy tunes. Many common words are shown and the unfamiliar brand names (e.g. "Ban," "Sominex") are usually short or easy to pronounce. It seems possible that from commercials a child could get a start on a basic vocabulary and make a few inferences about phonics, extend his reading knowledge through phonics, use the redundancy of language in simple books, ask occasional questions and be corrected by an adult.

Description of Reading

The tutoring situation made possible a number of direct observations of John's verbal skills. His spontaneous speech gave the basic data on his use of language. All the sessions were taped. He resisted any lengthy reading for me on the reasonable grounds that I was able to read things for myself. However, if he had to read something in the context of a game or other task, he never hesitated. Most samples of his reading were obtained in this way. Another kind of evidence came from his dictating, which occurred when he asked me to type things that were too hard for him to type himself. He took great pleasure in seeing his words emerge in print. His style of speaking changed considerably in this context from his spontaneous speech. His grammar and articulation were at their very best in dictating and it was rarely necessary to ask him to repeat or spell. It was as though he were conforming to the special style of language as it normally occurs in print.

John's oral reading was fast and confident. He showed no sign of word calling, but always read with normal sentence intonation. He could sound out words, but preferred to ask about those he did not know. Although the material might contain unfamiliar words and very unusual grammatical constructions, he was frequently able to grasp the sentence structure. For example, two rather unusual verses he read with correct sentence intonation were

> The bunny now gets twenty hops,
> While in the woods the lolly pops.

and

> Two more hops for the bunny and then
> Look out for the Pipsissewah in his den.

Although he asked for help with the words "hops" and "Pipsissewah," he read the sentences without hesitation, including the noun-verb intonation of the phrase "the lolly pops." I interpret this kind of performance as indicating that John treated written language as a natural alternate version of spoken language. He seemed to expect that print represented sentences and words with meaning. Two other kinds of behavior seemed to support this view. One was his silent reading, evidenced by the fact that he could quickly fill in blanks in written sentences without pronouncing either what he read or what he wrote. Given pictures as guides, he filled in the underlined words below without reading aloud or mouthing.

Here are some <u>flags</u>.

These are <u>shoes</u>. They belong to a <u>lady</u>.

The other evidence of his "natural" use of the written medium was his writing. Nearly all of his written production was in sentences and conveyed direct messages to me, although some were more or less on a fantasy level in that he did not expect compliance. Examples include

Put candy in the machine.
Touch the candy. Touch the jar of candy, John.
Look under the table.
Pour candy out the jar. (sic)
Jump rope.

Once, when I had been pestering him to read aloud, he printed "Get out."
In print he seemed not to be afraid of offending me or provoking his
mother. Although he used upper case letters wherever possible, he was
capable of printing as well as reading lower case. He rarely misspelled a
word, but did ask how to spell some words, for example, "laugh," apparently knowing it was a peculiar one. His grasp of the English writing system
obviously went far beyond any simple sound-symbol association.

John's oral spelling was also fast and confident. Although his articulation
was frequently so different from mine that I could not understand his words
even when he tried very hard, he could readily spell anything he could say.
For example, on one occasion, there was the following conversation,
transcribed as well as possible.

John: They were tired of shopping over there. Buying toys for Christmas
for the ch???s.
Me: Toys for the what?
John: Ch???s.
Me: Oh, churches.
John: Uh-huh, ch???s.
Me: Turkey?
John: Uh-uh, chrns. (Louder and very carefully articulated.)
Me: Can you spell it?
John: C.H.I.L.D.R.E.N.

Although he pronounced a final /s/ clearly, his spelling was the correct
plural without "s." On another occasion he asked for help in finding one of
a set of chips bearing single words. The word he wanted was /uh/, a single
schwa vowel pronounced very clearly. He rejected the word "a," as in
"a boy." Asked to spell what he wanted he said:

Uh, A. R. E., uh.

It is obvious that John found little difficulty in the fact that standard
English spelling was not perfectly consistent with his pronunciation. Although his own dialect of English lacked many of the sounds, especially
terminal consonants, of more standard English, sounds that correspond to
letters in traditional orthography, he was apparently able to take these
inconsistencies in stride, along with the many others that exist for even the
most articulate speaker of standard English. John's lack of difficulty raises
a question about the need for some kinds of language training as preparation
for reading. Although a single case cannot prove that careful articulation

of standard English is irrelevant to reading, it does demonstrate that it is not a necessary precondition. John's accurate reading of sentences whose grammar deviated radically from anything he would say himself is an example on the syntactic level of this same adaptation to the peculiarities of the language found in print.

John's spelling does not convert all aspects of his language into standard English, however. At one time he dictated an unusually long sentence to be transcribed on the typewriter. Asked to make clear what one of the words was, he responded by spelling the entire sentence, pausing briefly between words. It came out as follows:

Gregory put a candy in Johnny and the baby face.

Standard English would have inserted "'s" after "baby" and possibly also after "Johnny." John's dialect typically omits this possessive inflection. This particular dialect feature was carried over into his writing.

John's language development seemed not to be advanced for his age. The mean length of his utterances in morphemes at 62 months was equal to that of Brown's male subject, Adam, at 43 months. (Brown, 1967). In grammatical development, he was also somewhat behind Adam. Brown found that when Adam was about 44 months old, he did not normally transpose the subject and verb in forming a wh question. For example

Adam's Question	*Standard English*
What John will read?	What will John read?
Where it goes?	Where does it go?

When the original sentence contains an auxiliary, the auxiliary is transposed with the subject in forming a question in standard adult English. Without an auxiliary, an inflected form of "do" is placed before the subject in forming a question. By John's age (63 months) Adam was transposing nearly all such questions, but John produced the following:

What CBS stands for?
What they say?

John rarely transposed in casual speech but in dictation he did transpose.

Where do you live at?

In reading questions with "do," he commonly omitted the word, thus producing a question in the form he would have used. Here are some sentences with his reading.

John's Reading	*Text*
When you eat breakfast?	When do you each breakfast? (sic)
When you go to school?	When do you go to school?

In other cases where "do" appeared, he misread in other ways.

John's Reading	*Text*
What does he after school?	What does he do after school?
Do he goes to school?	Does he go to school?
Does he can read books?	Does he read books?
Can he write?	Can he write?

John's handling of "may" was parallel to his use of "do." He rarely or never used either in casual speech, but did dictate correct sentences with both. He dictated the following sentences, clearly enunciating "may."

May I go outside?
May I play with the blocks?

However, in reading he avoided or stumbled over the word.

John's Reading	*Text*
Help Uncle Wiggly a hop along.	You may help Uncle Wiggly a hop along.
You have to go . . .	You might have to go . . .

Several of the misreadings shown above seem to deviate from the text in the direction of conforming to John's own language. These errors suggest that John expected to find in print the things that he would normally say, that is, that writing to him was firmly understood as a natural alternate form of language. It was as though he read, not the words, but the meanings, and then expressed that same meaning his own way. John's ability to see the meaning of forms he did not use casually would be harder to account for if it were not for the evidence from his dictation showing that he did have some speaking knowledge of these forms.

Test Data

The Metropolitan Readiness Test was given to John when he entered kindergarten, four months before I first saw him, and again when he entered first grade a year later. Table 1 shows his scores.

Some observations of John in the tutoring situation seem consistent with his pattern of scores. He was preoccupied with letters, words, and numbers and not at all interested in nonsense shapes. Although he took great pleasure in digits, his concept of the quantities they represented was very limited. For example, although he could count as high as needed or identify any number, he was not able to determine the number of objects put before him by counting them. Only after several weeks of training with counting solid objects, was he able to play a parchesi type game in which a counter moves a certain number of spaces. He could write the sequence "$6+6=12$,"

Table 1 Metropolitan Readiness Test

	Kindergarten	First Grade
Total	59	51
Percentile	59	42
Word meanings	7	6
Listening	9	8
Matching	10	8
Alphabet	16	16
Numbers	9	9
Copying	8	4

but showed no sign of understanding that if you saw three elephants and then two more elephants, you could say there were five elephants. Similarly with words, he cheerfully read words from a French picture dictionary, pronouncing them as if they were English and showing no concern about their meaning. It is consistent, therefore, that John's high performance should be on the alphabet with scores of average or below on other aspects of readiness. Table 2 shows John's performance on the Wechsler Pre-Primary Scale of Intelligence, given to him at exactly six years, after he had entered first grade. There is no evidence here that his extraordinary reading ability is a matter of unusually high intelligence, or of extraordinary verbal ability. Block design is his high point, with performance scores generally above verbal scores. On the Bender-Gestalt Visual Motor Test he showed superior visual motor ability. He drew the required figures quickly and surely, retaining the form in all but the last two figures. He drew the diamond correctly as only about 50 per cent of seven year olds can do. On the Benton Visual Retention Test, whose norms begin at eight years, his ability to reproduce figures from memory was high average to superior.

Three other tests were administered. On the Peabody Picture Vocabulary Test his IQ score was 111. On the Wide Range Achievement Test his read-

Table 2 Wechsler Pre-Primary Scale of Intelligence

Verbal		Performance	
Information	7	Animal House (colorform matching)	7
Vocabulary	11	Picture Completion	11
Arithmetic	9	Mazes	12
Similarities	14	Block Design	16
Comprehension	6	Geometric Design	13
Verbal IQ	96	Performance IQ	111
Full Scale IQ	104		

ing at age six after two months in the first grade was 4.8 and spelling 5.0. However, his arithmetic achievement was 1.0. His Draw-A-Man was average for his age, done quickly and labeled "A man."

Conclusions

The following "conclusions" are presented, not as research "findings" from a single case, but rather as hypotheses suggested by the unusual aspects of the case. Reading for John seems to have been learned but not to have been taught by anyone who was consciously aware of teaching him. He appears to have asked just the right questions in his own mind about the relation between language and print and thus to have been able to bridge the gap between his own language and the printed form. His case may have some implications for the more general task of teaching and learning reading.

1) Reading is learned, not taught.

Even in school the teacher can only provide guidance, motivating circumstances, and answers to questions. No teacher has time to tell each child everything he has to learn, much less to drill him enough times on each element. The key for learning to read may be the child's asking the right questions of his environment. If the child does that, he will be able to get the answers from a variety of sources, not necessarily including a consciously teaching older person.

2) The key question is "How does something I can say look in print?" or, vice versa, "What does that print say?"

Effective reading ultimately requires that these questions refer to whole utterances, not to phonemes and graphemes or even words. John's phonic knowledge and his word attack skills were strictly subordinate to the task of reading what is said. I interpreted his intonation patterns in reading to signify that he understood that strings of printed symbols represented language as it is spoken, not a series of sounds or words. When he did not understand what he was reading, he slurred over it, skipped words, converted it into something that was normal for him to say or just rejected the task of reading it. He never did anything remotely like sounding letter by letter a sequence that wasn't a word he knew or calling word by word a sentence whose meaning escaped him. He read as though he always expected it to say something understandable.

3) However useful high verbal ability and high cultural privilege may be in stimulating reading, neither is necessary.

John has no more than average tested verbal ability and perhaps even less than average cultural stimulation in the direction of reading. The key factor in reading therefore must be something else. Large vocabulary, sophisticated thinking, accurate articulation of standard English, active encouragement and instruction in reading skills, may very well help a child learn to read. However, even a single case like John's shows that they are not indispensable, that is, that neither success nor failure in reading can be predicted in individual cases from these factors alone.

The above comments are based on the assumption that the test scores represent a fairly accurate measure of John's intellectual ability. It may be, however, that the tests, which are based on a different cultural milieu from John's, actually underestimate his ability. For example, the Otis Quick Scoring Mental Ability Test, Form A, contains a sample item consisting of pictures of a hammer, saw, chair, and pliers. The subject is supposed to pick out the object that is "different" and name the concept represented by the three that are alike. John pointed to the pliers and asked what they were. When I pointed to the saw and asked him if he knew what it was, he said yes, it was a knife. Obviously the point of the item is lost on a child who can identify only one of the "alike" objects. Since many standardized test items assume vocabulary and knowledge that John does not have, it is quite possible that his true abilities are higher than his test scores indicate, but we have no direct evidence that this is so.

References

Brown, R. The development of Wh questions in Child Speech, *Journal of Verbal Learning and Verbal Behavior, 7,* 2, 1968, 279–290.

Durkin, D. *Children Who Read Early* (New York: Teachers College Press, 1966).

14

Analysis of Oral
Reading Miscues:
Applied Psycholinguistics

——KENNETH S. GOODMAN

A reader who makes a mistake, says Goodman, is not necessarily behaving randomly, or guessing recklessly. He may be paying more attention to the semantics and syntax of the passage than to the visual information on the page. Words may be left out or put in, but the general meaning of the passage will stay unchanged. In other words the reader— and Goodman is specifically not excluding children learning to read— regards the comprehension of meaning as more important than the identification of words; he does not "decode" to sound.

In this chapter Goodman outlines a taxonomy he has developed for classifying the kinds of errors readers make. He calls the errors "miscues" in an attempt to avoid some of the stigma frequently attached to words like wrong". He also derives some theoretical conclusions from the miscues that he has examined. In his abstract he says, "The reader is viewed as a user of language who processes three kinds of information, grapho-phonic, syntactic, and semantic, as he reacts to the graphic display on the page. In comparing unexpected responses in oral reading to expected responses, the psycholinguistic reading process is revealed."

The chapter first appeared as an article with the same title in Reading Research Quarterly, *1969, 5, 1, 9–30, and is reprinted by permission of the author and publishers.*

Though it is only recently that attention has been given in reading research to linguistic and psycholinguistic insights, reading research has always dealt with linguistic questions if only by ignoring them. Every study of reading materials, reading instruction, the reading process, and reading errors has involved decisions about language units, language sequences, and the explanation and categorization of linguistic behavior.

The reader, whether proficient or beginner, is a user of language. During the reading process this user of language responds to a graphic display, physically no more than patterned ink blotches, and works at reconstructing a message encoded in the graphic display by the writer. No matter how this process is fractionated or atomized, linguistic and psycholinguistic questions are always involved. Understanding of the process must depend on understanding how language works and understanding how language is used, that is, how language and thought are interrelated. Psycholinguistics is the study of these relationships. Until now, researchers in reading have been but dimly aware of the fact that research in reading is applied psycholinguistics. It is the contention of this paper that, just as the solution of problems in space exploration would be impossible without applied physics, so research in reading is impossible without scientifically based psycholinguistics.

This article presents a psycholinguistically based analysis for use in the study of oral reading. The research in which this analysis has been used is basically descriptive, the goal being to describe what happens when a reader, at any stage of proficiency, reads orally.

Researchers and classroom teachers have known that the errors readers make provide insights into reading development. Although for decades oral reading errors have been subjected to scrutiny, this scrutiny has been atheoretical. Without a theoretical framework in which to deal with errors and other oral reading phenomena, many insights into the reading process have been lost.

Spache (1964) summarized a number of studies (Barbe, *et al.*, Daw, Duffy & Durrell, Fields, Gilmore, Payne, Swanson, Wells) and a number of analytical systems in a discussion of informal reading inventories. It is clear from his summary that analysis of oral reading errors has been characterized by establishment of arbitrary, often nonparallel, and overlapping, categories such as Fluency, Word Attack, and Posture, posture being hardly a reading error.

Spache (1964, pp. 104–105) attempted to compare the findings of ten studies of reading errors in terms of frequency rank of error types, but since all investigators did not use the same categories in the same way with the same definitions, the results were really not comparable. For example, what one classified as substitution, another called mispronunciation.

Weber (1968, pp. 96–119) summarized the classification systems used in studies of reading errors and the deficiencies in these systems. She found that most systems focused on words or letters or some combination of both. The variability among definitions of categories from researcher to researcher, however, made comparison very difficult. Furthermore, many classification systems included overlapping categories. Also confusions over the function of oral reading introduced a bias which caused the researcher to be distracted by extraneous phenomena (poor enunciation, hesitation, inadequate phrasing, posture), and a number of studies viewed reading errors as simple misperceptions of words and letters. Another recurrent shortcoming, Weber found, was the lack of concern for the linguistic function of the errors. Often errors were lumped together which were by no means of equal significance. Lastly, legitimate language differences due to the dialect of the reader were treated frequently as mispronunciations.

The analytical system presented here begins with the premise that all responses to the graphic display are caused and are not accidental or capricious. In every act of reading, the reader draws on the sum total of prior experience and learning. Every response results from the interaction of the reader with the graphic display. Responses which correspond to expected responses mask the process by which they are produced. But observed responses (O.R.'s) which do not correspond to expected responses (E.R.'s) are generated through the same process as expected ones. By comparing the ways these miscues differ from the expected responses we can get direct insights into how the reading process is functioning in a particular reader at a particular point in time. Such insights reveal not only weaknesses, but strengths as well, because the miscues are not simply errors, but the results of the reading process having miscarried in some minor or major ways. The phenomena to be dealt with will be called miscues, rather than errors, in order to avoid the negative connotation of errors (all miscues are not bad) and to avoid the implication that good reading does not include miscues. After a series of studies, the present author is convinced that only in rare special circumstances is oral reading free of miscues and that silent reading never is miscue-free. In fact, it appears likely that a reader who requires perfection in his reading will be a rather inefficient reader.

A few other researchers have also recently moved away from prior error studies. Weber (1967) studied errors of first-grade readers in Ithaca, New York. Clay (1966) in studies in Auckland, New Zealand, also looked at reading errors of beginners using linguistic criteria. Y. Goodman (1967) used the taxonomy presented here to look at first-grade reading development whereas Kolers (1969) analyzed the errors of adult readers.

During several years of research on miscues, an analytical system and a theoretical base have evolved in order to accommodate the actual observed reading responses of subjects. A theory must explain and predict and a taxonomy must provide for all phenomena without loose ends and with a minimum of arbitrary decisions. Both the theory and the taxonomy begin with psycholinguistic theory and are modified and explicated in terms of reality. In such a way the research does not stop with the description of superficial behavior, but goes beneath it to the competence which it involves. It is not enough to say that readers sometimes substitute *a* for *the*. It must be seen that such behavior can only result from the linguistic competence of the reader which makes it possible for him to produce a determiner where one is needed. It must also be seen that something more than word recognition or letter perception is involved.

Applications of Linguistics to Reading

Early applications of linguistics to reading have been narrow. Bloomfield (1963) concentrated almost exclusively on phonemics. He went only as far as seeking phoneme-grapheme regularity in materials. He did not study the process of reading nor make a full application of linguistics to it. Fries (1964) looked at reading theoretically, but he also focused on a narrowly defined method of reading based upon spelling patterns and the descriptive linguistic principle of minimal contrast. Lefevre (1964) in a theoretical work, partially developed a sentence approach to reading instruction which included attention to syntax and intonation. Educationists, with a few rare exceptions, have either completely accepted or completely rejected one or another of these methodological points of view.

Strickland's (1962) research was an exception because she studied the structure of children's language and compared it with the language in basal readers. Loban (1963) used similar analysis in his longitudinal studies of children's language development. Bormuth (1965) conducted studies of the relationship of linguistics to readability, using a transformational count. Bormuth also carried out psycholinguistically based research on reading comprehension. Hunt (1965) studied grammatical structures in children's composition and identified differences in complexity at successive ages, as indicated by increasing use of transforms. Hunt dealt with written expression, an encoding process. Reading is basically decoding, but oral reading also involves at least some encoding, since the reader must produce an oral version of what he reads.

The narrowness of early applications of linguistics to reading has led to the development of two unfortunate misconceptions: (*1*) that a linguistic method of teaching reading exists and (*2*) that linguistics can be applied to reading only to explain phoneme-grapheme correspondences. The first is patently untrue. There can be no linguistic "method" of reading instruction any more than there can be a "psychological" method. The second misconception is even more unfortunate because some linguists have written "linguistic" reading texts building on this unexamined assumption rather than doing the research necessary to determine the full scope of linguistic and psycholinguistic implications for reading.

The Theoretical Base

"The major deterrent to research on the reading process is the inefficiency of techniques for investigating the problems," says Helen M. Robinson (1968, p. 400). She suggests that "a wealth of information about processes could be secured from carefully planned . . . examination of children's reading behavior." (Robinson, 1968, p. 401).

With no theory underlying the detailed descriptions Robinson has called for, much could be added to the existing collection of data without making any contribution to coherent understanding of the reading process. Although researchers such as those associated with Project Literacy (Project Literacy Reports, 1964–1966) have taken a broad view of reading, they have been content to look at one portion of the reading process at a time, applying insights from psychology, linguistics, and psycholinguistics. Useful knowledge has been produced, but it has not contributed to a theory which could generate hypotheses and predict and explain reading behavior.

One of the best known theories of reading, Holmes' substrata factor theory, is not a theory at all, but rather an artifact of manipulation of statistics generated by a set of reading tests (Holmes, 1965). As Clymer (1968) points out, it is not possible to explain or predict cause and effect relationships on the basis of the Holmes' analysis, nor does it generate testable hypotheses.

Theories in reading have been thinly built on partial views of the process of reading. Notably missing has been any awareness of the nature of language and language use. Research programs designed to test such theories have been nonexistent, unless one includes classroom testing of materials based on theoretical assumptions. Such studies, however, have rarely been designed to yield any direct evidence about the validity of the underlying theory.

In the theory of the reading process which is evolving, reading is seen as information processing. The reader, a user of language, interacts with the graphic input as he seeks to reconstruct a message encoded by the writer. He concentrates his total prior experience and learning on the task, drawing on his experiences and the concepts he has attained as well as the language competence he has achieved.

In this process, thought and language interrelate, but they are not the same. Reading can be described as a psycholinguistic process, in which meaning is decoded from a linguistic medium of communication rather than a thinking or linguistic process. Furthermore, while reading, the reader may experience cycles of reflective thinking in response to the reading; these cycles cannot be considered part of the reading process itself any more than following directions after having read them can be considered a part of the reading process.

It is important, therefore, to draw a line between reading and the results of reading.[1] But, such a line should not be drawn short of meaning, because the entire reading process should be geared to the reconstruction of the message. Fractionating the process into constituent bits or skills for the purpose of research or instruction qualitatively changes not only the process, which through its interrelationships is much more than the sum of its parts, but also changes the nature of the parts since they normally function as part of a complex process.

Recent attempts by Chall (1967) and others to justify the separation of "code-breaking" from reading for meaning have been based on misunderstandings of how the linguistic code operates and is used in reading. A language is not only a set of symbols (phonemes for oral language, graphemes for written) it is also a *system* of communication in which the symbols are patterned to create sequences capable of carrying an infinite variety of messages. The system of language is grammar. In the process of acquiring his language in pre-school years, each language user acquires control over the rules by which his language is generated. These rules make it possible for him to generate original language utterances which are grammatical and understood by his listeners.

Though it is convenient to think of utterances as composed of units which are basic symbols, these units are themselves affected by their settings. Compare these words for example: *site, situate, situation*. Note that the affix creates a sequence which requires the final consonant in *site* to shift to /č/ in *situate* and the final consonant in *situate* to shift to /š/ in *situation* (Halle, 1969). Furthermore, constraints are imposed in all languages on the permissible sequences so that *lamp* is a possible English word, but *mpal* is not. The language user learns not only the symbols, but the rules by which they adapt to their settings and the constraints on them. He learns the small number of significant differences in sounds which differentiate the units, and he also learns to ignore differences which are not significant in his language. He must ignore these differences or those which are significant will be lost in a maze of irrelevant noise.

Two key facts have thus been overlooked by those arguing for code-emphasis programs: (*1*) Phonemes do not really exist outside of the full system of constraints in which they are found. (*2*) Oral language is no less a code than written language.

Those who argue that one may think of reading as matching oral units with written units have frequently labeled such an operation decoding. But decoding is a process of going from code to message in information theory.

Going from code to code is recoding (Goodman, 1967a). One may think of a hypothetical stage in reading in which the fledgling reader recodes

[1] For an extended discussion of this point, see Gephart (1969).

graphic input as speech which he then treats as aural input and decodes for meaning as he does in listening. Research has indicated that this view is not appropriate for proficient readers (Goodman & Burke, 1968) and may not fully apply even to beginners (Y. Goodman, 1967). Rather, proficient reading can be seen as direct decoding of graphic input. But even in this stretched out view, the reader must operate in response to real, meaningful, grammatical language if he is to have all the information available to him in proper interrelationship, and he must be able to eventually reconstruct and comprehend a message.

Even in an alphabetic system, the interrelationships between the oral and written forms of the language are not simple phoneme-grapheme correspondences, but are relationships between patterns of sounds and spelling patterns. The concept of regularity, i.e., consistent representation of oral language by written units, should be seen in relation to constrained sequences. *S* is a regular representation of /š/ in *sure* and *sugar*, just as *t* is a regular representation of /š/ in *action*. The correspondence is consistent, though it operates in limited circumstances (Venezky, 1967). Many of these minor-pattern regularities are so firmly based in the operation of the language as the user of language has come to know it, that they cause no particular problem in reading.

The most basic reason why the reading process cannot be fragmented is that the reader does not use all the information available to him. Reading is a process in which the reader picks and chooses from the available information only enough to select and predict a language structure which is decodable. It is not in any sense a precise perceptual process. As Kolers has indicated, it is only "incidentally visual" (Kolers, 1969). It is not a process of sequential word recognition. A proficient reader is one so efficient in sampling and predicting that he uses the least (not the most) available information necessary (Goodman, 1965).

All the information must be available for the process to operate in the reader and for the sampling strategies it requires to develop in the beginner.

Three basic kinds of information are used. They are:

1. *Grapho-phonic information.* This is the information from the graphic system and the phonological system of oral language. Additional information comes to the reader from the interrelationships between the systems. Phonics is the name for those relationships.

2. *Syntactic information.* This is the information implicit in the grammatical structures of the language. The language user knows these and, therefore, is able to use this information before he learns to read his native language. Reading, like all language processes, involves a syntactic context.

3. *Semantic information.* As he strives to recreate the message, the reader utilizes his experiential conceptual background to create a meaning

context. If the reader lacks relevant knowledge, he cannot supply this semantic component and he cannot read. In this sense, all readers regardless of their general reading proficiency are incapable of reading some material in their native language.

Since the value of any bit of the three types of information must be related to the other available information, the choice of which bit to select can only be made in full context and the strategies for making those selections can only be learned in response to real language materials (not flash cards or spelling matrices or phonics charts). Also, the reader cannot judge the effectiveness of his choices unless he has subsequent input which can tell him whether his choice fits the semantic, syntactic, and grapho-phonic constraints.

Consider Betts' (1963, p. 135) primer story paragraph as it was read by a first grader:

> Mrs. Duck looked here and there.
> But she did not see a thing
> under the [old] apple tree.
> And on the [she] went
> for a walk.

By omitting *old*, the child produced a sequence which was still acceptable both syntactically and semantically. Furthermore, he corrected a minor flaw in the writing. The phrase, *the big old apple tree*, was used early in the story. Subsequently, the phrases *the tree* or *the apple tree* were used. In connected discourse, a rule operates which generally requires the speaker to delete descriptive adjectives from subsequent references to the same noun. Perhaps the writer or editor of the story wanted to provide one more use of *old*. In any case, the child omitted it and did not correct or indeed appear to be aware of the miscue.

On the next line, the child substituted *the* for *she* and attempted to read on, but found that subsequent choices were not syntactically or semantically consistent. He then returned to the beginning of the line and reread the entire sentence, this time correctly. *The* and *she* are graphically similar (though phonemically, totally dissimilar). But, this reader was evidently concerned that what he reads be decodable, that is, make sense. The omission of *old* did make sense, but the *the* substitution resulted in an unacceptable sequence which he corrected. The process would have been totally different if he had encountered *old* and *she* on word lists.

A Taxonomy of Cues and Miscues in Reading

The taxonomy presented here enables one to analyze miscues, i.e., each instance where a reader's observed response (O.R.) differs from the expected response (E.R.) in order to observe how the reader is operating with the various kinds of input and to become aware of the strategies he is using.

The taxonomy provides a number of questions to be asked about each miscue, since the reader has, in every case, produced his response through the use of the wide range of information available to him in the reading process. Each question is to be answered on its own merits and the analyst is not forced to choose between possible cues and causes. Indeed, in any individual miscue, it is rare that one can say with strong assurance what exactly has taken place. But the patterns which emerge produce a picture in depth of the reading process in the reader.

1. *Words in the miscue.* The extent of the miscue is defined as the minimum text that can be included without leaving anything out. The word count is made on the E.R. or the O.R., whichever is longer. When substitution, insertion, or omission cause a change in function of an adjacent word, that word is included in the count. If a series of attempts is made on the same word or phrase, the last one is arbitrarily chosen as the miscue. In some cases, complex miscues require that sub-miscues be coded separately in some categories.

Example: E.R.: *or a monkey*; O.R.: *of monkeys*

2. *Correction.* Perhaps the most significant factor in analyzing any miscue is whether or not it was corrected. Analysis of which miscues are corrected and under what circumstances has been most revealing. It is also necessary to distinguish between successful and unsuccessful attempts at correction (though the vast majority of such attempts are successful). On rare occasions, correct responses are abandoned in favor of incorrect ones.

3. *Repeated miscues.* To avoid inflating certain types of miscues (particularly those involving unknown words or phrases) when the same miscue occurs repeatedly, only the first occurrence is counted for the purpose of analysis. A tally is kept, however, of the number of repetitions. Care must be exercised to make certain that the miscue is in fact the same in each occurrence. Successive attempts at producing oral equivalents of *philosophical* or continuous substitution of *topical* for *typical* are examples of repeated miscues. But the omission of *the* or deletion of terminal *d* in verbs under varying circumstances cannot be treated as instances of a single miscue.

4. *Word-phrase identification.* Closely tied to No. 3, word-phrase identification is concerned with the instance, after repeated miscues, of success. It is not uncommon for readers, after several unsuccessful attempts to produce a correct response, to subsequently experience no further difficulty. On rare occasions, readers will inconsistently vacillate between correct and incorrect responses.

5. *Observed response in periphery*. It is always possible that miscues may be partially the result of processing visual cues in the periphery, out of sequence. To deal with this question, two ovals around the miscue are arbitrarily defined as the peripheral field. The near field is defined as the line in which the miscue occurs and one line above and below. The extended field is two lines above and below.

6. *Habitual association*. Readers, particularly beginners, will form strong associations between words which then influence their reading. Two main types can be defined: substitution association as in: E.R.: *in the pail*; O.R.: *in the bucket*; sequential association: E.R.: *a happy occasion*; O.R.: *a happy birthday*.

Since habitual associations can only be inferred from overt behavior, for the purpose of the taxonomy they are defined as two or more occurrences of the same substitution. No distinction is made between long-term and temporary associations.

7. *Dialect*. Initially, in order to test hypotheses about dialect differences and reading, any O.R. which deviated from the E.R. in the present author's dialect was defined as a miscue. However, it became apparent that dialect miscues so defined are not like miscues in any real sense since they are the reader's own E.R.'s; thus, a much more inclusive line has been drawn so that a wide range of responses such as *sof* for *soft*, *fella* for *fellow*, *runnin* for *running* are not considered miscues at all. These are, in general, miscues which would go unnoticed since they are such common variants. Syntactic differences, e.g., *we was* for *we were*, semantic differences such as *bucket* for *pail*, and such dialectal variants as *punkin* for *pumpkin*, *pitcher* for *picture*, *feller* for *fellow* are still counted as dialect miscues. Whether a researcher chooses to draw his lines where the present author has or at some other point depends on the purpose of his research.

8. *Graphic proximity*. A scale is used to measure the graphic similarity of the E.R. and O.R. with the numbers 0–9 representing increasing similarity. This requires, of course, the creation of a graphic representation of the O.R. The most likely spelling and the one closest to the E.R. is chosen if there are alternate possibilities.

For purposes of comparison, the word is considered as having three parts, a beginning, a middle, and an end, and a number is assigned to each part. It is assumed that the beginning is more important than the end and the end is more important than the middle. Configuration is considered an additional point of graphic similarity. The following examples, moving from no similarity to homographs or words identical visually, are representative of the points of the scale.

0—(any with no similarity); 1—*zoom/cook*; 2—*helped/moved*; 3—*perceive/perhaps*; 4—*went/wanted*; 5—*pets/puppies*; 6—*quickly/quietly*; 7—*saw/was*; 8—*batter/butter*; 9—*read/read*.

The average of the graphic proximity scores for all miscues is the *graphic mean*.

9. *Phonemic proximity.* A similar scale is used to represent the phonemic similarity between E.R. and O.R. In this case, it is necessary to assume an oral equivalent for the E.R. In using these scales, graphic and phonemic aspects must be kept from contaminating each other. Here are examples, again moving from no similarity to homophones which are distinguished usually by intonation.

0—(any with no similarity); 1—*saw/was*; 2—*kite/cap*; 3—*pets/ puppies*; 4—*quietly/quickly*; 5—*unusual/usually*; 6—*miss/Mrs.*; 7— *grow/grew*; 8—*went/wint* (schwa); 9—*two/too*.

The average of the phonemic proximity scores for all miscues is the *phonemic mean*.

10. *Grammatical function of O.R.* Words or phrases are coded as noun, verb, adjective, adverb, function word, or indeterminate. Non-words are categorized according to inflectional ending and intonation, as well as syntactic pattern, if that is possible. The category is chosen entirely on the basis of actual function and not "part of speech."

11. *Function word O.R.* If the O.R. is a function word, it is classified here as: noun marker, verb marker, verb particle (in discontinuous verbs as: *pick up*), question marker, clause marker, phrase marker, intensifier, conjunction, negative, exclamation (including *well, now, oh*).

12. *Grammatical function of E.R.* The classifications are the same as in 10.

13. *Function word E.R.* The classifications are the same as 11.

Levels

The nature of the miscue is considered on each level from sub-morphemic (the miscue involving a shift *within* a morpheme) through sentence. It should be pointed out that an omission on one level can be a substitution on another level. For example, the omission of the consonant phoneme in *held* results in a sub-morphemic omission, but it is a substitution, *head* for *held*, on the free morpheme and word levels. Another problem to reckon with is that reading involves units of oral and written language. The word is a unit of written language, but the free morpheme and bound morpheme are units of oral language and must also be considered. Under each level involved, the miscue is classified as substitution, insertion, omission, or reversal. An example of each is offered below: (E.R./O.R.)

14. *Sub-morphemic level.*
Substitution: *bit/bat*; Insertion: *tanks/tranks*; Omission: *tracks/ tacks*; Reversal: *saw/was*.

15. *Bound morpheme level.* Included here are miscues involving all inflectional, derivational, and combined form morphemes.

Substitution: *televised/television**; Insertion: *usual/unusual*; Omission: *predetermined/determined*; Reversal: *small worker/smaller work.*

> * When an inflectional suffix such as *s* is not present in the O.R., but is in the E.R., e.g., *dogs/dog*, we count it as a substitution, since the absence of an inflectional suffix is itself a null element in the inflectional system.

16. *Free morpheme level.* This is a phonological category.

Substitution: *looked/jumped*; Insertion: *the boy ran/the young boy ran*; Omission: *the chicken pecked rapidly/the chicken pecked*; Reversal: *the boy ran happily/happily the boy ran.*

17. *Word level.* This is a graphically determined category.

Substitution: *the train was/the toy was*; Insertion: *the baby cried/the little baby cried*; Omission: *that the fish . . ./the fish . . .*; Reversal: *the crying child/the child crying.*

18. *Phrase level.* This category is marked when the miscue causes a syntactic change at the phrase level. It may either be change within the structure or a substitution of one phrase structure for another.

Substitution: *the yellow dog/the dog started toward the rimrock/ started to work the rimrock*; Omission: *plants that grew under water, snails, and . . ./plants that grew underwater snails and . . .*; Reversal: *pick the sticks up/pick up the sticks.*

19. *Clause level.* The category is marked when the miscue causes a change at the clause level. A transformational definition of a clause is used: a sentence at the deep structure level.

Substitution: *the book which you gave me was exciting/the book you gave me was exciting*; Insertion: *the flowers were for the party/ the yellow flowers were for the party*; Omission: *the book which you gave me was exciting/the book was exciting*; Reversal: (This must involve a clause of more than one word. It is a resequencing or reorganizing of existing elements.) *when I arrived he was there/I arrived when he was there; . . . , "mother said/ . . . Mother said, "No. . . .*

20. *Sentence level.* A graphically defined unit.

Substitution: *Now Skippy was gone./Now Skippy was gone?*

Reading through the terminal punctuation is coded as substitution of one sentence for two: *. . . bands of geese had flown over. Joel's father . . ./Bands of geese had flown over Joel's father . . .; Tom helped father. Then he went . . ./Tom helped father and then he went. . . .*

Insertion: No examples exist in our data. Omission: *Tom helped father. Next he helped mother. Then he went to the store/Tom helped father. Then he went to the store.* Reversal: *Tom helped father. Then he helped mother./Tom helped mother. Then he helped father.*

21. *Allologs.* Frequently the reader chooses an alternate form of the word. Examples include: O.R. is contracted form of E.R. (*cannot* becomes *can't*); O.R. is full form of E.R. (*won't* shifts to *will not*); O.R. is a long or short form of the E.R. (*airplane/plane*); O.R. is variant form (*pitcher/picture*); Shifts to or from idiomatic forms: *spreading over/spreading all over*; and articulation difficulties: *aluminum/alunimum.*

22. *Bound or combined morphemes (types).* Miscues that are classified as bound morphemes are here sub-classified according to whether they are: inflectional suffixes; non-inflected word form shifts (as *men/man, come/came*); allomorphs (*breakfast—s/breakfast—iz*); contractional suffixes; derivational suffixes; prefixes; parts of compounds; shifts in suffix types (*televised/television*); base form problems (*drowned/drownded*).

23. *Syntactic proximity.* In this category it is necessary to determine how much the syntax of the O.R. diverges from that of the E.R. This assessment is made primarily by looking at surface structure. The scores 0–9 represent increasing similarity. The mean score for all miscues is the *syntactic mean.* In dealing with syntax, it is important not to be distracted by any semantic shifts which accompany syntactic ones.

Here are the basic definitions of the points on the syntactic scale and examples to illustrate each.

0 The syntax of the O.R. and the E.R. are unrelated.
    E.R.: *Oh, good, . . .*
    O.R.: *Who . . .*

1 The syntax of the O.R. and the E.R. has little in common.
    E.R.: *A policeman stared at them.*
    O.R.: *I . . .*

2 The syntax of the O.R. has a key element which retains the syntactic function of the E.R.
    E.R.: *. . . had flown over. Joel's father . . .*
    O.R.: *. . . had flown over Joel's father . . .*

3 There is a major change in the syntax of the O.R.
    E.R.: *Inside there was usually . . .*
    O.R.: *Inside there were unusual . . .*

4 There is a change in phrase structure of the O.R., which is accompanied by an intonation change.
    E.R.: *. . . that grew under water, snails, and . . .*
    O.R.: *. . . that grew underwater snails, and . . .*

5 There is a syntactic change occurring within the phrase structure of the O.R.

E.R.: *. . . most of them came from jungle rivers where . . .*

O.R.: *. . . most of them came from Jungle River where . . .*

6 There is a change in person, tense, or number of the O.R.

E.R.: *How he wanted to go back.*

O.R.: *How he wants to go back.*

7 There is a change in choice of function word or another minor shift in the O.R.

E.R.: *There was a dinosaur.*

O.R.: *There was one dinosaur.*

8 The syntax of the O.R. is unchanged from the syntax of the E.R.

E.R.: *The windows were full of puppies and kittens.*

O.R.: *The windows were full of pets and kittens.*

24.   *Semantic proximity.* This category measures the similarity in meaning between the O.R. and the E.R. The scores 0–9 represent increasing similarity. Again, it is important not to confuse syntactic and semantic change. It is important also to keep in mind that meaning is always contextually determined. Words and phrases only mean the same thing in limited circumstances.

0 The meaning of the O.R. and the E.R. are unrelated.

E.R.: *One side of the store was covered with rows of smaller tanks.*

O.R.: *One side of the store was covered with rows of smaller tranks.*

1 The meaning of the O.R. is vaguely related to context.

E.R.: *"Let's go!" said Danny. A policeman . . .*

O.R.: *"Let's go!" said Danny. I . . .*

2 The meaning of the O.R. is appropriate, but unrelated to the E.R.

E.R.: *Lan Ying stared across the river.*

O.R.: *Lan Ying started across the river.*

3 The meaning of the O.R. is semantically associated with either prior or subsequent portions of the text.

E.R.: *—and yet he, too, . . .*

O.R.: *—and yet he knew, . . .*

4 There is some association between the meaning of the O.R. and the E.R.

E.R.: *Her sense of routine told her . . .*

O.R.: *Her sense routine told her . . .*

Or, there has been a meaning change resulting from a shift in intonation.

E.R.: *. . . under water, snails, . . .*

O.R.: *. . . underwater snails, . . .*

5 The E.R. and the O.R. are antonyms.

E.R.: *Inside there was usually . . .*

O.R.: *Inside there was unusual . . .*

6 The O.R. has an associated meaning with the E.R.
   E.R.: *Danny had to hold up the wires for him.*
   O.R.: *Danny had to hold up the telephone . . .*
7 The O.R. involves a slight change in connotation.
   E.R.: *. . . to think of her baby brother . . .*
   O.R.: *. . . to think of her new baby brother . . .*
Or, a similar name substitution.
   E.R.: *Mr. Barnaby was . . .*
   O.R.: *Mr. Barnberry was . . .*
8 The E.R. and the O.R. are synonyms.
   E.R.: *The lady's wig was . . .*
   O.R.: *The lady's fake hair was . . .*
9 There is no change in meaning between the E.R. and O.R.

25. *Miscues involving transformations (grammatical restructuring).* In many miscues the O.R. looks like a grammatical transformation of the E.R. This is theoretically possible if one acknowledges that in reading a reader may be inducing a deep structure more or less the same as the writer's and then generating his oral response from that deep structure. The surface structure of the O.R. in that case will differ from the surface structure of the E.R. to the extent that the reader's deep structure differs, to the extent that the rules that he uses in generating it differ from the writer's, and to the extent that he makes different optional choices. Indeed it is not possible to explain some miscues on the basis of a closer relationship between the print and the oral responses of the reader.

For current purposes, it is necessary only to ask whether or not a grammatical transformation is involved. Later studies may lead to a closer examination of the nature of the transformations.

Below are examples of miscues involving transformations:
   E.R.: *It would be nice to play with a dinosaur.*
   O.R.: *It would be nice to play with one.*
   E.R.: *The dinosaur was so tall Danny had to hold up the wires for him.*
   O.R.: *The dinosaur was so tall that Danny had to hold up the wires for him.*

26. *Intonational miscues.* Virtually every miscue involves intonation to the extent that there is at least some shift from the expected intonation. But, the range of acceptable intonation is quite wide in most cases, and recording every minor deviation would confuse the picture. Therefore, under this heading intonation is dealt with only where it is central to the miscue or may be causative.

There are miscues involving shifts within words as in: *próject/projéct.*

There are also miscues involving intonation between words: *jungle rivers/Jungle River.*

Relative intonation within a sentence may be involved: *that grew under water, snails, and/that grew underwater snails, and . . .*

Sentence terminal intonation may be involved: *had flown over. Joel's father . . ./had flown over Joel's father. . . .*

Or a conjunction may be substituted for a terminal punctuation: *The boys fished and then they cooked their catch./The boys fished. Then they cooked their catch.*

27. *Syntactic acceptability.* Syntactic shifts were mentioned earlier. Syntactic acceptability deals with the degree to which the resulting grammar of the O.R. was acceptable. This acceptability can only be judged in terms of the dialect of the reader and not on any standard or grammar book basis, since each reader is functioning within his own grammatical system.

Various degrees of acceptability are recognized: not acceptable, acceptable with the prior portion of the sentence, acceptable with the subsequent portion of the sentence, acceptable in the sentence, but not the passage, acceptable within the total passage.

28. *Semantic acceptability.* In judging whether the meaning is acceptable, similar degrees of acceptability are used. Again, it is important not to confuse meaning and grammar. The meaning of a passage is always contingent on its grammar, but meaning is carried over much longer sequences, whereas grammar is rarely ever affected by the grammatical patterns more than a few sentences away. A sentence pattern need only agree in person, tense, and sequence with the preceding sentences. But, a semantic interpretation which fits well within the immediate paragraph may be entirely inconsistent with the story line and developing plot.

Potential of Analysis of Miscues

It should be clear from the detail of the analysis that studies using the taxonomy are depth studies and the number of subjects in any single study must necessarily be quite small. It is a technique most suitable for seeking to thoroughly understand how a few readers use the reading process. It stands in sharp contrast to statistical studies of many subjects on a few key, isolated variables.

The studies which have utilized the taxonomy (Goodman, 1965; Goodman & Burke, 1968; Y. Goodman, 1967; Allen, 1969), have sought to understand the reading process and perfect the theoretical model of the process. They have compared small groups of children at different levels of proficiency, have studied children over time to see how the reading process changes, have looked at some phenomena such as substitutions and transformations in considerable depth. Continuing research aims at understanding the full range of variation in the operation of the reading process and of the strategies that readers use.

Reading has been focused on, but analysis of reading miscues offers some interesting possibilities for linguistic and psycholinguistic research in general. Such analysis, for instance, utilizes natural language rather than contrived quasi-linguistic tasks. It also provides an expectation model (the E.R.) with which to contrast the actual performance of the subject (the O.R.). It can make possible the more scientific use of reading tasks in psychological, linguistic, and psycholinguistic research. Ironically, use of the reading tasks in such research is quite common, but the influence of the task on the results has frequently been ignored. Reconsideration of the results of such research and replication of the research may throw considerable new light on the findings.

Though the current analysis is complex and time consuming, limited application of the concepts and insights involved may provide new classroom and clinical diagnostic procedures. Y. Goodman and Burke (1969) have already suggested an informal classroom procedure based on the taxonomy.

The descriptive research now being carried out hopefully will generate hypotheses about the reading process which can be empirically tested and lead to new insights into methods and materials for reading instruction.

Ultimately, the test of the value of this research, like all reading research, is in the contribution it makes to more effective learning of reading.

References

Allen, P. A psycholinguistic analysis of the substitution of miscues of selected oral readers in grades 3, 4 and 6, and the relationships of these miscues to reading process, a descriptive study. Unpublished doctoral dissertation, Wayne State University, 1969.

Betts, E. A., & Welch, Carolyn M. *The ABC Up the Street and Down.* (3rd ed.) Betts Basic Readers, The Language Arts Series. New York: American Book Company, 1963.

Bloomfield, L., & Barnhart, C. *Let's Read Series.* Bronxville, New York: C. L. Barnhart, Inc., 1963.

Bormuth, J. R. Readability: a new approach. *Reading Research Quarterly*, 1966, *1* (3), 79–132.

Burke, Carolyn L. A psycholinguistic description of grammatical re-structuring in the oral reading of a selected group of middle school children. Unpublished doctoral dissertation, Wayne State University, 1969.

Chall, Jeanne. *Reading: The Great Debate.* New York: McGraw-Hill, 1967.

Clay, Marie M. Emergent reading behavior. Unpublished doctoral dissertation, University of Auckland, New Zealand, 1966.

Clymer, T. What is 'reading'?: some current concepts. In Helen M. Robinson (Ed.), Innovation and change in reading instruction. *Yearbook of the National Society for the Study of Education*, 1968, *67*, Part II, 7–29.

Fries, C. C. *Linguistics and Reading.* New York: Holt, Rinehart and Winston, Inc., 1964.

Gephart, W. Application of the convergence technique to reading. *Occasional Paper No. 4, Phi Delta Kappa*, January, 1969.

Goodman, K. S. A linguistic study of cues and miscues in reading. *Elementary English Journal*, 1965, *42*, 39–44.

Goodman, K. S. *The Psycholinguistic Nature of the Reading Process.* Detroit: Wayne State University Press, 1967. (a)

Goodman, K. S. Reading: a psycholinguistic guessing game. *Journal of the Reading Specialist*, 1967, *4*, 126–135. (b)

Goodman, K. S., & Burke, Carolyn. *Study of Children's Behavior while Reading Orally.* (Report of Project No. S425) United States Department of Health, Education, and Welfare, 1968.

Goodman, Yetta M. A psycholinguistic description of observed oral reading phenomena in selected beginning readers. Unpublished doctoral dissertation, Wayne State University, 1967.

Goodman, Yetta M., & Burke, Carolyn. Do they read what they speak? *The Grade Teacher*, 1969, *86*, 144–150.

Halle, M. Some thoughts on spelling. In K. Goodman & J. Fleming (Eds.), *Psycholinguistics and the Teaching of Reading.* Newark, Delaware: International Reading Association, 1969.

Holmes, J. A. Basic assumptions underlying the substrata-factor theory. *Reading Research Quarterly*, 1965, *1* (1), 4–28.

Hunt, K. Grammatical structures written at three grade levels. *National Council of Teachers of English Research Report*, 1965, No. 3.

Kolers, P. A. Reading is only incidentally visual. In K. Goodman & J. Fleming (Eds.), *Psycholinguistics and the Teaching of Reading.* Newark, Delaware: International Reading Association, 1969.

Lefevre, C. A. *Linguistics and the Teaching of Reading.* New York: McGraw-Hill, 1964.

Loban, W. D. The language of elementary school children. *National Council of English Research Report*, 1963, No. 1.

McCullough, Constance M. Linguistics, psychology, and the teaching of reading. *Elementary English*, 1967, *44* (4), 353–62.

Project Literacy Reports. Ithaca, New York: Project Literacy, Cornell University, No. 1–8, 1964–1966.

Robinson, Helen M. The next decade. In Helen M. Robinson (Ed.), Innovation and change in reading instruction. *Yearbook of the National Society for the Study of Education*, 1968, *67*, Part II, 397–430.

Spache, G. D. *Reading in the Elementary School.* Boston: Allyn and Bacon, 1964.

Strickland, Ruth G. The language of elementary school children: its relation to the language of reading of selected children. *Bulletin of the School of Education*, Indiana University, 1962, *40* (4).

Venezky, R. English orthography: its graphic structure and its relation to sound. *Reading Research Quarterly*, 1967, 2 (3), 74–106.

Weber, Rose-Marie. Errors in first grade reading. *Unpublished manuscript.* Cornell University Library, 1967.

Weber, Rose-Marie. The study of oral reading errors: a survey of the literature. *Reading Research Quarterly*, 1968, *4*, 96–119.

15

On the Psycholinguistic Method of Teaching Reading

——with KENNETH S. GOODMAN

This chapter is more of a plea than an argument. Science is frequently expected to stand aside impartially while the rest of the world makes what it will of its discoveries. I shall not go into the more obvious consequences of this neutral attitude. But I see two justifications for taking a stand on the matter of psycholinguistics and reading instruction. The first is that psycholinguists are frequently invited, if not challenged, to comment upon how their insights are relevant to instruction. The second is that the very name of the discipline is at stake; whether psycholinguists like it or not, their name is being taken to give authority to instructional methods which may be the very opposite of what psycholinguistics would recommend.

Goodman and I, therefore, decided that the best form of defense was attack. We might not be able to prevent misuse of the word "psycholinguistics", but at least we might try to warn teachers of what was happening. Teachers, after all, would be the primary target of "psycholinguistic" technology. We struck while the irony was hot.

The paper with the title of this chapter was published in Elementary School Journal, *1971, 177–181, and is reprinted by permission of the publishers.*

Our concern is with an imaginary monster—the "psycholinguistic method." At the time of this writing, it is as mythical a beast as the phoenix, the unicorn, or the hippogriff. But we have no confidence that in the near future this monster will not show its face upon the earth. In fact, we would put such a method into the same category as female presidents of the United States—a logical possibility that happens only temporarily to be an empty set.

We must declare our interest. Each of us is responsible for a book about reading that has the word "psycholinguistic" in its title (1, 2), and we are both anxious not to have the term associated with a particular instructional dogma. To be blunt, we regard the development of "psycholinguistic materials" as a distinct threat, not just to us but to the entire educational community. Already we think we detect perturbations in the publishing underworld indicating that a new vogue word is about to be launched into reading pedagogy. Therefore we have decided on this pre-emptive strike. Our objective is to destroy the phoenix of "psycholinguistic instruction" before it can arise from the methodological ashes of the 1960's, although our expectation of success is slight. Our numbers are small, and we have nothing but reason on our side.

The value of psycholinguistics lies in the insights it can provide into the reading process and the process of learning to read. As such, a "psycholinguistic approach" to reading would be the very antithesis of a set of instructional materials. As we shall argue, psycholinguistic analysis formally confirms what we have all known intuitively for years—that the key factors of reading lie in the child and his interaction with information-providing adults, rather than in the particular materials used. Materials most compatible with such interaction are those that interfere the least with natural language functioning.

Obviously we write with some feeling. This would not be the first time that the reputable name of a scientific discipline had been used with marginal justification as a label for classroom fads. The new science of psycholinguistics has much to offer the study of reading, and its contribution could be sullied by the first comer to attach its name to a souped-up package of classroom impedimenta.

Psycholinguistics, as its name suggests, lies at an intersection of psychology and linguistics. As an independent discipline, it is about fifteen years old. Its central task, according to Miller, is to describe the psychological processes that go on when people use language (3, 4*). From linguistics, the new science derives insights about the system that is language—about the competence that individuals acquire when they become fluent users of their language. Some of these insights are incompatible with hypotheses about language-learning that psychologists have held for decades.

Linguistic analysis, for example, shows that it would be impossible for a child to learn to speak simply by imitating adult sentences. The number of sentences possible in a language is infinite—at least a hundred billion billion different grammatical twenty-word sentences could be constructed, and practically every utterance we make or hear is unique. Therefore language must be a system, a set of rules that is capable of generating an infinite number of sentences.

We are all capable of learning what these rules are, because we are all capable of distinguishing acceptable from unacceptable grammatical constructions in our language (even if our own individual grammars vary a little from one person to another). The rules must be learned; they cannot be taught, partly because no one can say what they are.

Not even linguists can describe with any adequacy the rules by which grammatical and ungrammatical sentences can be distinguished; if linguists could, we would have computers that could converse and translate with the facility of human beings.

Linguistic analysis also shows that language has two levels—a surface structure—that is, the sounds or written representation of language—and a deep structure—that is, meaning. These two levels of language are related in a complex way through the system of rules that is grammar, or syntax. Without these rules we could never understand a sentence because the meaning of a sentence is given not by the individual words, but by the manner in which the words interact with each other. (If it were not for syntax, "man bites dog" would mean the same as "dog bites man" and a Maltese cross would be indistinguishable from a cross Maltese.)

Psychology contributes insights about how language must be learned and used. Psychology shows that there are severe perceptual limitations on the amount of acoustic (or visual) "surface structure" that we can process to comprehend language. Psychology shows that our working memory is so constrained that we could not possibly comprehend speech or writing if we analyzed individual words. Psychology also provides a wealth of data about human learning, showing, for example, that negative information can be as valuable as positive information. It can be just as instructional to be wrong as to be right, although all too frequently we are conditioned to avoid the "error" of our ways. Psychological studies show that all human beings have preferred strategies that use a small and apparently innate range of capacities for acquiring new knowledge. These studies also show that learning is rarely the result of a passive exposure to "instruction" but rather the result of an active search for specific kinds of information, which is another reason why rules can be learned but not taught.

At the intersection of these areas of psychology and linguistics lies the growing and fascinating field of psycholinguistics. Already there is an imposing body of knowledge about how fluent language-users construct and perceive sentences. Psycholinguistic research confirms, for example, the linguistic insight that language is processed at deep structure levels. We remember meanings, not individual words. We distinguish elements and relationships that are not actually represented in the surface structure but are constructed from the meanings that we derive from the hidden deep structure.

Some of the most exciting advances made by psycholinguists have been in their studies of how children acquire the rules of adult language (2). Studies show that these rules are developed rapidly between the ages of eighteen months and four years, and appear to follow a similar pattern of development in all children. This pattern, so systematic and invariant, is nothing like a miniature or deformed version of adult language. This fact has led to the suggestion that children have an innate predisposition for discovering the rules of language. The view is supported by the fact that no one can verbalize these rules to tell them to a child.

Insights of the kind found in linguistics and psychology appear to be leading to a profound review of long-held beliefs about reading and how it is learned. It is becoming clear that reading is not a process of combining individual letters into words, and strings of words into sentences, from which meanings spring automatically. Rather the evidence is that the deep-level process of identifying meaning either precedes or makes unnecessary the process of identifying individual words.

Psycholinguistic techniques are beginning to be applied directly to the study of learning to read. They show that the type of information a child requires is not best presented in the form of stereotyped classroom or textbook rules and exercises. Rather, a child appears to need to be exposed to a wide range of choices so that he can detect the significant elements of written language. Experiments have shown that even beginning readers look for and use orthographic, syntactic, and semantic redundancy in written language—but whoever thinks of trying to "teach" a child about that? The child learning to read, like the child learning to speak, seems to need the opportunity to examine a large sample of language, to generate hypotheses about the regularities underlying it, and to test and modify these hypotheses on the basis of feedback that is appropriate to the unspoken rules that he happens to be testing (5, 6).

None of this can, to our mind, be formalized in a prescribed sequence of behaviorally stated objectives embalmed in a set of instructional materials, programmed or otherwise. The child is already programmed to learn to read. He needs written language that is both interesting and comprehensible, and teachers who understand language-learning and who appreciate his competence as a language-learner.

The value of psycholinguistics, we are firmly convinced, lies in the new understanding it can give us all—researchers and practitioners—about the reading process and learning to read. If we were given to slogans, we might well be among the first to assert (with the publishers and the publicists) that this is the dawn of the psycholinguistic era in reading instruction. But we appeal for caution for two reasons. First, because the discipline of psycholinguistics is new, especially in its application to reading. It is far too early to derive rigid practical conclusions from the data that have been collected. Second, because the data clearly indicate that the "revolution" that psycholinguistics might create in reading pedagogy lies in a richer understanding of what the child is trying to accomplish and of his superb intellectual equipment.

We do not deny that there might be a psycholinguistic approach, or attitude, toward reading. In such an approach, the adjective "psycholinguistic" would be synonymous with "objective," "analytical," or "scientific." But in phrases such as "psycholinguistic primer" or "psycholinguistic kit" the adjective would be devoid of meaning.

Nor do we deny that materials for reading instruction could be improved both in their construction and use by the insightful application of psycholinguistic knowledge. But enlightened teachers do not need to wait for new materials. They can make much more effective use of existing materials simply by viewing the reading process as one in which the developing reader functions as a user of language. It may well be that such teachers will find themselves rejecting large portions of the materials and the accompanying guide books as inappropriate, unsound, and even destructive.

We stated earlier that our fears about the misuse of the word "psycholinguistic" were based on precedent. We are thinking of what has already happened to one half of the psycholinguistic partnership.

The study of reading was advanced significantly when linguists turned their attention to the subject. They contributed a number of profound and important insights that continue to serve the discriminating reading researcher and the teacher. But the name of linguistics also became associated with a particular clutch of instructional materials and that is a different kettle of fish. The attachment of the label "linguistic" to reading materials had two disadvantages. The first disadvantage was that any material or procedure that could be associated with the label gained a spurious authority, as if anything that bore the trademark "linguistic" carried a scientific seal of quality. The second disadvantage was that the word "linguistics," and the science itself, became devalued in many circles because of a kind of Gresham's Law that operates among instructional materials.

We shall not speculate about reasons why no instructional materials have ever been characterized as the "psychological" method for teaching reading, although such a label would seem to be as justified as "linguistic." Whatever the reasons for the inhibitions about using the word "psychological," they do not appear to apply to "psycholinguistic," which is gaining growing prominence in the promotional literature of the education industry.

Our plea is simply that the term be used with respect. . . .

References

1. K. S. Goodman (ed.). *The Psycholinguistic Nature of the Reading Process*. Detroit: Wayne State University Press, 1968.

2. F. Smith. *Understanding Reading: A Psycholinguistic Analysis of Reading and Learning To Read*. New York: Holt, Rinehart and Winston, 1971.

3. G. A. Miller. The psycholinguists, *Encounter, 23* (July 1964), 29–37.

4. G. A. Miller. Some preliminaries to psycholinguistics, *American Psychologist, 20* (January, 1965), 15–20.

5. K. S. Goodman and C. Burke. Study of Children's Behavior while Reading Orally. Final Report. United States Office of Education Project S425, 1968.

6. K. S. Goodman and C. Burke. Study of Oral Reading Miscues That Result in Grammatical Retransformation. Final Report. United States Office of Education Project 7–E–219, 1969.

16

Twelve Easy Ways
To Make Learning
To Read Difficult*

*and One Difficult Way To Make It Easy

With reservations, because I still believe strongly that teachers should not expect to be told what to do, my final chapter responds to the frequent challenge to indicate how psycholinguistics is relevant in the reading classroom. I do not spell out a sequence of simple steps for teachers, because the question is not as easy as that. There is no psycholinguistic recipe to guarantee that the cake of reading will rise. But I do indicate how teachers might question many of the things they are often exhorted to do, and thus suggest how the ideal conditions for learning to read might be approached.

I have been asked to stress that my "Twelve Rules for Reading Teachers" should not be taken seriously. I have been warned not to leave them lying around at conferences of reading specialists, where they might be picked up and put to use. And it has been suggested that some teachers fresh out of training college might already have learned the rules by heart.

But I doubt whether any teacher could follow my twelve rules and stay in the business. In fact I conclude the chapter and the book with what I consider to be a defensible upbeat note. Many teachers are—or could be—far better at their jobs than they are often given credit for. And psycholinguistics can help to assert the right of children to learn to read with the aid of people rather than procedures.

I have collected a dozen precepts on the topic of how to teach reading. The list is set out, concisely tabulated in a form suitable for framing, in the table on the next page. I make no claim to originality for my specimens, in fact I have chosen them because they have such widespread currency; they are part of the conventional wisdom. They might not be considered out of place displayed on the staff room wall as a model of exemplary practice, or enshrined in the pages of manuals for teachers (which is where I found most of them in the first place).

Some of my twelve precepts are venerable to the point of senility. I propose to examine them one by one, and to indicate why each in its own way may be regarded as a potential and powerful method of interfering in the process of learning to read.

1. *Aim for early mastery of the rules of reading.* This rule is absurd because there are no rules of reading, at least none that can be specified with sufficient precision to teach a child. All proficient readers have acquired an implicit knowledge of how to read, but this knowledge has been developed through the practice of reading, not through anything that is taught at school. The learning process is identical with that by which infants develop a set of internal rules for producing and comprehending spoken language without the benefit of any formal instruction. And just as no linguist is able to formulate a complete and adequate set of grammatical rules that could be used to program a computer (or a child) to use spoken language, so no theorist has yet achieved anything like an adequate insight into the knowledge that people acquire and use when they become fluent readers.

But even if we did have a clearer understanding of the reading process, it would be doubtful whether anyone should try to give this understanding directly to children. After all, millions of children have learned to read in the past without any profound insight on the part of their instructors into what the children were learning to do. There is absolutely no evidence that teaching grammar helps a child to learn to speak, and none that drills in phonics or other non-reading activities help the development of reading. It is not difficult to argue that mastery of phonics develops only to the extent that reading proficiency is acquired, just as grammar is a meaningful and useful subject (if at all) only to those who already know how to use language.

Typically what are called "rules of reading" are hints or slogans for reading instruction. Learning to read is not a matter of mastering rules. Children learn to read by reading.

2. *Ensure that phonics skills are learned and used.* A prominent aspect of the "reading by rules" fallacy is the notion that reading ability depends on a knowledge of spelling-to-sound correspondences. (In its less sophisticated form, this notion merely asserts that children must learn the "sounds of letters", without any realization of just how complex and unpredictable spelling-to-sound correspondences are.) But reading is not accomplished by decoding to sound—meaning must usually be grasped before the appropriate sounds can be produced, and the production of sounds alone does

TWELVE RULES FOR READING TEACHERS

1. Aim for early mastery of the rules of reading.

2. Ensure that phonic skills are learned and used.

3. Teach letters or words one at a time, making sure each new letter or word is learned before moving on.

4. Make word-perfect reading the prime objective.

5. Discourage guessing; be sure children read carefully.

6. Encourage the avoidance of errors.

7. Provide immediate feedback.

8. Detect and correct inappropriate eye movements.

9. Identify and give special attention to problem readers as soon as possible.

10. Make sure children understand the importance of reading and the seriousness of falling behind.

11. Take the opportunity during reading instruction to improve spelling and written expression, and also insist on the best possible spoken English.

12. If the method you are using is unsatisfactory, try another. Always be alert for new materials and techniques.

not give meaning. Decoding directly from letters to sound is unnecessary as well as inefficient.

It quickly becomes obvious to anyone who gives more than passing attention to the actual process of reading that a fluent reader does not translate written symbols into sound in order to understand what he is reading. Nevertheless it is frequently argued that a mastery of phonics must surely be essential for children, otherwise how would they ever learn to recognize words that they had not met in print before, words that are not in their "sight vocabulary"? There are two good reasons why the last resort of a child in such circumstances should be to turn to phonics.

The first objection to phonics as a way of reading is that it is conspicuously unreliable and cumbersome. Let me repeat what I said in Chapter 7. Studies at the Southwest Regional Laboratory for Educational Development showed that 166 rules would be required to account for the most frequent correspondences in just 6000 one- and two-syllable words in the vocabulary of six- to nine-year-olds—and these 166 rules would still not account for over ten percent of the most common words which would have to be excluded as "exceptions". There is no rule for predicting which of many alternative rules should apply on any particular occasion, any more than there are rules for determining which words are exceptions. The rules often cannot be applied unless one is aware of the meaning and syntactic role of the word and the way it carries stress. In other words, phonics is easy—provided one knows what a word is in the first place.

The very complexity and indeterminacy of such a system makes it remarkable that anyone should expect children ever to try to learn it. Nevertheless many educators, including the instructional product developers at the Southwest Regional Laboratory, believe that teaching at least an arbitrary part of the system is the answer to "the reading problem". But even if a child were gifted and gullible enough to learn such a system, there is absolutely no evidence that he could ever actually use it in the process of reading. Quite the reverse, it is easy to show that any attempt to read by translating letters to sounds through the application and integration of phonic rules could result only in catastrophic overloading of short-term memory. Besides, the use of spelling-to-sound rules to identify words is as absurd as clipping a lawn with nail scissors. Far more efficient and economical alternatives are available.

This leads to the second objection to the phonics fallacy, namely that sounding out words letter by letter (or the even more complicated task of identifying and articulating "letter clusters") is the last resort of the fluent reader—a fact already known by most children whose natural perception of reading has not been distorted in the process of reading instruction. I have discussed the alternatives in Chapter 12.

3. *Teach letters or words one at a time, making sure each new letter or word is learned before moving on.* There is a widespread misconception that

many children have trouble learning the names of objects and words and letters, and that only constant repetition will help to fix a name in a child's mind. This view is based on an oversimplification of the learning process. There are two quite distinct aspects of any name-learning task, the first being to discover how to differentiate the named object or type of object from all other objects—which is essentially a concept formation problem— and the second to discover and associate that concept with its name. By far the more difficult of the two parts of the task is the first—discovering the rules that differentiate categories. Name associating itself seems so easy as to be almost trivial. Children in the first six years of life learn perhaps half a dozen new words, most of them "names", every day, often in a single trial.

The manner in which a child learns how to define the category to which a name belongs is instructive. He looks at the situation in which the name seems to be applied, and tries to extract some features that will mark the situation so that he will recognize it in future. He looks for—but does not ask to be told—some *rules* that will specify the defining characteristics of the category. He constructs "hypotheses" about what the concept is. We can get an idea of what these hypotheses are by looking at the errors that a child makes. If for example he calls all and only four-legged animals "dog" then we may conclude that his current hypothesis is that "dog" simply means four-legged animals. If he applies the name to four-legged animals and tables we can assume that animation is not one of his hypotheses. If he calls only his own dog "dog" he is undergeneralizing.

A child can generate hypotheses only by comparing examples of the category being named with non-examples of the same category. It is as important to be aware of four-legged animals that are not called "dog" as to see some others that are. A child can modify his hypotheses only by testing them and receiving feedback. He learns practically nothing if he is simply shown a dog and is told "That is a dog", except perhaps that a category named "dog" exists. He learns only when he can compare what is a dog with other objects that (to him) might be but are not dogs. More specifically, he learns when he discovers that objects that he would not call "dog" (according to his hypotheses) are in fact dogs, and that objects that he would call "dog" (according to his hypotheses) are in fact not dogs.

A similar situation applies when a child approaches the task of learning the names of letters or words. Simply to be shown the letter *H* over and over again, while being told "This is an 'h'" is not going to help him discover what *H* is. He is still quite likely to call a *K* "h" and perhaps *H* "k". Instead he must find out how *H* and *K* are different, which means first that he must see them together (or at least have a chance to hypothesize what makes *H* different from *K*) and second have a chance to test his hypotheses about the differences between the two.

The manner in which letter and word names are learned is just one of several critical issues involved in understanding the task confronting a child when he learns to read. Learning to distinguish among letters and words is an obvious case in which there are "rules" to be learned in reading, but these are not rules that we can teach. They are like the rules we learn for distinguishing cats and dogs, or for spoken language—rules that we have acquired without instruction and cannot talk about. Instead a child learns by being given the evidence—positive and negative—and also the opportunity to test his theories for himself.

4. *Make word-perfect reading a prime objective.* There is another reason why emphasis should not be put on the learning or identification of words in isolation, and this is that it is the most difficult way to do it. All fluent readers use other cues when they are required to read letters or words. It is much easier to identify a letter when it occurs in a word, or a word when it appears as a meaningful sentence, than when it is standing alone. As I have already pointed out, the identification of individual words is not the most important part of reading. Far more visual information is required to identify words standing alone (or as if they were standing alone) than to identify words in a sentence. Because of the information-processing limitations of our visual system and working memory, it is the handling of large amounts of visual information that makes reading difficult. One of the most important parts of learning to read is learning to use as little visual information as possible.

Fluent readers do not read words, they read meanings. Reading for meaning is far easier than reading words. Children seem to know this instinctively, no doubt because of the strain that reading every word puts on their information-processing capacities.

5. *Discourage guessing; be sure children read carefully.* I have already referred to the role of guessing in the identification of unfamiliar words. I have also referred to the need to spend as little time as possible lingering over every word. Efficient readers make maximum use of a minimum of visual information. Reading for meaning is easier than reading for words. There is another critical factor that I have not yet mentioned—reading quickly is easier than reading slowly. What all the preceding distills down to is that "reading carefully" is not efficient reading, and reading without guessing is not reading at all. Goodman has aptly termed reading "a psycholinguistic guessing game". In order to read one must guess, not recklessly, but on an informed basis. Informed guessing means by making the best use of nonvisual information, of what one already knows. More precisely, in order to read one must constantly form expectations that reduce the uncertainty of what one is reading, and therefore reduce the amount of visual information required to extract its meaning.

We all know that when reading an unfamiliar or difficult text, whether a complex novel, a technical article, or something in a fairly unfamiliar foreign language, it is impossible to read and simultaneously refer to a dictionary, or to slog through a sentence at a time. We may be tempted to slow down, but the only efficient strategy is in fact to speed up, to read on. When it is necessary to "read carefully" for one reason or another, we do not try to do it cold. Instead we take a quick scan through the material "to see what it is about"—which means to get the essence of the meaning—and then read through a second time still relatively fast, to get the details.

An important generalization reveals itself through a number of the observations that I have made so far—that *reading provides its own cues.* The best way to discover the meaning of a difficult passage is to read more of the passage. The best way to identify an unfamiliar word in text is to draw inferences from the rest of the text. The best way to learn the strategies and models for identifying new words "by analogy" is to read. Any instructional method that interferes with reading must almost certainly interfere with the process of learning to read.

6. *Encourage the avoidance of errors.* Learning cannot take place without error. We cannot learn to use names correctly, for animals, letters or words, unless we accept the possibility of being "wrong". A child must take the risk of using a word incorrectly in order to find out whether the rules he has for identifying or using that word are correct; he must use his rules in order to get feedback. I have also argued that reading is highly dependent on guessing, and that reading for meaning is both far easier and far more important than reading to identify words. Again it is obvious that a child must be prepared to make errors, in fact one of the greatest difficulties that a child can face in the process of learning to read is to be inhibited from responding because of the risk of being wrong.

There is no need for scientific evidence to demonstrate that learning is not possible unless we accept the chance of being wrong. If a child already knows he is right before he says something, then the feedback that he is in fact right provides him with no information at all—he already knew he was right. But if a child makes a response, if he names an object or ventures an opinion about meaning, knowing that it is possible he might be wrong, then he will learn something whatever the outcome. If he happens to be "right" then he has confirmed his existing hypotheses. If he happens to be "wrong" then he has acquired some equally important information; he has learned that he must modify his hypotheses. That is the way a child naturally tries to learn—by testing hypotheses—provided of course that he has not been taught that society places a high premium on being right and that it is better to stay quiet than to be wrong. Adults who treat, or who encourage other children to treat, misreadings as stupidities, jokes or transgressions do more than misperceive the basic nature of reading, they also block the principal way in which reading is learned.

7. *Provide immediate feedback.* Chapter 6 pointed out that both good and poor beginning readers make errors, but they differ in the type of errors

that they make. One difference between the good beginning reader and the one heading for trouble lies in the overreliance on visual information that inefficient—or improperly taught—beginning readers tend to show, at the expense of sense. The words they read may not make sense but they look pretty much like the words on the page. The good reader on the other hand will get the sense of the passage but may omit, insert or change a number of words. It is clear that the better reader barely looks at the individual words on the page—he minimizes his use of visual information. The problem for the teacher is to distinguish between the two types of reader. It is easy enough for the teacher (or other children in the class) to jump on a child and give him immediate feedback if he reads a word incorrectly, but this feedback has no relevance if the child is not reading to identify words in the first place, but reading for meaning.

"Immediate feedback" is a dangerous rule to apply indiscriminately— it is necessary to know what feedback is being given for. Feedback implies answering a specific question. If the child is in fact practising individual word identification, if he wants to know "Is this word 'elephant' "? then immediate feedback may help (with a qualification that I shall mention in a moment). But if he is reading to get the general meaning—which means reading fluently—then immediate feedback on words is more than just misplaced or irrelevant, it is disruptive.

There is a second important difference concerning the errors of good and poor beginning readers. Even good readers make occasional errors of meaning; they read anomalously. But a difference lies in what happens at the end of the sentence or passage, at the point where the anomaly should become apparent. The better reader will go back and self-correct; he has been paying attention to the meaning of what he reads. But the word-by-word reader will have no reason to go back and self-correct even if he has been producing absolute nonsense. He was not reading for meaning in the first place. There is a simple strategy, then, for distinguishing the child who is reading for meaning from the others. Wait and see if he self-corrects errors of meaning. Of course, the teacher who pounces on every misread word as soon as it is uttered will not have the opportunity of finding that out.

The preceding discussion leads to a second important generalization, that *reading provides its own feedback.* Provided we read for meaning, we can always check whether errors of interpretation, and even of word identification, have occurred.

8. *Detect and correct inappropriate eye movements.* An inappropriate eye movement means the reader is looking in the wrong place. This rarely occurs because there is something wrong with the reader's eyes, but rather because he does not know what he should be looking for. Unless a child has a gross visual deficiency that manifests itself outside reading, there is little justification for blaming reading difficulties on visual defects or bad habits. Any child who can recognize a character on a television screen or

spear a pea on a plate has the visual acuity and control necessary to be able to read. But that does not mean he will know where to look. Knowing where to look depends on the nonvisual skills of reading. Drilling the eyes to move blindly from one meaningless position to another is a pointless exercise.

9. *Identify and give special attention to problem readers as early as possible.* Very often far too much is required of early readers; they are expected to demonstrate skills beyond the capacity of fluent adult readers. Relevant examples that I have already mentioned concern the identification of unfamiliar words on the basis of spelling-to-sound rules alone and the requirement that reading aloud should be word-perfect. A third factor lies in the type of material children are often expected to read. Many primers bear absolutely no relevance to a child's particular life or language, and short sentences barely connected by a story line place a premium on word identification and provide little support for intelligent guessing. Subject matter texts that children are later expected to comprehend and appreciate often present an even worse obstacle. Teachers and other adults frequently expect children to read and learn from "resource material" so opaque and dull that it is doubtful whether the adults themselves could bear to read it, let alone learn from it. Furthermore, expectations about comprehension itself are far too high to be realistic. The proper distinction is not drawn between *understanding* what a sentence or passage or book is about, which means grasping the author's meaning, and *recall* of what was said, which is quite a different matter. While recall and understanding are related, in the sense that the former can rarely occur in the absence of the latter, committing detailed information to memory and retrieving it on a later occasion is a complex cognitive task that depends on much more than mere reading skill. There are very stringent limits on how much information can be put into long-term memory at any one time. In fact the requirement that a reader try to store in memory an unreasonably large amount of the information in a passage is a sure way to interfere with the process of reading altogether.

I mention the preceding points because there is a risk that children will be classified as reading problems when the only problem that exists lies in the unreasonable expectations of a parent or teacher, or of the system in which the teacher and child interact. Sometimes the problem lies in a complete misunderstanding of what constitutes good reading: "Johnny is above average at comprehension but he persists in making careless errors with individual words". Reading and diagnostic tests are a very poor guide to reading ability in this respect. The materials and methods used to "measure" reading in fact only measure what can be measured—facility in an assortment of drills, rules, and "power" tasks that at best bear only a tangential relation to fluent reading.

Treating a child as a "special case" always carries a number of unpleasant side effects, particularly damaging in the case of reading. Being singled out all too often adds to a child's anxiety, increases his tension, makes him concentrate on detail and become even more apprehensive about errors. Involvement with clinics and consultants scarcely contributes to the confidence required to read with the flexibility that makes comprehension possible. And if a child continues to fall short of expectations despite the special attention that he gets when identified as a "problem", then the only way he can go is in the direction of further confusion, ultimately with the risk of being labelled minimally brain damaged (which means "We really cannot understand why he does not benefit from our instruction").

I do not want to dwell on the moral, social or personal implications of acting rashly in labelling a child as inadequate. But there is one practical consideration that should be taken into account. The remedial measures taken when a child is identified as a reading problem frequently result in the child reading less than he was before. He spends more time on exercises, drills, tests and interviews; more time trying to boost his "conceptual skills" and general language ability (and even his pronunciation) and less time actually reading. The difficulty before his "problem" was identified might well have been that he was not doing enough reading in order to learn to read, yet the "cure" turns out to be even less reading experience.

10. *Make sure children understand the importance of reading and the seriousness of falling behind.* The only way to learn to read is with confidence and enjoyment. Once again I make the point not as a moral judgement but for purely practical reasons. Anything that makes reading difficult, or unpleasant, or threatening, makes learning to read more difficult. Lack of confidence, unwillingness to risk errors, a reluctance to become *involved* in reading, will all contribute to making learning to read impossible.

There is nothing reprehensible in falling behind one's classmates in reading instruction, and absolutely no damage can be done, except in terms of the school schedule and the expectations (and sometimes the egos) of adults. Reading is not learned competitively, and no convincing evidence exists that there is a critical age for learning to read. The most that can be said about a seven-year-old who is a year behind is that he reads like an average six-year-old. This one-year lag may be disconcerting for parents and teacher, but there is no sound psychological reason why it should be regarded as a precursor of educational catastrophe for the child. The notion is absurd that because 20 percent of a class or school read less fluently than the other 80 percent, remedial action should abolish the bottom 20 percent. The aim should obviously be that all children progress toward fluent reading, not that they should change place in relative ranks.

As I have indicated, tests are poor indicators of reading ability, partly because they are limited in what they measure, but largely because they are almost invariably based on a total misunderstanding of what reading involves. (My precepts 1, 2, 4, 5, 6 and perhaps 11 could be interpreted as a large part of the test-maker's creed.) The purpose of reading is not to score high on reading tests, and progress in learning to read does not require keeping up with the neighbors.

11. *Take the opportunity during reading instruction to improve spelling and written expression, and also insist on the best possible spoken English.* Writing and reading involve quite different systems of knowledge and skill, as I have indicated in Chapter 10. Knowledge of spelling is never used in the process of identifying a word, and words are frequently read for which the spelling is not known. (For this reason some reading skills, such as the visual knowledge of how words should look, may be used to test whether a written word has been spelled correctly.) Reading may assist writing, but not vice versa. Apart from anything else, writing is too slow to do anything but interfere with the process of reading, just as the mechanics of the writing act can interfere chronically with a child's expression of his thought. Even so, instruction in written language, which aims at being primarily concerned with getting well-articulated thoughts on to paper, very often finds itself more concerned with such disruptive side issues as "correct" spelling and grammar, formalized layout, page and paragraph numeration, and neatness of fist. But the analogies between the disruptive precepts of "good reading instruction" and those of "good writing instruction" are too extensive to pursue here.

I am not saying that the obvious relations between reading and writing should be concealed, but only that the fragile process of learning to read—of achieving that delicate balance between fidelity to the printed page and overcoming the strain that an overload of visual information places on eye and brain—should not be further complicated by introducing worries about handwriting or spelling.

Similarly, spoken English is largely irrelevant to reading. There can only be interference with learning to read if the child must worry about how he pronounces what he reads—literally a superficial aspect of reading. A child who reads *I do not have any candy* as "I don't have no candy" has picked up all the significant features of meaning from the text and succeeded in translating them into his own thought and language. Expecting him to read "word-perfectly" not only confuses pedantry with reading, it will probably convey to the child a completely distorted notion of what reading is about. He may be deluded into requiring far more visual information from the text than any mature reader would be able to cope with.

One of the great advantages of conventional English spelling is that it appears to be maximally efficient for all dialects (Chapter 8). The particular dialect that a child speaks makes no intrinsic difference to the basic task of learning to read (Chapter 11). Printed materials are rarely anyone's spoken language written down. Of course, discrepancies among dialects may lead to communication and even sociocultural conflicts within the classroom, especially if the teacher expects the child to read word for word (which the teacher himself would probably find it difficult to do), or if he uses every reading lesson as an occasion for undermining a child's native spoken language expression.

12. *If the method you are using is unsatisfactory, try another. Always be on the alert for new materials and techniques.* The belief that improvement in reading instruction lies just around that corner in the form of another kit of drills, some new basal readers, or a cabinet of technological trickery, is based on an egregious educational fallacy. The belief rests upon the naive assumption that an ideal method of teaching reading exists for every child, and that all a teacher need do is find the right method, or wait for the educational industry to provide it—together of course with the infallible "test" that will match every child with the best method.

There are trivial but quite valid objections to any random, trial and error, hit or miss imposition of materials in the hope that one will brush the child with the magical dust of reading. There is no guarantee that any method will be an improvement on the one before, and there is no test, no set of evaluation procedures, to help teachers make reliable choices. We tend to overlook the damage and despair that constant exposure to different instructional methods, and repeated failure, can produce in a child. We tend to forget that many millions of children learned to read without the benefit of the techniques and technology we have today, let alone those we hope to have tomorrow. Many children have learned in classrooms at least as large as many around today, with desks nailed down in rows, and using abysmally printed and sanctimoniously written material.

Rather than devote so much time—and sanguine hope—to how children will learn to read in the great new days of the future, it would be more instructive to examine how children learned to read in the bad old days of the past.

A more serious objection to dependence on methods and materials than the fact that it is unrealistic is that it reflects a totally distorted view of what is required to improve the quality of instruction. The focus is all wrong— it should be on the child, not on the instructional materials. In fact the common critical inadequacy of all my twelve precepts is that they fail to take any account of what a child's needs might be. They are all directed to the question of what the teacher ought to do, not what the child might be trying to do.

I hope to make my point clearer as I turn from the negative and attempt to summarize in a positive way the alternative I have to offer—difficult though I promise it will be.

One difficult rule for making learning to read easy. Moving from the soothing bath to the cold shower can be profoundly numbing, so I propose to introduce a brief transitional stage in my progression from the easy to the difficult. I offer a guideline, a bridge to my one rule for making learning to read easy.

The guideline is this: The only way to make learning to read easy is *to make reading easy*.

My guideline may appear banal to the point of meaninglessness but it must be justified before I go on to the difficult rule, which otherwise might appear even more pointless.

Learning to read is a complex and delicate task in which almost all the rules, all the cues, and all the feedback can be obtained only through the process of reading itself. Children learn to read only by reading. Therefore the only way to facilitate their learning to read is to make reading easy for them. This means continuously making critical and insightful decisions —not forcing a child to read for words when he is, or should be, reading for meaning; not forcing him to slow down when he should speed up; not requiring caution when he should be taking chances; not worrying about speech when the topic is reading; not discouraging errors . . .

But I do not intend to offer a collection of proscriptions in exchange for the prescriptions that I have so destructively criticized. The simple point is that the twelve easy rules all make reading more difficult, and reading is a difficult enough task already. The twelve golden rules are dross.

The skill of riding a bicycle comes with riding a bicycle. We do not offer a child lectures, diagrams, and drills on the component skills of bicycle riding—we sit him on the saddle and use a guiding hand or training wheels to make sure he does not fall off while he teaches himself the precarious art of keeping balance. Forcing him to worry about laws of motion and centers of gravity would obviously confuse him.

Making learning to read easy means ensuring cues at the time a child needs them, ensuring feedback of the kind he requires at the time he requires it, providing encouragement when it is sought. Making learning to read easy requires an understanding of the reading process, and of what the child is trying to do.

Now I have reached my one difficult rule, the antithesis of the twelve easy rules: *Respond to what the child is trying to do.*

To my mind this rule is basic. There is no alternative. The rule recognizes that the motivation and the direction of learning to read can only come from the child, and that he must look for the knowledge and skills that he needs only in the process of reading. Learning to read is a problem for the child to solve. Glance back at all my twelve easy rules, and you will see that none of them is really concerned with what the child is doing—at the most only with what a remote authority suggests he should be doing.

Obviously, my one rule is difficult. It requires insight, tolerance, sensitivity, and patience; it demands an understanding of the process of reading, a rejection of formulae, less reliance on tests, and more receptivity to the child. Its main demand is a total rejection of the ethos of our day—that the answer to all our problems lies in improved method and technology—and of the emphasis on method that pervades almost all of teacher training.

One final point. The last thing I want to do is imply that teachers have been doing everything wrong. Quite the reverse, my interest is in the fact that for so long, with so many children, teachers have been doing things that are obviously right.

Nothing I have said can change the world as it was yesterday. Any method, any approach to reading instruction, that worked before this chapter was written is obviously still going to work after it has been subjected to a critical review. Yesterday's methods might even work a little better if we get some insight into what really made them effective.

Most teachers are eclectic—they do not act as brainless purveyors of pre-digested instruction (that is why there is the frightening trend these days to produce "teacher-proof" materials). In short, teachers—at least the best of them—are good intuitively. They are effective without knowing why.

The word "intuitive" may sound vague and unscientific—it is a word that is widely discredited—but mainly I think because the quality of intuition is not well understood. Here is an off-the-cuff definition of intuition: a responsiveness to the intangible forces and motivations that largely determine the manifest nature of events. Put in psycholinguistic terms, intuition implies access to underlying structure without awareness of the grammar relating this structure to the physical events that impinge directly upon our senses. More colloquially, intuition is a feel for what is really going on. In terms of reading instruction, intuition is a sensitivity for the unspoken intellectual demands of a child, encouraging and responding to his hypothesis testing.

The good intuitive teacher, in other words, is one who instinctively ignores the twelve easy rules.

Suggested Further Reading

Psycholinguistics

Booksellers' shelves are beginning to be crowded with introductory volumes on this topic. Recent and authoritative additions are:

Peter Herriot. *An Introduction to the Psychology of Language*. London: Methuen, 1970.

James Deese. *Psycholinguistics*. Boston: Allyn and Bacon, 1970.

Hans Hormann. *Psycholinguistics*. (translated by H. H. Stern). New York: Springer Verlag, 1971.

Harold J. Vetter. *Language Behavior and Communication*. Itasca, Illinois: Peacock, 1969.

Roger Brown. *Psycholinguistics*. New York: The Free Press, 1970.

Some psycholinguistics texts emphasize particularly the development of language:

David McNeill. *The Acquisition of Language*. New York: Harper & Row, 1970.

Paula Menyuk. *The Acquisition and Development of Language*. Englewood Cliffs, New Jersey: Prentice-Hall, 1971.

Also relevant is:

Eric Lenneberg. *Biological Foundations of Language*. New York: Wiley, 1967.

197

For a completely opposite point of view to the psycholinguistics of this book, look at:

B. F. Skinner. *Verbal Behavior.* New York: Appleton-Century-Crofts, 1957.

And for a swinging attack on the previous volume, see:

Noam Chomsky. Review of B. F. Skinner's *Verbal Behavior. Language,* 1959, *35,* 26–58.

Recent topics of central interest in psycholinguistics may be explored in:

David L. Horton and James J. Jenkins (Eds.). *The Perception of Language.* Columbus, Ohio: Merrill, 1971.
John R. Hayes (Ed.). *Cognition and the Development of Language.* New York: Wiley, 1970.

A book that surveys its topic from a historical point of view is:

Arthur Blumenthal. *Language and Psychology.* New York: Wiley, 1970.

Psychology

Two excellent volumes, both of which will be rather technical for the uninitiated but which contain much of the basic cognitive psychology underlying the psycholinguistic approach to reading are:

Eleanor J. Gibson. *Principles of Perceptual Learning and Development.* New York: Appleton-Century-Crofts, 1969.
Ulric Neisser. *Cognitive Psychology.* New York: Appleton-Century-Crofts, 1967.

A number of relevant papers are included in:

Donald C. Hildum (Ed.). *Language and Thought.* Princeton: Van Nostrand, 1967.

An informative article on some of the limitations of memory is:

R. C. Atkinson and R. M. Shiffrin. The control of short-term memory. *Scientific American,* August, 1970, 82–90.

Linguistics

Good introductory volumes are:

John Lyons. *Introduction to Theoretical Linguistics.* Cambridge: University Press, 1968.
H. A. Gleason. *Linguistics and English Grammar.* New York: Holt, Rinehart and Winston, 1965.
Roderick A. Jacobs and Peter S. Rosenbaum. *English Transformational Grammar.* Waltham, Massachusetts: Blaisdell, 1968.

Collections of papers on language, the first particularly psycholinguistic in emphasis, are:

R. C. Oldfield and J. C. Marshall. *Language*. Baltimore: Penguin, 1968.
John Lyons. *New Horizons in Linguistics*. Baltimore: Penguin, 1970.

For an interesting and relevant book about a linguist, read:

John Lyons. *Chomsky*. London: Fontana, 1970.

Analyses of spelling-sound correspondences of English are contained in:

Richard L. Venezky. English orthography: its graphic structure and its relation to sound. *Reading Research Quarterly*, 1967, *2*, 75–106.

Two outstanding collections of papers on dialect and sociolinguistic questions, representing major research efforts and areas of concern, are:

Frederick Williams (Ed.). *Language and Poverty*. Chicago: Markham, 1970.
Roger W. Shuy (Ed.). *Social Dialects and Language*. National Council of Teachers of English, 1964.

Reading

Recent books on reading reflecting a psycholinguistic point of view include:

Kenneth S. Goodman (Ed.). *The Psycholinguistic Nature of the Reading Process*. Detroit: Wayne State University Press, 1968.
Kenneth S. Goodman and James T. Fleming (Eds.). *Psycholinguistics and the Teaching of Reading*. Newark, Delaware: International Reading Association, 1969.
Harry Levin and Joanna P. Williams (Eds.). *Basic Studies on Reading*. New York: Basic Books, 1970.
Frank Smith. *Understanding Reading*. New York: Holt, Rinehart and Winston, 1971.

And with more of a linguistic emphasis:

Ronald Wardhaugh. *Reading: A Linguistic Perspective*. New York: Harcourt, 1969.

There is a multitude of books on reading, mostly written from the point of view of method. One deservedly popular book that looks at method from a theoretical point of view opposite to the themes of the present volume is:

Jeanne S. Chall. *Learning To Read: The Great Debate*. New York: McGraw-Hill, 1967.

A classic originally published in 1908 containing insights widely ignored for over half a century is:

Edmund B. Huey. *The Psychology and Pedagogy of Reading.* Cambridge, Massachusetts: M.I.T. Press, 1968.

Among papers emphasizing perceptual and cognitive aspects of learning to read are:

Eleanor J. Gibson. Learning to read. *Science*, 1965, *148*, 3673, 1066–1072.
Eleanor J. Gibson. The ontogeny of reading. *American Psychologist*, 1970, *25*, 2, 136–143.

A paper examining much of the same evidence and coming to conclusions similar to those in several chapters of this book is:

Ellen B. Ryan and Melvyn I. Semmel. Reading as a constructive language process. *Reading Research Quarterly*, 1969, *5*, 1, 59–83.

In Chapter 8, Carol Chomsky remarked that the "underlying lexical level of representation" of words has a psychological reality for the language user. A remarkable study of pre-school children's invented spelling showing how sensitive children are both to the sounds and underlying structures of English is reported in:

Charles Read. Pre-school children's knowledge of English phonology. *Harvard Educational Review*, 1971, *41*, 1, 1–34.

At a wholly nontechnical but insightful level is:

S. H. Sebasta. My son the linguist and reader. *Elementary English*, 1968, *45*, 233–242.

Several review papers on the topic of language development and reading appear in the Fall 1971 issue of *Reading Research Quarterly*.

Name Index

Subject Index